SOTHIS PRESS

Sothis Press aims to completely reimagine the public domain book with an emphasis on universal access to captivatingly designed print editions. We believe that technology will enable every single book ever published to be perpetually accessible in beautiful print form. Sothis is beauty in ubiquity.

www.sothis.press
1 Waterhouse Square, London, ECIN 2ST

Men and Mysteries of Wall Street

James Knowles Medbery

SOTHIS PRESS

ISBN 978-1-83548-180-6

Men and Mysteries of Wall Street
is in the public domain.

This edition is published by
Sothis Press © 2023. The company
is registered in England and Wales.
The Company Number is 14900389.

D MYSTERIES

OF

L STREET.

BY

K. MEDBERY.

WITH O IGINAL ILLUSTRATIONS.

OSTON:
OSGOOD, & CO.
1870.

MEN AND MYSTERIES

OF

WALL STREET.

BY

JAMES K. MEDBERY.

WITH ORIGINAL ILLUSTRATIONS.

BOSTON:
FIELDS, OSGOOD, & CO.
1870.

UNIVERSITY PRESS: WELCH, BIGELOW, & CO.,
CAMBRIDGE.

TABLE OF CONTENTS.

CHAPTER IX.

CHAPTER X.

CHAPTER XI.

CHAPTER XII.

CHAPTER XIII.

CHAPTER XIV.

CHAPTER XV.

CHAPTER XVI.

CHAPTER XVII.

LIST OF ILLUSTRATIONS.

MEN AND MYSTERIES OF WALL STREET.

CHAPTER I.

PRELIMINARY.

THE farthest reach of audacious speculation in our day is not without a definite background of conservatism. An age of steam has stringent need of immense balance-wheels. The sharp and fevered struggle for wealth has created a necessity for secure investment; and no man, however gigantic may be the balances of his ledgers, feels himself safely over the bridge of fortune until his assets assume the shape of quickly realizable values. Hence the ease with which national debts are now funded and joint-stock enterprises are set on foot. With an instantaneous exchangeable value for all kinds of property in the world's market, and an average certainty of return to invested capital, mankind would deem itself not far from the threshold of the millennium. And it is because civilization has as yet failed to make adequate progress in this direction with reference to the products of agriculture and machinery, that great money-marts have arisen and expanded into paramount importance.

Cotton is good, corn is good, real estate is very good; but none of these have the beautiful qualities of 3 per cent British consols or United States 5-20s. Commodore Vanderbilt can convert the bulk of his vast property into money in a day. There is no similar market ready to perform a like service for William B. Astor. The Spragues of Rhode Island are slaves to their factories. The heavy cattle-raisers of Texas, the great farmers of California and Illinois, the mill-owners of New England, are not merely subject to fluctuations in the prices of their products, they are the veriest victims of circumstance whenever they attempt to turn their property into coin, or the equivalents of coin. Daniel Drew, the drover, had come to comprehend this serfdom very thoroughly before he took up his quarters at the Bull Head Tavern and mastered the subtleties of Erie speculation. Up and down the human gamut it is everywhere the same, even to the affairs of the most modest of capitalists. The clergyman whose ten years' faithful ministry has resulted in the painful saving of a thousand dollars is very much at the mercy of his parish if his money is in land, and quite his own master if it be locked up in bonds or shares, merchantable at once in the great city which lies an hour's distance from his village. The tradesman in extremity is keenly aware of the advantage of collaterals over mortgage. Gloucester fishermen know the difference between sloops in the Bay of Fundy and a package of Boston and Maine R. R. stock stowed away in a bank-vault.

Nor is the proverbial sensitiveness of paper values any considerable bar to their popularity. Over all the rumor of fraud, of " street " artifices, of the perils of open market, and of whirlwind crises, is the mighty fact that the main bulk of securities in the great stock boards bear annual fruitage in interest, and are assured of instant sale at current prices. If we glance across the water to the great centres of finance, — London, Paris, Frankfort, — we perceive what immense consequences follow in the train of this modern tendency for convertible investment. In those controlling money-marts, the major portion of the assets of all the large houses are in paper evidences of sunken value. This paper, it is true, has a gold edge. The marginal annual worth, its interest-bearing dividend property, is coin. By virtue of one of the grandest outgrowths of our present civilization, — that profound yet strangely misunderstood instrumentality of finance, the share market, — it is indeed practically all coin up to the accepted limit of its selling capacity. The forms which it assumes are manifold. It lies in British consols, French *Rentes*, in all those weighty mortgages which nations in sore strait have executed over the whole property of their subject populations; in shares, bonds, — those representatives of absorbed wealth which have created English railroads, mines, banking-houses, and insurance companies, Credit Foncier and Credit Mobilier, transtlantic steam lines and subatlantic telegraphic cables, placing the locomotive in Russia and the far East, and joining the Mediterranean and the Red Sea by ship-canal. Curiously, — or what, at least, would be curious if the fact were not a part of education, — the most desirable of these assets lack one of the main essentials of conversion. Were all the capitalists of Europe to combine to-day, they could not compel England to redeem its national debt. And in degree, a like rule holds regarding all these securities. Interest in due season is certain. The principal in season or out of season is hard to reach. Nevertheless, for every purpose of life, this property is available. It has bought crowns. It has sustained governments. It is a perennial flower of auriferous bloom, whereby all that is splendid or solid or beautiful in Europe is made possible. The magnificence of courts, the glories of art, the permanence of industries, the serenity of humble firesides, the open hand of organized and consecrated charities, depend upon the stability of these values. In sum total they can only be estimated by billions. A shadowy frost-blight on the confidence of Capital, a tremor of doubt affecting these investments in slight per cent, is like the sudden engulfment of a vast fleet, home-laden with specie to the quarter-deck. It is a lightning annihilation of definite wealth, not less terrible because temporary, comparable only to a conflagration wrapping some imperial city, or the fitful prostration of whole industries. A most facile instrument of foreign exchange, the best possible groundwork for business loans, the safest vehicle of testamentary bequests, they have become the stanchest and pre-eminent bulwark of commerce. Yet without the interposition of the stock market, they would be the most volatile of values. Those startling variations in prices between almost contiguous centres of trade which characterized all the prime commodities of life in pre-railroad and pre-telegraph days would equally appear in the transactions of the kings of finance, if they were without the restraining influence of mutual consultation and the test of mutual desire afforded by the great Exchanges. The large economies consequent upon the symmetric working of the various Bourses and Stock-Marts of Europe compensate a hundred-fold for all excesses of speculation. On that intimate monetary sympathy which the wide connections of the principal bankers and the agency of the telegraph has brought about in England and on the Continent, the steadiness of the whole social fabric of the Old World may be justly said to hinge.

In America, up to the point when the exigencies of civil war compelled to a vast expansion of the national debt, there was nothing that could fairly admit of European comparison. We had our pivotal money-mart. We had minor Exchanges in certain important seaboard cities. In some particulars there had been an actual decline in the international influence of these financial centres. When Nicholas Biddle entered upon his gigantic scheme of making the Southern cotton yield the basis of a broad national credit, and our State legislatures had ventured into the London market with bonds as yet untarnished by the whisper of repudiation, foreign exchange was largely influenced, and the New York Stock Board assumed a dignity which the crisis of 1837 could not wholly efface. Thereafter, however, Wall Street concerned itself almost wholly with securities whose quotations were limited to this side the Atlantic. The tendency to become borrowers still inhered in the country.

but the creditor class was made up from among our own citizens. Municipalities provided for the wants of the future, in costly aqueducts, in spacious city-halls, in grand parks and generous avenues. States constructed imperial water-ways, and rendered themselves debtors for the assured education of the young, for the care of the insane and imbecile, for the protection of the law-abiding from the criminal, and through a proud solicitude for the quick development of their multitudinous domestic resources. The people themselves, conscious of the splendid promise of the great agencies of steam and electricity, supplemented the not wholly selfish purposes of capital by magnificent subscriptions to railroads, to telegraph companies, and to every form of industry which avails itself of the joint-stock principle.

The shares and bonds resulting from these growing necessities of a young and daring nation had everywhere a local market, and in large proportion were the subject of daily dealing at the New York Stock Exchange. That consciousness of the manifold uses of this form of investment which already filled Europe had seized upon the mind of every intelligent class in this country. It was a popular medium for the employment of the meagre savings of men on salaries, or the week's earnings of mechanics. It was not less the favorite with that more fortunate portion who sought security for surplus wealth. That current finance was already deeply affected thereby was notably made evident in the depressed days of 1854 and the subsequent revulsion of 1857, when the fact that the banks were more and more in the custom of lending money to brokers and merchants on security of stock was one of the most alarming revelations of the time.

Ever and anon, also, in the columns of the daily press it became apparent that these paper values were the instrument of speculative tactics, some of them as old as the Mississippi Land Scheme and 'Change Alley, while others, if not of purely American origin, yet had received their first definite nomenclature in our domestic share-mart. A degree of public interest attached to the proceedings. The morality of the United States, more effective, if not more earnest, than in recent years, launched forth invectives which carried force and in partial ways affected public opinion. A stock operator was regarded somewhat as lottery dealers are at present. In rural cities and villages the summer visit of brokers was an occasion of suspicion. At watering-places solid merchants warned their dames and daughters against these *ignes fatui* of wealth in the same terms of denunciation which opulence assumes toward social adventurers. And although the great capitalists of the nation, through whose agency railroad shares, State bonds, and other securities had become marketable, were well aware that in this epoch there cannot be a great people without a great stock exchange, and that, in comparison with the essential advantage of an open mart for the equalization of values, the chance profits of speculation were as naught, they nevertheless so far acquiesced in the prevailing opinion as to seek to cloak their intercourse with what was already known as "the Street." The great majority of brokers made it their pride that they performed a purely commission business. However much in the secret ledgers of their offices the outward assumption lacked confirmation, they claimed to be high-priests of the ideal in stock-market transactions.

In the final years of the last decade a palpable change began to disclose itself, both in opinion and action. Nice distinctions perceptibly crumbled. Railway directors were less chary of their reputations. Brokers had familiarized themselves with the idea that speculation was a necessity of their calling. The general public had apparently ceased to regard the stock market as something that could be overthrown by sentimental outbursts, and from accepting it as a fixed fact there was an evidently growing disposition to overlook its shortcomings in its larger usefulness.

Then came the terrible apparition of war, with swift-succeeding consequences. An enormous national debt was created, absorbing more than a billion and a half of dollars. Large emissions of greenback currency took the place of gold, and by its immense volume stimulated production and gave the loyal sections of the nation an aspect of sudden opulence. The earnings of all the great share companies were rapidly augmented. Railroad stocks began a succession of gigantic upward strides in the market, and through the deceptive appearance of increased values, a pretext was afforded for a notable expansion of paper capital. The mining corporations, operating in the distant West, declared unusual dividends. The genuine wealth, foreshadowed by the rich yield of Petroleum in Pennsylvania and Western Virginia, opened a new avenue for investment. And the excitement naturally growing out of the excessive demands upon reserved capital by the vast varieties of new securities was lifted to flood-tide by the exaggerations of speculation and the rumors of millionnaire fortunes disappearing and reappearing in the vortex of Wall Street.

In one form or another every citizen throughout the country was affected by the changed condition of affairs. Money always has a tendency to concentrate itself, and stocks, bonds, gold, rapidly accumulate at those points where the most considerable financial activity prevails. The greater the volume of floating wealth, the more conspicuous is this peculiarity. It resulted from this law that New York City became to the United States what London is to the world. Eminent before, this chief metropolis of the seaboard now assumed an absolute financial supremacy. Its alternations of buoyancy and depression produced corresponding perturbations in every State, city, and village in the land.

A strange sympathy exists between all descriptions of paper securities under a common monetary system. The reason may not always be apparent, but the fact never ceases to be apparent. A fall in one class may lead to a fall or rise in another class; there may even be a want of congruity between the date of the cause and the date of the effect; but the sympathetic relation remains constant, however perplexing its developments. Potent, therefore, through these subtle influences, over even the municipal and county bonds, — the shares and manifold securities of remote and insignificant communities, — the paramount money-mart exercised peculiar control over those larger values with which the share market especially concerns itself. The holder of Governments in Wisconsin or in Vermont sought the money value of his property, not on the face of his bond, but in the telegraph report of Wall Street transactions. Administrators of estates gauged their worth by multiplying each budget of State bonds, or railway shares, by the last "quotation" from New York. The Baltimore merchant who had made a shipment to Brazil when gold was 150 saw his venture return not only with the fair margin of commercial profit, but with the additional gain incident to a rise of specie to 260. Country traders found their local banks perpetually influenced by the ease or stringency of money in a city perhaps many hundreds of miles distant. Retail city dealers averaged the probabilities of the incoming month by the stock barometer, and expanded their orders with the rise of the market.

Moreover, these conservative considerations were not the only ones that formed the interest of Wall Street. Flushed with greenbacks, and influenced by the varying fortunes of our armies, the whole population of the North gave itself up to a speculative frenzy. Brokers were overwhelmed with orders. The slang of the stock-board found its way to the drawing-room. Everybody made ventures. Gold was the favorite with ladies. Clergymen rather affected mining-stock and Petroleum. Lawyers had a *penchant* for Erie. Solid merchants, preferring their customary staples, sold cotton or corn for future delivery, or bought copper and salt on margins. Some of the strange episodes of that period may be glanced at hereafter, but our present object is rather to indicate their existence, and to remark that the consequences of that excitement are likely to be permanent. The war, which made us a great people, made us also a nation in whom speculative ideas are predominant. The events of ten years have educated us into a certain scientific appreciation of hazards, into a greater degree of foresight, into a habit of action which combines conservatism with an aptitude for risks. To-day the wires of our telegraph companies are constantly burdened with orders to brokers from gold or stock operators, thickly scattered throughout every State in the Union. Many of these persons are large capitalists; the majority are salaried men, small merchants, individuals who deem it an averagely safe business to divert their surplus to the chances of the market. In sum total, the number is unquestionably one of high figures. Nor if we take into our reckoning the enlarged proportions of the values naturally the vehicle of speculation, and the inevitable fluctuations to which they are subject, is there any just reason for anticipating a decline in this tendency?

As a matter of fact, that power which, for lack of a better name, common usage denominates Wall Street, has become of overshadowing importance. The variations of its share market affect the whole volume of capitalized indebtedness the country through. Its loan market holds the keys of trade, and invigorates or depresses all our domestic industries. Its daily sales of gold influence our entire international commerce. Indeed, if the United States holds steadfastly to the prosperities of peace, in three decades it will be the controlling financial force of the world. At present, London, Frankfort, Paris, retain a certain supremacy, but the element of longitude is against them. The New York broker by high noon knows the aspect of the London stock market and the European Bourses. He scans their closing prices, while bids and offers are still resounding through the halls of our home Exchanges. Thus far the Cables serve only in respect to purely American securities, but the set of foreign speculative Capital is westward, and there is needed nothing but the growth of confidence to secure us the enormous advantage of the active employment of the accumulated wealth of England and the Continent.

To exhibit in all its profound aspects the working of our money centre, whether in its international relations or its influence upon our multiplex national life, would be an achievement of incalculable value. That no such work has yet appeared is doubtless due to the great embarrassments of the subject. It is needless to add that the present volume has far humbler pretensions. Its purpose is limited to a very incomplete survey of some of the more obvious phenomena of Wall Street, and with especial reference to its speculative transactions. What these phenomena are we shall now proceed to consider.

CHAPTER II.

THE NEW YORK STOCK EXCHANGE.

THE year 1835 was one of high speculation in New York. In January the famous Morris Canal and Banking Company "corner" culminated. The stock jumped from almost nothing to 185. In July and August Wall Street had so far forgotten the lesson that 64,000 shares of Harlem were sold for future delivery, although the whole capital stock was only $ 7,000. Incidental to this immense activity were corresponding "irregularities." Bartow, Cashier of the Commercial Bank of Albany, was a defaulter to the extent of $ 130,000. Wilding, an operator from London, disappeared with $ 45,000 worth of shares. Some of the members of the State Legislature were involved in the transactions, and one was expelled from the Senate. At Buffalo, Benjamin Rathbun had reached the climax of his land and house ventures, and was just on the eve of a $ 3,000,000 failure, with half his liabilities in bills bearing forged indorsements!

Does any one know how much Wall Street was worth in those days? It is a hard question, — to be solved only by inferences. There was a Jew operator, for example, who made occasional bank deposits of $ 500,000 in a day, and men spoke of it under their breath. Three years before a block of a million dollars in United States funds had been purchased, and the transaction was still town talk. The Stock Exchange itself was so far unequal to its young ambitions that it twice refused to enforce contracts in the case of brokers caught in the "corners," and on a test vote, in a week of unparalleled excitement, could only muster fifty-two members.

The lapse of thirty-five years has certainly wrought changes, and the contrast is as wholesome as it is remarkable. To-day the New York Stock Exchange includes in its roll-call over one thousand names. It eclipses all other stock organizations in the world for wealth. The daily credits and deposits of brokers in city banks and trust companies are estimated in hundreds of millions, and the par value of annual sales, made at the boards and "over the counter," are computed as considerably exceeding $22,000,000,000. This notable increase in financial importance has been attended by corresponding results. Speculations, which, in former times, swept over the street like a monsoon, now produce mere ripples. Defalcations, forgeries, bank robberies, disappear from sight and thought, as the sea closes over wrecks. A healthy conservatism and a profound sense of responsibility lie at the base of the vast proportion of operations, and whatever may be the vicissitudes of individual members, there is an unvarying enhancement of permanent collective wealth.

The present has another triumph over the past. In that very year 1835, just ten days before Christmas, occurred the great conflagration which must ever remain one of the dark memories of New York. The Stock Board, then meeting at the old Merchants' Exchange, became suddenly houseless, and from that day, for thirty years, it flitted hither and thither about the neighborhood, now in an attic over the Corn Exchange Bank, and again in rooms reached by obscure passage-ways off from William Street, — always without permanent abiding-place, and with none of the surroundings essential to give dignity and character to such a body. The energy of a few public-spirited and far-sighted members has changed all that. Through a building committee, incorporated under State law, a fund was subscribed, the result of which now appears in the fine and admirably ordered edifice, standing on the west side of Broad Street, a few steps off from Wall. Perfectly fire-proof, with a stately marble façade, free from any of the shams and flauntings of the "American" style of architecture, a magnificent vaulted basement, where property of vast value is held secure from theft or flame, and with spacions halls furnished forth with all the fitting appointments of an imperial business, the New York Stock Exchange is one of the most substantial and noteworthy structures in the metropolis.

Before entering the spacious Broad Street portal and surveying the interior, it is highly essential that the organization of the Board and the salient features of its daily routine should be thoroughly comprehended. On the 29th of July, 1869, the consolidation of the Government and the Open Boards with the old historic Stock Exchange, which had been provisionally completed for the space of two months, received its final confirmation by the passage of a revised Constitution and By-Laws. This new organic law is marked by a conservatism that cannot fail to impart a character and strength to the Association, such as its high representative position demands. As before, there is a President, whose office is mainly perfunctory, and there is a Treasurer of semi-annual importance; there are two Vice-Presidents, a Secretary with his Assistant, and the Roll-Keeper,— all intrusted with the duties naturally incumbent upon similar officers in every organization of men, and with the special and extremely arduous work incident to the daily sessions; but the real Executive control now rests with a Governing Committee, consisting of forty members, selected from the whole body, together with the President, Secretary, and Treasurer, in their unofficial capacity. All duties of administration, of legislation, of police, devolve upon this *imperium in imperio.* Divided into classes of ten, one of which goes out each year, the Committee, like its associate officers, is subject, in a certain degree, to the will of its constituency. But beyond its right of election at the annual meeting the Board is nearly powerless. The Governing Committee may make or unmake, suspend, expel, re-admit. It may even alter the entire letter of the Constitution or By-Laws, and unless two thirds of all the members of the Association disapprove thereof within one week, the changes become final law. So full an attendance of the Board as is required by this rule is almost unexampled, and the Committee is, therefore, practically as autocratic as the Venetian Council of ten. It is scarcely possible to overrate the excellence of this revolution, which has transferred the essential power from that impulsive, volatile, centrifugal aggregate of forces which meets daily "round the table," to a select and authoritative body, who combine with a great experience the sense of a great responsibility.

This Governing Committee, in reference to its varied functions, consists of seven subdivisions, whose duties correspond to the distinct objects for which the Association was created. The most vital of these objects are:—

First, the rigid scrutiny of all securities liable to be dealt in by the Exchange.

Second, a proper surveillance over members in respect to their fidelity to contracts, and a stringent examination of the good character and responsibility of candidates for membership.

Third, a systematization of the whole business of brokerage, so far as it relates to the intercourse of member with member.

No stock, bond, or other security can be dealt in by the Board, unless all the financial conditions, capital, number of shares, resources, etc., have been searchingly examined. As an additional safeguard, the Exchange binds itself to exclude any active speculative stock of any company which fails to keep a registry of shares in some responsible Trust Company, Bank, or kindred agency, and to give due public notice of every intention to increase its capital, either through the conversion of bonds or by direct issue, with the grounds for such increase. This exceedingly conservative provision owes its origin to the stock-jobbing improprieties of the directors of the Erie and other railway companies, whose manœuvres during the past decade have brought more discredit upon Wall Street operations than all other causes combined.

The rules for the admission of members, and for the government of those already enrolled in the organization, are necessarily very strict. In an arena where a mere nod may seal a contract involving hundreds of thousands, and a whisper is as binding as the longest and most cunningly phrased agreement of all the lawyers, men must have keen heads, vast experience, spotless business reputation. Every debt, every offer made and accepted, must be rigidly fulfilled. A member who fails must notify the President at once; he, in turn, announces it to the Board; the Secretary records the name on the fatal list; the stock which has occasioned the default is sold or bought in open market *under the rule;* and the broker loses every privilege of the Exchange until his creditors are satisfied, and the Governing Committee consents to his reinstatement. The reader has only to consult the Constitution to discover how carefully the Exchange has guarded itself against the hazards of failure, compelling "weak" members to supplement their contracts by heavy money deposit, punishing fraud by expulsion, rendering suspension a severe penalty by its network of rules framed out of extreme solicitude for the rights of the creditor. Not less exacting are the provisions for new membership. Brokers' clerks,—representing that alert, quick-witted, sure-footed class, which has grown up under the rough tuition of the street, knows its laws, comprehends the abiding sacredness of its verbal contracts, — find the doors of admission open much more readily than do men whose experience is limited to two or three years as capitalist brokers or bankers. The latter, indeed, must show a very clean record, and submit to a scrutiny in its very nature extremely irksome. In former years the black-ball played an efficient part in winnowing out candidates, and the new regimen, although probably more free from the influences of personal dislike, is likely in other ways to be not less exacting.

That portion of the government which concerns itself with the terms of each several class of contracts, and the regular order of business, can, in many respects, be more properly explained hereafter. It is a curious blending of law and usage, the latter being enforced as strictly as the former, although finding no place in the By-Laws. There is one point, however, demanding particular consideration. In all the great European share-marts there is a general executive organization differing only in local details from that by which the New York Exchange is regulated. But the functions of the officers cease at the moment when the real business of a stock-market begins. The syndic of the Paris Bourse, it is true, presides over the daily sessions ; but his duties are wholly subordinate, and the *agens de change* in the Corbeille — that basket-like chamber where the *parquet* assembles — direct the market quite at their pleasure. In the London Stock

Exchange even this semblance of authority is wanting. The daily meetings are simply the confluence of a mob, in which everybody bargains with everybody, in which there is no order, nor system, nor record of transactions.

The New York Stock Exchange, in this regard, has a completeness to be found in no similar transatlantic organization. The securities dealt in by the Board are divided into two classes, known respectively as the Regular and the Free List. No bond or stock can be or has been enrolled in either of these classes without due scrutiny in committee, and the ground of separation is simple: The Regular List must be called in sequence by the Vice-President in the chair: the Free List may or may not be called at the option of members. Of course, the former is the important class, and includes some two hundred and seventy-eight distinct securities, comprising all the great railway shares and bonds, State and city securities, bank-stock, and a curious *mélange* of express, telegraph, mining shares, etc., which is enumerated as "miscellaneous."

Every day, at half past ten in the morning, the First Vice-President ascends the rostrum, in the official chamber of the Stock Exchange, and goes through with the selected list in the subjoined sequence:—

FIRST. — Miscellaneous Stocks.

SECOND. — Railroad Stocks.

THIRD. — State Bonds.

FOURTH. — City Stocks.

FIFTH. — Railroad Bonds.

The assembled brokers, with their budget of orders, wait expectant; and the instant a stock is reached that is in their day's book, they spring into the arena with a bid or an offer. When a "speculative" or favorite stock is called, the excitement deepens, and the air is rent with rival cries. The presiding officer repeats the transactions to the Assistant Secretary at his side, who at once records them, while the "marker" or black-board clerk writes off the prices upon the tablet at the head of the room. Where there is a doubt regarding buyer or seller, the Vice-President decides, subject to immediate appeal in case of dissatisfaction; such brokers as witnessed the transaction voting and generally upholding the Chair.

As soon as the Regular Call is completed, the Free List is in order, and the Vice-President repeats the name of such stocks as the members may select for dealings, the Assistant Secretary recording every bid and the accompanying details. After this the session closes, unless the members in attendance wish to call up anew particular stocks on the Regular List; this provision allowing of dealings in those securities which were slurred over in the routine morning call.

At one o'clock the afternoon session is held, over which the Second Vice-President usually presides. The usages of the Morning Board apply here as well. The Vice-President holds the market in his hands, directs all movements, announces each transaction, and arbitrates in all disputes. The Assistant Secretary also renews his record of all biddings, and in his book, at the close, the whole history of the day's work appears.

Fifteen minutes before the first meeting at the Regular Board, the Government Board begins its sessions in an adjoining chamber. The same routine is observed: a Vice-President directs the market; an Assistant Secretary notes down against each class of national securities, as it passes the gantlet of the brokers, the prices offered and demanded, and every important feature of a transaction in case of positive sale. Were the stock-dealings of Wall Street limited to these two rooms, an efficient safeguard would exist against some of the most perilous phases of speculation. But it has happened, partly on account of the great volume of daily business, partly from a desire to avoid, for speculative reasons, this very registry, that a chamber is provided at the Exchange, where members may bargain with members at any hour throughout the day. This is known as the Long Room. Practically, then, the daily routine of brokers at the Boards might be classified, as follows:—

Government Securities.	All other Securities, Shares, Bonds, etc.
Government Board.	*Regular Board.*
Sessions 10¼, 12¼, 2¼.	Sessions 10½ A. M.; 1 P. M.

Every class of Speculative Stock on any list of the Stock Exchange.

Long Room.

Sessions Continuous, from the moment brokers come down in the morning, till night arrives to relieve them.

It is apparent, from what precedes, that the really important officers of the Stock Exchange are those in active duties at the daily sessions. The Vice-Presidents perform all the work which is not ornamental, with the Secretary and his Assistant as active coadjutors. Next in usefulness is the Roll-Keeper. He records the fines, and no body of men are to all appearance more fond of breaking over minor rules, and promptly meeting the penalty, than New York stockbrokers. The annual dues of the Exchange are only fifty dollars, but the fines of individual members not seldom mount up to nearly ten times that sum. Any interruption of the presiding officer while calling stocks renders a broker liable to a penalty, "not less than twenty-five cents" for each offence. To smoke a cigar within the Exchange costs five dollars. Non-attendance at special meetings subjects one to a fine of anything under five dollars. A broker cannot stand on a table or chair without paying a dollar; or innocently fling a "paper dart" at a neighbor without being amerced ten dollars. It costs twelve and a half cents to call up a stock not on the Regular List, and all the way from one to five dollars to do anything not enumerated in these offences which may be deemed indecorous by the Presiding Officer.

Besides the register of fines, there is another officer whose name has no place in the publications of the Board, but whose services are perpetually called into requisition by almost every member, and whose presence is an inevitable and formidable apparition to a chance visitor at the Exchange. Concerning his *rôle* we shall presently have occasion to speak somewhat fully, for the now sufficiently instructed reader will

CHAPTER III.

A DAY AT THE BOARDS.

THE first impression on entering the Stock Exchange is upon the tympanum. A genuine tourist almost inevitably has a dreamy reminiscence of Niagara. The visitor finds himself in the vestibule of a vast chamber, which stretches a furlong deep from Broad to New Street. At the farther end, shut off by successive iron barriers with narrow gateways under watch and ward, is a huge basin-like enclosure, filled with wild human tumult. Peering down through the high-vaulted, dim-lighted space, the eye sees nothing but excited faces, arms flung wildly in air, heads appearing and disappearing, — a billowy mob, from which surges up an incessant and confused clamor. The straining ear distinguishes ever and anon an individual voice rising in shriller pitch or heavier volume, only to be drowned by fifty other cries booming and echoing out from the abyss. This chaos of plunging sound and deafening roar is the Long Room. To comprehend it, one must approach nearer. Previons to such visit, however, a stranger should instruct himself by mounting the staircase at the left and studying the more orderly proceedings of the regular sessions.

Just at the head of the stairway are the private and public approaches to the Regular Board. At ten in the morning we can take a leisurely survey of the architectural peculiarities of the room. Opening the nearer door, we suddenly confront the mild-mannered Cerberus of the Stock Exchange. The reader has already been forewarned of this unescapable phenomenon. His duty is to challenge every stray-comer. Properly introduced by officers or members, you can pass. Without these credentials, there is no ingress. His guards are stationed at every doorway. They rise up before you at all the avenues to the Long Room. They stand athwart the threshold of the Government Board. One might as well attempt to visit the Kabla at Mecca without swearing by the Prophet, as to enter the sacred arena of the brokers, when lacking satisfactory introduction. Besides his sterner function, "Peter," the door-keeper, acts as a sort of general factotum. When telegraphic messages arrive for brokers inside, he shouts the name with a resonant voice rolling high above the clangor of the stock market. In fact, with his leash of page-boys who assist him in distributing the incoming telegrams, he is one of the most remarkable institutions of the room. Sixteen years at his post, he has grown into his place, and the broker guild could no more do without him than they could speak of him other than by his Christian-name. Showing our permit with the authentic signature of President Neilson, Peter nods his head graciously, and we walk forward. We are now in a hall some seventy feet long and fifty broad. The lofty walls are lined with heavy green damask. At the base of the room, and running round the most of two sides, is an iron railing behind which there is ample accommodation for that motley throng which daily gathers in the strangers' gallery. Within this enclosing balustrade, in the space reserved to brokers, the floor slopes gradually toward us in terrace after terrace of arm-chairs, until it reaches the interspace in front; then it falls sharply right and left into a series of semicircular steps leading to a hollow in the middle, where stands an elongated table at right angles to the official rostrum. This is the point where the excitement of the Board fuses to white heat, the central centre, the maelstrom, the mid arena of the combat. Above is the platform of the officers, with the President's pulpit-like elevation flanked on the left by desks for three secretaries, on the right by that of the Roll-Keeper. Two black tablets on either side against the wall slide up through easy grooves, at the will of the recording clerk. On these the prices of the more active stocks are marked off as rapidly as made. At the extreme west corner is a telegraph key-board, and on the east the gold indicator. Installed in gilded frames, the keen faces of old John Ward and Jacob Little overlook the transactions of a generation whose daily dealings eclipse those of these giant veterans in a lifetime.

All the time that we have been glancing about us the floor has been filling up. Some twenty or thirty members are standing round the table, others are chatting idly among the arm-chairs. Peter watches at the entrance with four or five page-boys around him. The blackboard clerk is looking over his crayons. Shrewd-eyed, wide-awake Secretary Broadhead has just seated himself in his throne-like chair, and is already surrounded by half a dozen brokers. The Roll-Keeper is opening his book, and the Assistant Secretary is adjusting himself to his desk. Lithe, light-haired, pleasant-faced Vice-President Wheelock, who has borne the honors and ardor of office full thirteen years, every May-day more alert and popular, bends over his stock-jobbing pulpit, and sharp at the half-hour calls the Board to order. As there was no official business at yesterday's session, there are no minutes to be read, and the day starts abruptly with the Regular List.

V. P. "Delaware and Hudson Canal. Any bids ?"

As no broker makes an offer, the mallet rings down upon the desk, and the call proceeds —:

"Pennsylvania Coal, Central Coal, Cumberland Coal, American Coal, Spring Mountain Coal, Canton Company, Western Union Telegraph —"

Voice. "I 'll give '5 for a hundred, — '5 for a hundred, — '5 for a hundred."

Other Voices. "A hundred at ⅝." "Five hundred at a ½." "Any part of five hundred at a ¼."

First Voice. "I 'll take a hundred."

V. P. "At 5¼. A hundred at 5¼. Any bids ?" *Rap. Rap.* "That will do for that stock. — Quicksilver."

Robust Bidder. "12 for a hundred,' — "12," —' "12½," — "13," — "14" —

Voice. "Sold."

Simultaneous Second Voice. "I take that stock."

V. P. "One hundred to Snow at 14."

Second Voice. "I claim that lot, Mr. President."

V. P. "The Chair decides that Snow made the purchase."

Second Voice. "I appeal."

V. P. "Is the appeal seconded?"

Fresh Voices. "Second the motion."—"Second the appeal."

The Vice-President brings the question before the Board, and Broker No. 2 has but three votes to show for it.

V. P. "The Chair is sustained. Go on with the stock. Mariposa. Any bids?—Pacific Mail."

And so the mill grinds on. Nigh a billion and a half of bonds and shares will be flung into the swaying crowd, before the list is ended. Old prices disappear; new prices come forth, and the click of the telegraph is already helping the financial world to go over its ledgers anew, and record the shrinkage of a hundred million dollars, or twice that sum of fresh new wealth born of a buoyant market, and destined perchance to untimely death before the sun has swept twenty-four hours farther through the eternities.

As the moment for the call of Railroads approaches, the chamber assumes a vast access of life. A fresh stream of brokers pours through the private passage, and eddies round the President's desk, or swirls off toward the base of the room, where eager crowds are discussing the terms of loans, or are improvising private markets for the various shares. Behind the public railing a motley throng has gathered,—the curious or the anxious, small speculators, merchants from the country down town to see the sights, all sorts of persons from all sorts of places, by dozens on quiet days, in shoals of hundreds on hundreds when the rumor of a great speculative campaign is abroad. Through this dense aggregate of inquisitiveness, intermittent messenger-boys twist in and out, carrying hurried whispers back to offices, or dashing forward with emergent orders for brokers whose names are shouted by the page-boys in shrillest treble.

The roar from the cock-pit rolls up denser and denser. The President plies his gavel, the Assistant Secretaries scratch across the paper, registering bids and offers as for dear life. The black tablet slides up second by second with ever-fresh figures evolved from the chaos below. Every tongue in every head of all this multiform concourse of excited or expectant humanity billowing hither and thither between the walls, is adding its contribution to the general bedlam. The keenest weather-beaten operator of all that outside world in the gallery vainly strives to follow the biddings of the voices "round the table," — those voices of destiny, which he wishes most to hear, torn in a hundred tattered shreds of sound by the intervening shoutings, shrieks, and sibillations. Peter, now overworked by ever-fresh arrivals of telegrams and orders, bellows out "Smith," "Jones," "Robinson," in interminable succession, the names exploding in mid air with the crash of a forty-pounder. Failing of response, Peter discharges his pages like a sheaf of rockets into the tumult, and "Jones, JONES,

Jones, Smith, JONES," mingle with "Buyer 30," "A half," "Seven eighths," "Cash," the tara-ta-ta-tat of the auction hammer, and whatever else aids the confusion.

Suddenly the Chair shouts, "New York Central."

At this word a thrill of excitement permeates the room. A whirl as of a tempest carries every broker to the great interspace in front. The table has momentarily disappeared from sight. In its place is a tide of swaying hands and faces. The rattle of the President's hammer is like the falling of a pin in the immense confluence of shoutings. "I 'll sell five hundred at 95." No bid! "At 4½, buyer 10." "Take 'em." "Five hundred more." No bid! "Five hundred at 4." "Five hundred at 3, seller 30." "At 2, cash." "Any part of a thousand at 90." This last offer is as a huge stone flung into a geyser. A silence born of astonishment and dismay fills the multitude, followed by the plunging roar of a hundred voices.

Up in the eastern corner a grave-faced man has his fingers on the key-board, and is spreading the news of this fierce "bear" raid, by which Central has been hammered down five per cent, through four hundred bankers' and brokers' offices.

Down in the cock-pit the Commodore's "pups," as the merciless, cacophonic "street" argot denominates the broker friends of Vanderbilt, are making an ineffective rally. They have carried up Central to 91, 1⅛, 1¼, 1½, when the load proves too heavy, and the sliding downward scale begins, and again *Ursa Major's* voice sounds out like a bassoon, — "At 90, buyer 3 or 30; any part of five thousand."

V. P. "Any part of five thousand is offered at 90, buyer 3 or 30, — what 's bid ?" The hammer is poised for the fall which will clench Central at 90. Just on the second, however, a little wiry man, who has been wriggling through the contending gladiators with a crumpled bit of paper in his tightening hand, screams out in the face of the king bear: "I 'll take your lot, and five thousand more. 91 for a thousand, — '2 for five thousand, — '3 for any part of five thousand." A fusillade of voices follows the leader cry. The ear catches "3¼," — "⅞," — "4," — "5." "Take 'em." "Sold." "Two hundred more." "Sold." "A hundred more." No response. Down goes the gavel, and Central closes firm at 95. Hudson succeeds and Harlem after, the bulls now jubilant and holding the market. While the battle goes on in the cock-pit, a whisper spreads that the money-market is active and loans have risen to seven per cent, and ⅛, ¼, or ⅜ commission.

V. P. "Northwestern. What 's bid ?"

A voice like a sledge-hammer. — "A hundred at ⅞, five hundred at ¾, any part of a thousand at ½."

Half a dozen brokers. — "Give you ¼ for a hundred." "⅜ for five hundred !" "⅝ for a hundred !"

First Voice. "Sold. Five hundred more. Five hundred at ⅜; five hundred at ¼. A hundred at an ⅛; a hundred at '4. Help yourselves, boys, at '3¾, regular or buyer 3."

The market trembles. The bulls hesitate. The tightening money-market is doing its work. Other bears fling themselves into the *mêlée.* Northwestern plunges downward. Twenty hands are snapping out whole volleys of descending bids, — "Two hundred at '4." "Two hundred at '3$\frac{7}{8}$." "Take 'em," cries a bull, struggling to hold the market. "Five hundred more at $\frac{7}{8}$." "A hundred at $\frac{3}{4}$." "I'll give $\frac{1}{2}$ for a hundred!" "Sold." "Five hundred more." "Five hundred at $\frac{3}{8}$." "Take 'em at a $\frac{1}{4}$." A sudden lull at this last bid. The Vice-President seizes his opportunity. "That will do for that stock. No more offered. The stock" (turning to the "marker") "closes at 85$\frac{1}{4}$ – $\frac{3}{8}$."

"Rock Island, gentlemen!"

And so on and on, pausing for five minutes over some speculative stock or a new State bond, and racing forward at the rate of ten, twenty, or even twice that number in the same space, when the securities belong to the investment class. The Regular Call completed, the Free List is in order, and the President brings forward such stocks as the brokers present wish to deal in. Possibly the stock of some wild-cat oil company may be named, and a member, anxious to appreciate its value, will bid "15 for a hundred, — 20 for a hundred, — 25 for a hundred." Other brokers in irony shout: "A hundred at '5$\frac{1}{2}$." "Five hundred at $\frac{7}{8}$." The Vice-President cries, "Any more bids? Oilville Scrip. 25 bid." Up go all the hats, and the Board breaks out in a round of admiring cheers. Still more stocks, new bids and offers, now a light pattering, and anon a driving storm of cries.

Suddenly a Secretary mounts the rostrum. A silence as of the tomb overspreads the chamber. Every hat is lifted decorously from head. The death of a member is announced with a few appropriate words. Then back go the hats, bids and offers resound once more, and the coffin is forgotten in the coupon.

By this time the room is almost deserted. A straggling half-dozen spectators stand near the door. Perhaps twenty-five brokers are round the table. The Free List is rapidly finished off. If any member wish to bring forward a particular stock on the Regular List, which was hastily passed over at the first call, now is his season. Fortunately for the reader, the bidding today is very brief, and in a few moments the Board adjourns.

As we pass into the corridor, we notice a boy at a side-stand with the morning share-list for sale, printed in a private office up stairs almost on the second that the first call is finished. The Bankers and Brokers' telegraph, whose wires are just at the left, has, however, superseded this list to a great extent, and it is now useful mainly for files.

Before us, opening on the floor where we now stand, is the room of the Government Board. The bidding there is still going forward, but only a small portion of the members are. present. In fact, in order to see this chamber in full excitement, it is necessary to be on hand at the first call. The early Board meets at a quarter past ten.

Had we entered at that hour, we should have found ourselves in an apartment little more than a third of the size of that occupied by the Regular Board, with much the same appointments, but with this difference, that there is no cock-pit, and the sumptuously cushioned seats rise tier on tier from the floor to the green tapestry of the wall. In these chairs the Government Brokers sit. At the head of the chamber is the rostrum for the officers, and the order of proceedings is very little dissimilar from that which we have already witnessed. The Vice-President begins : —

"6s '81 registered, — '81 coupon. 5-20s '62 registered, — coupon. What 's bid ?"

Here and there from the flanking chairs come sputtering bids or offers : —

"Ten thousand at ⅜, buyer 3."

"I 'll give an ⅛, seller 3, for the lot."

"¼, buyer 30, for fifty thousand."

"¼, regular, for any part of five thousand."

First Voice. "Sold, — five hundred."

The presiding officer repeats the sale and terms, the Secretary makes his registry, and a new bond is started.

Sometimes when 5-20s are called, there is at first only one voice, which rings the changes on "I 'll give 115. I 'll give '15 for a thousand, — '15 for a thousand." Presently, however, before any response follows the offer, a member in a distant corner, either carelessly or maliciously, shouts out, "I 'll give '14 for a thousand, — '14 for a thousand."

The Vice-President plies his hammer. "Fine Irving, — fine Irving fifty cents." The Roll-Keeper proceeds to make his little note of it, and Irving, who has violated the rule, founded on common-sense, which forbids a member from making a bid below or an offer above the one which has the floor, immediately subsides amid the laughter of his neighbors.

Occasionally an interruption of a grosser character occurs, a member leaping from his seat on some slight provocation, and striking off the hat of the man who has offended. "Fine Harrison, fine Harrison again, *fine*, FINE him again, — FINE Harrison," cries the Vice-President, repeating the word without cessation until the broker's wrath has been appeased, and he returns to his chair with the disagreeable reflection that a heavy score is against him for the semiannual settlement-day. Every repetition of that fatal monosyllable was a fresh mark of fifty cents or a dollar against his name. Generally, however, the Government brokers are more orderly than their neighbors in the Regular board. Indeed, the whole proceedings are more decorous and respectful, the bidding, half the time, being carried on in a low conversational tone. At second call there is a brief excitement, but when "things are dull" throughout the street, this room peculiarly reflects the external influences.

Very different it is, however, on days when some special cause provokes great fluctuations. Then the members spring from their seats, arms, hands, excitable faces, rapid vociferations, all come in play, and the element of pantomime performs its part in assisting the human voice as naturally as among the Italians of Syracuse. To the uninitiated the biddings here are as unintelligible as elsewhere, sounding to ordinary ears like the gibberish of Victor Hugo's Compachinos. But the comparative quietude of this Board renders it easier to follow the course of the market, to detect the shades of difference in the running offers, and generally to get a clearer conception of this part of the machinery of stock brokerage. Nor is it only for grasping those special brevities of utterance with which sales are affected, — as condensed as the military vocabulary of Hardee's Tactics, — that this Board is a good school. One can study not less readily that other feature of the market, — the theatrical effects, the simulated eagerness which seeks to influence values by the energy with which offers are made, as if an immense money force were at work to crush down 5-20s to zero, or to tide them up to limitless heights. It is the skill of fencers, the false lunges, the flourish which may mean a parry or a thrust, a perpetual series of deceptions which never deceive. One slowly comes into a clear understanding that all these enthusiasms are stale; that, although in some instances the tactics are freshly evolved from the unexpected developments of the day, the main shaping of the register is very much like the results of a political caucus in which all motions and nominations have been previously arranged, and whatever is novel is due to the clashing of opposing cliques. If the visitor wishes to master one problem at a time, therefore, he will keep his seat in this chamber, and he will find abundant room for reflection in the thought that here around him are the men who daily gauge the value of a billion and a half of national debt, whose shouts are the annihilations of millions or a crest-wave of momentary fresh wealth, rippling through bank-vaults and the iron chests of the thrifty, east and west along the tremulous wire, to San Francisco at one end and Frankfort at the other.

In "doing" the Stock Exchange for the first time, however, it is well to content one's self with the merely outward aspects. Brokerage is a science, and, apart from the technical difficulties, the phenomena of the Boards depend upon a great number of distinct forces, all acting from without and only disclosing themselves vaguely in the prices of the daily share list. Here on the upper floor the official record has notched the last wave line of each billowing security, but below fresh elements are working, and in the heaving caldron of the Long Room is a changeful ebb and flow that has neither rule nor limit nor certainty. There, least of all, should one resort for a key to the mystery of the street; but, having visited it, the reader will have prepared himself for the explanations of subsequent chapters.

You can reach the Long Room from the antechamber on Broad Street, from the Gold Room by a side entrance, or from New Street, — the latter ingress affording a better opportunity to the spectator.* As we have before stated, it is a deep basin, broken up into circles of broad steps descending one below the other to a floor,

* The presence of a spectator in the Long Room must be understood as metaphorical. That theatre of finance cannot be approached, as we are informed by most eminent officials, except by payment of fifty dollars. This, to be sure, will purchase a season ticket. But as single admission is only possible on the same terms, it makes this dramatic performance the most costly in the world. The cause of this exclusiveness, which has, to say the least, an absurd aspect to mere sight-seers, is partly because of the incessant calls upon the courtesy of officers, but chiefly

THE LONG ROOM.

perhaps fifteen feet in diameter. When the Regular Board is convened, this room is usually deserted; but it can scarcely ever be called empty, and, frequently, long after half past ten the chamber seethes with a crowd unwilling to leave the perpetually fresh sensations of the free market for the slow routine of official sessions.

At all other hours the Long Room is thronged, sometimes densely thronged. Here the great bulk of purchases and sales are made. In the Regular Board an average of seven million dollars' worth of shares are sold in a day. In the Long Room, brokers roughly estimate that ten times that amount is bought or sold between sunrise and nightfall. On field-days the whole capital stock of a speculative railroad will be tossed from hand to hand in the financial shuttlecock. A hundred dollars become three millions, or a million lessens to a mill.

There are the same shouts, the same cries of messenger-boys, the same confusion of hands and arms, which one finds in the rooms above; but here everything is more intense, blinding, deafening. Every broker has a different mission. Two hundred and seventy-nine members may be bidding for two hundred and seventy-nine different stocks in the same breath. Just as in the Ni-

from the fact that the lobbies on both the Broad and the New Street sides have been found very valuable places of resort to "outside" brokers and speculators. The frequenters have nearly all the advantages of regular brokers, and though they are not permitted to join in the Long Room cries, there is nothing to prevent their making quiet bargains on the basis of current bids. Nearly all the old "curbstone" dealers now hold tickets, and are willing to pay the small annual charge for the privilege of warmth, use of room, and the superb chances for speculation.

agara whirlpool there are innumerable minor eddies, whirls within whirls; so here, also, there will be a little circle of Erie, another of Pacific Mail, New York Central, Rock Island, or any other great speculative stock, with the skirting swirl of fifty other stocks boiling up in spasms and flowing into a vast maelstrom of sound.

Orders of every description and of every conceivable amount come in from Philadelphia, Boston, Baltimore, from strange small towns in border States, from the regions of corn and cotton and iron, from where the spindle flies incessantly or the sugar-cane crackles in the mill, — from the capitals of Europe and the capitals of new-fledged States. No city would seem too great or village too small not to have some vivid interest in this smelting-furnace of values. Laden with these commissions, with the secret instructions of some king operator, with private schemes of their own, the brokers fling themselves into the *mêlée* with "What 's bid for Lake Shore?" "Five thousand Lake Shore at 89, buyer 30." "At '8⅞, cash." "Take 'em." "Who?—how many?" "Five hundred." "All right." "Hundred St. Paul at ½, buyer 3." "⅜, seller 3, for a hundred." "Fort Wayne." "Northwest." "Any part of a thousand at ½, *cash.*" "One hundred at ⅜." "Erie at ¼, *cash.*" "I want five hundred Reading." "Give '2⅞ for three hundred Central." "I 'll loan two hundred." "I 'll take a hundred *flat.*" "Fifty Rock Island at '4⅝." "Hundred at ⅝." "I 'll sell a hundred more." "Take 'em." "Give it for five hundred more."

Peaked faces, rosy faces, faces like sunshine, and faces

over which ripple all forms and shadows of expression. Voices like a church-organ and voices like a bag-pipe; stridulous, whooping, screeching, deep-toned, piping voices, — voices like a trip-hammer crashing through all other cries, and carrying the whole market down by an offer as tremendous as the lungs which gave it birth. Every step and crevice jammed with men. Note-books, arms, fists, dexter fingers, hats, heads, tossing, swaying, darting hither and thither with nervous eagerness, and suggesting a perpetual explosion of bomb-shells from below. Now concentrating upon a single stock; again breaking out into twenty different markets. Supple youths loom up above the level, with feet apparently planted upon nothing and standing firmly there, snapping up an odd lot of Pacific Mail here, and selling five thousand Michigan Southern there, buying a "put," making a loan, doing it all in the same moment like flashing lightning, and then like lightning disappearing in the broadcloth darkness. Dante, gazing down into this human craze, would have added another book to *Il Inferno.* Men might go mad here and no one know it. In this hot air and reeling life they *would* go mad, were it not for that great undercurrent of humor which bubbles up continually through the earnest confusion. In the old days when buying Erie was not like pumping out the Atlantic Ocean, and Daniel Drew was wont to send in a legion of brokers with cross orders of "carry it up to 90," or "sell it down to 80," and the Long Room would lurch and roll under the tornado of perplexing orders and bids, a lank face once emerged from the crowd with a rocket-like cry of "I'll buy any part of half a million Erie at 33!" Smash went the man's hat down over his eyes. "Give us a power of attorney on your brandy-bottle at Delmonico's," shouted somebody. A roar of laughter followed, and, the fit of fun still on, a broker with rich, mellow voice struck up, —

"John Brown's body lies a mouldering in his grave";

the whole assembly beating time with feet and hand, and joining uproariously in the chorus.

Such transitions are of daily occurrence, and the immense flow of ready gayety perpetually relieves the tense and jaded brains of the *habitués* with some fresh and lively outburst.

Usually the Long Room begins to thin out by four in the afternoon, but in periods of high speculation the session prolongs itself till five, the flickering jets of gas from the pillars throwing a ghastly flare over the pale and weary faces.

In the feverish days of the war, night brought no rest to the stockbrokers. Scarcely was dinner well through than up at Madison Square, first in a cellar beneath the Fifth Avenue Hotel, afterward in Gallaher's Exchange at the Broadway corner of Twenty-Third Street, the members came together anew, and carried on their hoarse and frantic biddings far into the small hours. The Jenkins and Ketchum defalcations fortunately checked this human madness; but even at present, during every access of speculative excitement, throngs gather in the corridors of the Fifth Avenue Hotel, and country guests can hear on every side the confusing street slang, with its subdued but significant utterances of "Take 'em!" "A thousand more!" "Closed at a quarter!" Should we follow the individual broker through a single twenty-four hours, we should have a still more startling conception of the engrossing character of this profession. At waking, he calls for his morning paper and reads once more the "quotations" of yesterday. His breakfast is a sandwich of toast and Fort Wayne, or Central, or 5-20s. He talks stock all the way down town in the stage. He bids from nine till five; he whispers of street incidents to his neighbor in the up-town car; he dines upon stocks, he mingles stocks with the smoke of his post-prandial cigar, he crams his "book" in his pocket and saunters up to the Fifth Avenue, and when finally he consents to retire, he dreams of stocks the whole night long. This ceaseless tread-mill would seem to be quick murder. Yet, averagely, a healthier class cannot be found than that of men who deal in stocks. They are robust, cheerful, bubbling over with animal spirits. One reason, undoubtedly, is that they are thoroughly good livers. They dine well and dress well. But beside this, the luck of the market compels them to a sensible philosophy. None know better the fickleness of fortune. None bear up more bravely under reverses. The very variety of their life is healthful. Routine itself is poisonous to brain and body, but the technicalities and small details of brokerage soon become a sort of second nature, and the mind is left free to enter into all the absorbing intricacies of speculation, replete with dramatic episodes, and so fascinating that the gains or losses would be as nothing, were they not essential elements in the successful issue of the game.

To understand the real life of the broker, and to acquire a clear perception of the daily features of the Stock Boards, one must be content to begin with the alphabet and master the language. It is impossible to comprehend the business of Wall Street unless all the conditions of sale and purchase are accurately set forth, unless broker's terms are rendered thoroughly intelligible, and the main forces which group around the market are distinctly grasped. Some of these details, however important, are not the less notably dry and a weariness to the soul. But without a proper apprehension of all the cog-wheels and running gear of speculation, the game itself will be only a delusion and a snare.

CHAPTER IV.

THE MACHINERY OF SPECULATION.

THAT portion of the world at large whose evil genius has borne it, willingly or unwillingly, into court-rooms and lawsuits, is probably familiar with that sublimity of humbug known as Legal Fiction. Its cardinal idea is that things are not what they are. The New York Stock Exchange has a pleasant hallucination of this kind. All its members are supposed to be brokers till proved to be otherwise. This proof is diligently not sought for.

The absurd hypothesis has an advantage. It enables us to consider the theoretical as the practical. The New York Stock Board, then, according to the presumption of its constitution, is an organization of agents who purchase or sell stocks or bonds on commission. This commission, when a customer buys for regular investment, is one quarter of one per cent on the par value of securities. In case of speculative transactions, one half of this is charged. Recently a saving clause has been adopted, making these rules binding *where no agreement has been made to the contrary*. There is an immense meaning in those italics. They can be understood better, however, if disregarded just at present.

Throwing out of view the question of regular investment, this broker's per cent amounts to twelve and a half cents, or a New York shilling, upon every transaction in shares whose par value is one hundred dollars. To the uninstructed reader this is a microscopic item. One and a quarter mills on the dollar is to the cent per cent of a Broadway loan office what infusoria are to the megatherium. The tax is certainly not exorbitant, but its sum total is worth considering.

We have before us the authorized list of shares, bonds, and governments dealt in by the Stock Exchange. Comparing this schedule with the published statements of the various incorporations, etc., as to the full volume and par value of all these securities, we find that the sum in gross is considerably above three billions of dollars. If the New York brokers should have this amount of values pass through their hands once only in the year, their profit as agents would be three million seven hundred and fifty thousand dollars. Moreover, it is to be noted that to every buyer there is a seller, and that on both transactions the commission is levied. Obviously, therefore, the real percentage is doubled, or two and a half mills on a dollar. In other words, the brokers would take seven and a half millions out of the whole every time the entire bulk is sold. How often does such a sweeping sale occur? Perhaps never, but its equivalent is sold on an average about every two months. This is ascertainable partly through the records of stock sales. In 1868, at the Regular, and the now non-existent Open boards, there were bought 19,713,402 shares. The bonds bought during the same period are stated at a par valuation of $245,245,240. Calling $100 the par of stock, and adding the two amounts, we have a sum total of two billions two hundred millions.

But we are only on the threshold of a proper estimate. Ask an intelligent broker where sales are chiefly effected. The answer will be, "Stocks, in the Long Room; governments, over the counter." At the official boards, we shall be told, there is scarcely one tenth of the real business of the stock market. Unfortunately, no registry is kept of these other transactions, and in reckoning them as ten times the whole sum we are liable to the danger attendant upon all conjectural calculations. Even on the supposition that the recorded sales are one eighth of the amount subject to the percentage we shall have a total of over seventeen and a half billions. The two and a half mills taken at the twofold sale and purchase of one dollar's worth of securities would give, if levied in similar proportions upon the entire bulk, a tax through commissions of forty-three million seven hundred and fifty thousand dollars.

There are not more than four hundred stockbrokers who do any considerable business on "the street." Dividing up this percentage among that number of members of the Exchange, we find that it will allow of a yearly income to each of about $109,000!

These figures explain by inference the secret of the rule, which makes the broker's per cent subject to modification, viz. in case of *agreement to the contrary.* Members naturally compete with each other, and a reduction to a half, or even a quarter, of the full commission is frequent street practice. There are the One-Sixteenth men, who take 6¼ cents on the hundred dollars; the One-Thirty-Second class, who are satisfied with 3⅛ cents; and even a One-Sixty-Fourth class, who make no objection to dividing the preceding profit by two. The larger the order, the greater the reduction.

This commission is levied upon the par value of stock. A share selling at 35 costs as much, in the matter of broker's per cent, as one quoted at 90 or 110. It is charged when the stock is bought, and again upon sale; and the greater proportion of really first-class houses adhere to the *one eighth of one* percentage, even in the case of old customers. This is, unquestionably, one of the most profitable features of brokerage, and there are firms whose yearly commissions amount to upward of a million dollars. The great rivalry for orders, however, has sensibly reduced the gain from this source, and the average of all transactions is probably not above $6.25 on 100 shares of stock, the par of which would be $10,000.

When a customer has arranged the terms of commission, the next question is how the stock is to be bought or sold. To approach this part of the machinery properly, it is desirable to concentrate the attention upon what may be styled "ideal brokerage."

The ideal of brokerage is the purchase or sale of securities for outside parties, where the object is an absolute acquisition of property, or absolute sale of property. Generally speaking, there must be in such case a deposit of the stock or of the money value of the stock.

Of course, this rule loses its rigidity where the customer is a heavy capitalist or a person of recognized responsibility; brokers, in such event, habitually buying on no further guaranty than a verbal or telegraphic order.

The first point necessary to know is when the customer wishes to receive or deliver the stock. He may prefer to-day, to-morrow, or a more distant date. Each of these methods of settlement has a special name.

Cash, in broker's language, means that the contract entered upon shall be fulfilled by payment and delivery of stock, at or before 2.15 P. M. of the day of sale.

Regular, or *Regular Way*, is the term for sale when the delivery is to be made at or before 2.15 P. M. of the day succeeding that of contract.

Buyer's Option, is where the purchaser has the right to require the delivery of stock upon any day within the time covered by the option.

Seller's Option, is where the day of delivery is at the convenience or pleasure of the person making the sale, within the time stipulated at the moment of sale.

In all cases, notice must be given by the holder of the option to the other party in the contract, on or before two o'clock of the day previous to that when delivery of stock is called for; but the stock is deliverable at the termination of the contract without notice.

The sharp elliptical offers and bids at the Boards express the options in such phrases as Buyer 3, Seller 10, Seller 30, Buyer 30, — the numerals standing for the number of days during which the option continues. So far as concerns the principle of this transaction, there is nothing to hinder contracts extending to any point in the year; but to brokers a sale buyer 7, buyer 9, buyer 11, 12, 21, etc., would affect the ear like a wrong note in music. Custom has made 3, 10, 30, 60, 90, the usual figures for both descriptions of options.

A broker receiving an order to sell 500 shares of the Chicago Rock Island and Pacific Railroad Company, at 105, would go to the Board, and, according to his instructions, shout out, "I 'll sell 500 Rock Island at '5' cash," "500 at '5' regular," "500 '5' seller 3," "500 '5' buyer 30," dependent upon the desire of his customer.

It is apparent that where the seller wishes money at once, he sells *Cash;* where he hopes to get a better price, or cannot make a delivery of stock until next day, he sells *Regular;* where a still longer time is required before he can make a delivery, he sells *Seller's Option,* or if ready for delivery at any moment, he sells *Buyer's Option,* and thereby gets a better price, as the buyer is willing to pay proportionately for the advantage which the advantage of time gives him.

Cash, Regular, and a three days' option bear no interest. Beyond three days' option six per cent interest *(per annum)* is paid by the buyer from the day of sale to the day of delivery. And this interest is due whether the sale be on buyer's or seller's option, the rule being that the actual holder of stock should be remunerated for the time during which his property lies dead in his hands.

Transactions either by Cash or Regular Way are carried through, usually, by verbal contract alone; and, in general, a nod of the head as well as word of mouth suffices to make a bargain binding on both buyer and seller. In options, however, it is customary to give acknowledgments after a set formula. Thus, if the firm of Takem and Makem had received an order to buy 500 shares of New Jersey Central on February 10, 1870, at 101, buyer's option, for 30 days, they might have sent a member of their house or some other broker into the Long Room. His first question would be, "How is New Jersey Central?" If answered, "'1 – '1⅛," he begins to shout, "I 'll give 101, buyer 30, for five hundred New Jersey Central." Possibly another broker, entering from New Street, with an order to sell New Jersey Central down to 100 if necessary, has commenced simultaneously to cry, "Any part of a thousand '1› seller 30." Broker No. 1 replies, "101, buyer 30, for five hundred." "Sold," screams the other. The two now come together, give the name of buying and selling firms, and the subjoined papers are subsequently exchanged, after 2.15 P. M., generally.

JONES & ROBINSON.

500 *Shares.* 101, *B.* 30.

NEW YORK, *February* 10, 1870.

We have SOLD to TAKEM & MAKEM *Five Hundred* (500) *Shares of the Capital Stock of the New Jersey Central R. R. Co. at One Hundred and One* (101) *per cent, payable and deliverable, buyer's option, within Thirty days, with interest at the rate of Six per cent per annum. Either party having the right to call for deposits of Ten per cent during the pendency of this contract.*

JONES & ROBINSON.

TAKEM & MAKEM.

500 *Shares.* 101, *B.* 30.

NEW YORK, *February* 10, 1870.

We have PURCHASED of JONES & ROBINSON *Five Hundred* (500) *Shares of the Capital Stock of the New Jersey Central R. R. Co. at One Hundred and One* (101) *per cent, payable and deliverable, buyer's option, within Thirty days, with interest at the rate of Six per cent per annum. Either party having the right to call for deposits of Ten per cent during the pendency of this contract.*

TAKEM & MAKEM.

These forms are now universally adopted in all "option" transactions, and through them a large proportion of speculative movements are effected. Since the Government tax of one cent on every purchase or sale of a hundred dollars has been enforced, the acknowledgments are frequently covered with revenue stamps, not merely upon the face, but down over the entire back of the paper.

"Cash," "Regular," and options comprise the ordinary terms heard at the Boards. A sale, however, may take place at a time when the transfer-book of the company is closed, either for dividend or for an election. In such event, a transfer of shares or the issue of new certificates is impossible. If the purchase is made *Cash,* the buyer receives the old certificate with a power of attorney, and upon the opening of the books the transfer-clerk makes the substitution if desired. *Power and Certificate* is the broker's term at such a sale, and in share price-lists was formerly printed *p.c.*

When similar sales are made for time, the phrase used

was formerly *At the Opening,* abbreviated in stock-reports to *o.p.g.;* the meaning of the seller being obviously that a delivery will be made as soon as the transfer-books are again at the service of the public. Many certificates of stock, however, pass from hand to hand without transfer.

The usage of the Stock Board forbids the sale of less than five shares. Ten shares is the real unit. Less than this amount is styled an "odd lot," and sells a trifle above or below the market price, according as one wishes to dispose of or to purchase. A broker, with a commission to buy three shares of a certain stock, goes to the Board, and when some one cries, "Any part of fifty," he shouts, "Take 'em." "How many?" "*About* five," is the answer; the broker holding up three fingers to signify the number purchased. In case of an option, where circumstances may delay delivery, the stock being in Philadelphia or London, the broker sells "*about* buyer 10,—*about* seller 30." In bids or offers, the usual fraction is an eighth, while, on the London Stock Exchange, one sixteenth is the habitual fractional unit. At the New York Board, however, on a close market sometimes an eighth and a sixteenth are bid or offered. With this occasional exception the bids run numerically, 1, $\frac{1}{8}$, $\frac{1}{4}$, $\frac{3}{8}$, $\frac{1}{2}$, $\frac{5}{8}$, $\frac{3}{4}$, $\frac{7}{8}$, 2.

At present, purchases or sales of this absolute character form but a small proportion of Wall Street business. When stock is bought for permanent investment, or when sold in order to change the employment of capital, this method is naturally adopted. Yet even for these ends it is not unusual for outsiders to make use of the element of credit, whereby stock operations can be conducted with even greater disproportion of capital to the volume of business than characterizes the ordinary transactions of trade. This expansion of money, by which a hundred dollars may perform the service of a thousand, is technically known as the "margin."

Still holding the idea of actual investment in mind, let us suppose that a young Pennsylvanian has just inherited a hundred and fifty thousand dollars,— most of it in manufacturing stock. He has come to New York with some ten or twelve thousand dollars, and goes to a broker,—perhaps an old family friend: "I notice that 5-20s '67 registered are selling at 109. Now I want you to buy $ 8,000 bonds; if it were only next month I 'd put ninety thousand dollars more in it, and then off to Europe. The bother is, I can't realize on that factory property just this moment, and meanwhile, of course, governments will rise." "That 's probable," replies the broker; "but if you can pledge your ninety thousand in thirty days, and will deposit ten thousand now, I 'll buy the whole lot to-day. You must pay me an eighth of one per cent commission, and interest of seven per cent on what I lend you. If money costs me more than that, you must make the extra interest good. I shall allow you seven per cent interest on what you leave with me, and you will be insured against the risk of a rise. If the stock falls, however, you must correspondingly increase your margin." "Done," responded the Pennsylvanian. "Buy $ 100,000, and if you want a trifle more of deposit you shall have it. The balance shall be here in thirty days sure."

The broker sends over to the Board and buys $ 100,000 registered 5-20s of '67, regular way; and then looks about him to see how he shall meet his new obligation. In twenty-four hours he will have to pay out $ 109,000. His customer finally deposited $ 11,000. There are $ 98,000 to be hunted up. Possibly he has ten thousand dollars at his bank, but the rest of his capital is tied up as completely as the property of his friend of the Keystone State.

Two usages of Wall Street make the problem easy. The New York banks allow broker depositors of reputable standing to draw checks for amounts immensely disproportionate to that actually to their credit. These checks, sometimes for two hundred thousand dollars, are promptly "certified," i. e. guaranteed as representing that sum of *bona fide* deposits, although the books may not show a real credit of even five thousand dollars. This species of accommodation is based on confidence in the giver of the check, who is bound in honor to make the whole amount good before 3, P. M., of the same day. On the other hand, banks and banking-houses freely lend money on good bond or stock security, within ten or twenty per cent of par or the selling or market value.

When, therefore, the bonds are presented, our broker gives a check on his bank for the full amount. The seller hastens to get it certified, and the buyer proceeds to one or more of the great loan houses or banks, and readily borrows $100,000. In financial language, the bonds on which the money is raised are called "collaterals," and the act of placing them in pawn is styled "hypothecation." There were ten thousand dollars previously to the broker's credit at his bank. He now despatches the hundred thousand, together with his customer's deposit, and thereby makes his check good, as well as insuring a slight balance in his favor.

The $11,000 originally exacted by the broker, and the difference between the cost of the bonds and what was borrowed upon them, are both called "margins." It is obvious that their necessity arises from the fluctuating character of stocks. Were the bonds to fall to 99⅞, the lending bank would be in the position of holding a pledge of less value than the money advanced upon it. Against such contingency the lender protects himself, first, by the margin, seldom less than ten per cent, often widening in case of certain stocks to twenty or even forty per cent; secondly, by furnishing money only on condition that it may be demanded at any moment. Such an arrangement is known as a "call loan." If the market falls, the bank either calls for the money or a proportionate fresh amount of stock. Now the broker's power to buy on a margin depends upon the certainty that the collaterals will have a definite borrowing capacity. If in a week the 5-20s are at 95, the loan may be recalled, and a new one must be made either with the same or different parties. Perhaps he succeeds in borrowing $90,000. But he has still the difference of $10,000 to make up, and if his bank account remains as before, he will be unable to meet his obligations. Of course, no broker would be willing to place himself in such a position, and the first clause of every contract for purchase by margin is that the relative per cent must be kept up. If a customer fails to do this on due notice, the stock is sold out at once. In the present instance, the broker, had the bonds shown signs of weakness, would have immediately telegraphed to Pennsylvania for more money. As a matter of history the bonds did not fall, but, on the contrary, rose steadily to 115. When the transaction was settled, therefore, the country buyer found that by paying some six hundred dollars' interest he had made six thousand dollars; since, had he waited until he could realize upon his home property, he would have had to give one hundred and fifteen thousand dollars for what he now receives at one hundred and nine thousand. Were he to decide to avail himself of the high market, and to sell out his bonds, the advantage of the margin would be still more apparent. He has been putting out his money all the while at seven per cent interest, and now receives it back with six thousand dollars additional, *minus* the charges of his brokers, which would amount, all told, to scarcely a bagatelle of the customer's profit.

This is a conservative illustration, but it would be easy to find a far more startling example in the every-day facts of Wall Street. On November 14, 1868, Erie sold in the morning for 36⅝. That day a man with thirty-seven thousand dollars of *borrowed* money, who had a premonition of what was coming, could have gone to a broker, arranged for a ten per cent margin on selling value, and simply said: "Buy at once not above 37, and sell to-night, regular, for the best figure you can get." That afternoon Erie was at 52¼. The speculator's account would have stood:—

Dr.		Cr.	
10,000 Erie at 37, .	$370,000	10,000 Erie at 52¼, .	$522,500
Margin, ...	37,000	Margin returned, . .	37,000
Two commissions at ⅛ of 1,	2,500		
Net profit,	150,000		
	$559,500		$559,500

He was paying perhaps but fifty dollars a week for the money which, in twelve hours only, had brought him the clean sum of one hundred and fifty thousand dollars.

Here we have an extension of the margin to its subtlest degree. The fifty dollars of interest, together with the borrower's credit, enabled him to command thirty-seven thousand dollars; this again secured the temporary control of ten times that amount, and the turn of the market not only cancelled every dollar of obligation, but created an immense new capital. Such a chain of fortuitous circumstances is rare, but any broker who has grown old in the street can recall very many incidents on a minor scale of similar disproportion between the risk and the profit.

The principle of the margin, probably the outgrowth of a legitimate desire to make use of the force of credit in ordinary stock transactions where the final object was investment, is now the mainspring of speculation. Even in the case of what may be styled, for the sake of distinction, solid purchases or sales, there is clearly an opportunity for availing one's self of the rise and fall of the market. In July, 1867, the shares of the Panama Railroad sold for 256; in September, for 300. The difference of $ 44 on each certificate could have been procured just as well by buying out and out, as by paying in only an instalment. Nor is there any dissimilarity between the conditions of purchase in complete and in marginal transactions. Supposing a customer be always lucky enough to buy lower than he sells, the margin enables him, if he operates on comparatively stable securities, to purchase in ten per cents just ten times what he could otherwise obtain, and thus make an equivalent increase in gains. If he be prudent, his margins will never be his whole property; and he will be prepared to make good the losses by fluctuations. As long as the man who thus acquires a thousand shares at par, conscientiously intends to add to his $ 10,000 $ 90,000 more if occasion demands it, he is engaged in a business no more speculative than purchasing real estate on mortgage.

The application of the margin to *bona fide sales* is less easy to comprehend, although it is really identical with purchases. A capitalist wishes to dispose of a thousand shares of a certain company at ruling prices, but cannot deliver them for thirty days. His broker would consent to do it upon the condition that ten or twenty per cent of the par value should be placed upon deposit, and that this margin should be increased in the event of an upward fluctuation. The necessity of money in this case will be apparent when the reader considers the problem before the broker. His order is to sell at "ruling prices." The stock might, for example, be Hudson; say 1,000 shares, worth, on the day the customer comes, just par. It can be sold either cash, regular, or on an option. If sold on a thirty days' seller's option, then the risk of the broker lies in the possibility of his customer's failing to deliver the stock at the time agreed upon. It may be in London or San Francisco. The steamer may founder, there may be an accidental delay, the property may be attached by sheriff's officers; there are a hundred contingencies. But the broker has pledged himself to deliver on a fixed day; he has, therefore, no alternative but to go into the market and buy, or, as is commonly styled, "buy in." The shares may cost 110 or 120, owing to either an artificial or natural appreciation of the security. In other words, he must pay $110,000 or $120,000 for what he presently receives $100,000. The object of the margin is to cover this excess in price at time of delivery.

Again, the stock would probably not have realized the same at option as if sold cash. As the order was "ruling prices," the broker may have felt bound to get the best rates. He therefore sells cash or regular, and borrows of Broker C the shares which he delivers to Broker B, who bought the lot of him at the Board. This places him as debtor to C for 1,000 shares, which can only be made good either by his customer's keeping to his agreement or by "buying in" the stock. Here, as in the option, the margin protects against the rising market.

Stock can almost always be obtained by borrowers, either *flat*, i. e. with no interest on either side, or with interest at market rates for the money advanced to the lender. In options, six per cent goes to the seller. The broker in the above transaction, therefore, charges his customer nothing on the difference between margin and selling rate. Seven per cent is generally allowed on margins, as well in sales as in purchases. The six per cent interest on sales on option goes to the customer; but where the sale is made for cash, and the broker borrows the stock, any interest he may get is his perquisite as a compensation for the trouble and risk in borrowing.

As a matter of fact, the use of the margin is even less frequent in solid sales than in solid purchases; but it is highly important that the underlying principle of this magnificent instrument of speculation should be rightly apprehended. Every conceivable transaction of Wall Street is based upon the presumption of an amount of actual capital equal to that which figures in the bargain. The mahogany may be veneering; but it is always genuine wood so far as it goes. Brokers take commission on sum totals, and interest on sum totals. If they sell billions of stock, they actually deliver it; if they buy billions, they pay over every dollar for which they have contracted. We shall presently consider more at large the immense expansive power of money as applied to speculation; but it may not be undesirable at this juncture to reconsider the *modus operandi* of stock-dealing with reference to the general public. The explanations of this chapter cover all the main features of buying or selling, whether the object be for investment or speculative. In any case whatsoever, where stock is purchased or disposed of, the broker buys or sells either

Cash,
Regular Way,
Buyer's Option, or
Seller's Option.

And demands of his customer either

> Solid deposit of money or stocks, or marginal deposit of money; the margin to be ten, twenty, or even forty per cent of the par value of the stock, and to be increased in proportion to any subsequent change of the market;—in sales, where the price of the security advances; in purchases, where the price falls.

Seven per cent a year is generally allowed on *all* margins advanced by customers.

If the transaction be either cash, regular, or a three days' option, it implies no interest.

If it be more than a three days' option, six per cent on the selling value of the stock is paid by buyer to seller.

If the stock is bought by the broker on a given day, and held for the customer until he is ready to take it or sell it, the former charges seven or even a higher per cent for the difference between cost and margin, this interest continuing from the day of purchase to the date of closing the transaction. The broker, in such cases, "carries" the stock.

In sales, no interest is charged to the customer, while he is always credited with interest on margin; and, if the operation be by options, he is entitled to six per cent, in addition, on the difference between selling price and margin. With regard to this latter point, however, usage differs.

Furthermore, the broker requires one quarter of one per cent on the par value of securities in case of solid purchase or sale, or one half of this where stock is bought or sold on margin; these conditions being obligatory "where no agreement is made to the contrary."

CHAPTER V.

MARGINS AND THE LOAN MARKET.

THE moralists of this and recent generations have been much concerned over what are called the speculative tendencies of the world, and an opinion is abroad that in this particular the old days were better than our own. A broker of the writer's acquaintance, who has a *penchant* for geology, claims, to the contrary, that mankind, since the beginning of things, has been doing a vast amount of business on a very thin margin indeed; and proves his point by stating the miles total of the earth's diameter and the total of furlongs making up the tenuous crust which keeps us all from instantaneous and fiery liquidation. The illustration is quaint enough, and not so very illogical. For the gist of all credit is that the creditor has something to stand on.

Take that eminently sound and responsible debtor, Great Britain. It has succeeded in borrowing some four billion dollars on a margin of not quite four per cent. This margin is put up anew each year, and the weight of consols is "carried" with an astonishing freedom from fluctuations. At bottom, this mountain of credit has not the substance of whipped-syllabub.* It is made up of

* Soame Jenyns neatly stated the case when he characterized the difference between laying out money in land and investing it in funds, as

notes issued by generations dead and buried, and indorsed by a small minority of the living population, called the governing power. To collect this debt, the only process possible is by what has always excited a shudder in the English citizen, whether it has taken place in classic or modern times. That process, which no army in Christendom is strong enough to enforce, is called "universal confiscation." There is about as much likelihood of this occurring as of the earth's crust breaking through. What, then, keeps up British consols? Simply a confidence in the national honor, and the clear fact that England owns more than it owes. The answer is sufficiently trite, but it embodies the principle which lies at the base of all modern finance. It is the groundwork of banking, the main-spring of commerce, the pivot around which the vast system of European and American speculation revolves.

Enter any broker's office in Wall Street. You have greenbacks and give an order. There is not a respectable broker in all that money quarter who will execute your commission even for ninety cents on the dollar, unless you are properly introduced and your responsibility vouched for. Establish a definite credit, and you may be able to buy the equivalent of a thousand dollars on a deposit of fifty. The nine hundred and fifty dollars represent the certainty that you are not only willing to

consisting, in the first instance, of principal without interest, and, in the other, of interest without principal. The delicate satire upon the disadvantages of English real estate will be less appreciated by the American reader than the other point in the definition.

meet your obligations, but that you have the ability to do so. What you pay down is called margin; but behind it lies your whole fortune. There is not an operation in the whole history of stock speculation that did not start with just such a background. The thinnest one per cent margin, allowed by personal friendship, and coupled with the understanding that if the market should fall below, no subsequent claim should be made against the customer, must some way, in valid manner, through broker's credit and the subtleties of stock, represent behind it ninety-nine per cent of the selling value of the shares before the machinery of speculation will touch it. To the outside world this statement may appear as mystical as the Swedenborgian theology; but its truth will become manifest as we advance. Preliminary to a further inquiry into this feature of speculation, however, it is essential to understand the phenomena of the loan market.

Out of all the incorporated banks in the United States, there are thirty situated in Wall Street and its neighborhood, whose office is not unlike that of the heart in the economy of animal life. Although less than half the full number of banks in the metropolis, these thirty have two thirds of the capital, and quite two thirds of the circulation. By a provision of statutory law, all outside National banks, numbering some sixteen hundred, are allowed to keep one half, and many three fifths, of their reserve balances in New York. In this way our great financial centre is rapidly acquiring the function of a National clearing-house. These temporary deposits bear a small interest, and are subject to be called for at a day's notice. They can only be used, therefore, by the employing banks on the same conditions. The stock market supplies these conditions. Bonds and shares bought to-day and sold to-morrow, endowed with all the properties of swift conversion, and held by men whose training has been one of incessant grappling with the new and unexpected, are the only class of property upon which money can safely be borrowed without a protection against sudden demands. On these securities, therefore, the down-town banks make call loans. The name implies the nature. The money which the thirty receive from without, together with their own reserves, is lent freely to stock-brokers, with the simple provision that it must be returned immediately upon notice, if financial exigencies require it. This vast volume of what may well be styled fluid wealth is difficult of estimate in figures. The published statements of loans made by city banks make no distinction between discounts of commercial paper and what is advanced on securities. In sum total, the thirty banks lend weekly about $165,000,000. Indeed, including all New York banks, the average is nearly $255,000,000. During the week ending September 18, 1868, these banks lent $266,496,024. The real meaning of these last figures will be better understood when it is known that they exceed the entire average loans and discounts of all the national banks of New England and New York State, with the exception, of course, of the city itself. Or, to take a more sweeping view, they surpass the total weekly loans of national banks in Maryland, Virginia, North Carolina, South Carolina, West Virginia, Georgia, Alabama, Texas, Arkansas, Kentucky, Tennessee, Ohio, Nebraska, Kansas, Missouri, Minnesota, Iowa, Wisconsin, Illinois, Michigan, Indiana, Delaware, and New Jersey. Nigh one hundred and eighty millions of the amount cited above were advanced by the downtown banks. What proportion of this was lent on stocks? Probably much over one third. As many of the other banks also make call loans, we may, perhaps, estimate that from seventy to one hundred million dollars are furnished daily to the brokers and operators of New York.

This, however, is but one element in the lending force of the city. There are five Trust Companies, with capitals amounting in the aggregate to five millions and a half, which lend, at times, sixty millions a week. There are also a great number of private banking-houses, of which Jay, Cooke, & Co. may be selected as representatives, that daily loan vast sums of money on security. The foreign houses alone, which, like Belmont & Co., Brown Brothers, Drexel, Winthrop, & Co., operate in Wall Street, employ not much less than two hundred million dollars of capital.

On this ocean of wealth, fed by tributary streams which flow from all America and ripple up from the far-off European capitals, along the strands of deep-sea cables, the fleets of the stock market ride with such security as is the luck of mariners the world over. For money, selected by mankind as the gauge of all values on account of its exceeding stability, has nevertheless its whirls and eddies, its calms and tempests, its heave and swell. To-day men will loan millions at four per cent. To-morrow it cannot be had for twice or thrice that payment. A certain degree of order, however, attends these fluctuations. In general, the money market may be said to be subject to periodic influences covering whole months, and repeating themselves year by year at nearly the same seasons. In spring and fall the crops are to be brought forward. Merchants need money. Those who have securities hypothecate them if they can; and sell, if they cannot borrow. Hence a universal call on banks and bankers, the tide of interest rising higher, and the amount of individual advances lessening in quantity and proportion. The financial chroniclers announce that money is "very active," and the loan market "stringent."

In midsummer the atmosphere changes. A tropical calm succeeds the trade-winds. The lender seeks the borrower. Money becomes a drug. Technically it is "easy" or "inactive." Then the broker can borrow more, and will have to pay less, than at any other season. Both these periods are subject to temporary cross currents, and in some years there seems to be no law whatever to the fluctuations. In one form or another, however, these two conditions are unfailing facts, and all stock speculation depends upon them.

For it cannot too frequently be iterated, that speculation means solid money. There cannot be a solitary transaction except upon this basis. Every departure from this principle flings the gates wide open to failure.

Now the groundwork of a purchase of stock is the customer's margin, the broker's capital, and the borrowing capacity of the security. The last of these three elements is the one which must be fully known, before the risk can be calculated.

Entering the loan market we find that the securities dealt in by the stock exchange classify according to description and value for loans very much as follows:—

Collaterals.	On which money is lent
Governments, gold-bearing State bonds, railroad bonds not open to question, bank shares, and generally all high-valued scrip held mainly for investment.	At par, or within 10 per cent of selling value.
Speculative stocks that average high dividends, and have an investment value, although heavily dealt in by operators.	Within 10 or 20 per cent of selling value.
Wholly speculative stocks, usually called "fancy," and of nominal real value.	Within 20 or 30 per cent, if at all.

This table necessarily implies a steady value in the securities. If, as not seldom happens from special causes, a stock sinks in selling worth after a loan is effected, the lender at once calls in his money, or requires a further advance of stock equal to the percentage of depreciation. How the machinery works practically can be best shown by an example.

Suppose a firm of brokers to have a customer, A, who desires to deal very largely in a particular stock upon which a loan can be effected within five per cent of par, the selling price being 110. Wishing to accept the whole order, and believing that the stock could not possibly fall below five per cent; they agree to buy, on a ten per cent margin, twenty thousand shares. Their capital is so far in use that they can only employ in the transaction $100,000. The order requires $2,200,000. They accomplish it as follows:—

Bought 20,000 shares @ 110, $2,200,000

Paid for it by

Hypothecation of 20,000 shares @ 95, .	$1,900,000
Customer's margin, ...	200,000
Broker's capital, ...	100,000
	$2,200,000

If the market sinks five per cent, the entire capital at command of the brokers instantly disappears. If it sinks six per cent, they are bankrupt. This bankruptcy may not appear because the banks *may* not call in their loan. Even at six per cent depreciation they hold securities valued according to the market price at $2,080,000. The possibilities of a fall we shall presently consider. At this point we wish to call the reader's attention to the great amplitude of credit open to brokers.

The firm in question had placed on deposit at their bank the customer's margin and their entire capital. When the purchased stock was presented, they gave checks for $2,200,000, which their bank certified, although there were but $300,000 to show for it, and they could not make this temporary deficit good until they had received the $1,900,000 as a loan on their collaterals.

The running scale of their credit, starting with the solid basis of $ 100,000, might be thus stated:—

1st. As margin, $ 200,000. (Customer's confidence.)

2d stage.
- $ 1,900,000 of certified checks based upon nothing but confidence.
- 1,900,000 lent on stock.
- 200,000 margin.

3d stage.
- $ 1,900,000 lent on stock.
- 200,000 margin.

The condition of credit at the second stage will appear more forcibly by the subjoined diagram:—

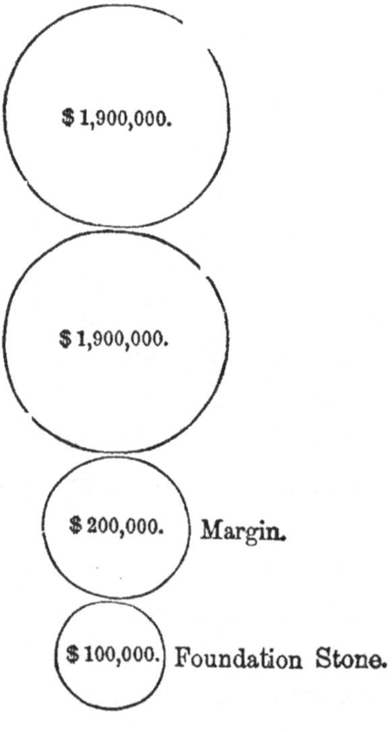

The bank credit through certified checks is really the only weak point in this pile of values. That existed merely for an hour or two, and was safe enough, if we regard the results of experience. The assertion may confidently be hazarded, that, taking known facts, the risks of mercantile houses in ordinary trade credits, or of operators through fluctuations of stock, are tenfold, if not fifty-fold, that of the banks in these temporary daily credits.

As long as money remains plenty, the firm can carry its immense load. Naturally, also, the buying public is disposed to pay even higher prices for stock. Quite possibly the shares may rise to 120. At this point, if sale is effected, there must be a renewal of the credit by certified checks. A has made a gross profit of $200,000. The brokers, at one eighth of one per cent commission, would receive $5,000, and they would also gain in the difference between the percentage on which they "carried" the stock, viz. seven per cent, and what they were obliged to pay. They might have borrowed at four per cent per annum. In 1867, when the Treasury report for April exhibited an expansion of currency to the amount of a million, call-loans were four per cent, and loans for thirty days were made readily for five per cent. In inactive times, such rates are by no means infrequent.

We have supposed an easy loan and a buoyant stock market. It may have chanced, however, that the shares fell, while lending rates remained as before. The brokers, in such a contingency, demand that the margin shall be increased in proportion to the decline. The bank is still ready to lend, but not at such liberal advances. As the stock depreciates the loan is called in.

The scale may be stated in this manner:—

Stock: 20,000. Selling Rates.	A's Margin.	Broker Capital.	Call Loan.	Cost of 20,000.
110	$ 200,000	$ 100,000	$ 1,900,000	$ 2,200,000
100	400,000	100,000	1,700,000	2,200,000
90	600,000	100,000	1,500,000	2,200,000
80	800,000	100,000	1,300,000	2,200,000
70	1,000,000	100,000	1,100,000	2,200,000
60	1,200,000	100,000	900,000	2,200,000
50	1,400,000	100,000	700,000	2,200,000
40	1,600,000	100,000	500,000	2,200,000
30	1,800,000	100,000	300,000	2,200,000
20	2,000,000	100,000	100,000	2,200,000
10	2,200,000			

At every stage of this descent it is A who stands in the gap. As against the street, the transaction presents a series of intrenchments in which both A and his brokers cover the bank, and in which A covers his brokers and increases the defences, step by step, as the danger becomes more imminent. The moment A's resources fail, the brokers sell. In fact, below 50 or 60 the whole illustration is pure hypothesis, as at that point neither broker nor lender would have faith in the security, and A would have to assume the whole burden or relinquish it.

We have supposed, in the above case, that the brokers borrowed from only one bank and kept but one bank account. Practically, however, such a large loan would be distributed through half a dozen banks or Trust Companies. The usual method is to place the securities in a long envelope with a printed form on the back, stating the amount hypothecated, and the money desired. Thus, if Black & White have a lot of Chicago and Northwest selling at 70, Rock Island worth 101, and Pacific Mail rated at 48, on which they wish to borrow within nineteen or twenty per cent, they would make up their budget, enclose it in an envelope, and fill out the blanks as follows: —

LOAN
$100,000
To BLACK & WHITE
Jan. 5th, 1870.
Interest *7* %.

SECURITIES.	
500 Rock Island	*$50,500*
300 N. W. Com.	*21,000*
1,000 P. Mail	*48,000*
	$119,500

In case the bank called for more stock, on account of subsequent depression, they would either make up the deficiency with other shares, or send over another envelope with the loan marked down to $ 90,000 or $ 80,000, proportionate to the decreased value. The former transaction would thus be closed up and a new loan commence.

As banks lend more freely to customers than to outsiders, the great broker houses make it a point to keep two, three, or even more bank accounts, proportionate to their capital. They also endeavor to leave daily deposits of as large an amount as the exigencies of business will allow, varying week by week, but with an average of from twenty to a hundred thousand dollars. It is the advantage which banks derive from these deposits of non-interest earning capital which makes them willing to certify checks to such enormous amounts, and to accommodate the speculative public with loans.

When the loan market is stringent, the question of interest becomes of paramount importance. Sometimes there is apparently no limit to the rates. The city banks halt at seven per cent, and the moment money rises above this, recourse must be had to private bankers. There is an impression, very current among a portion of the mercantile class, that the banks profit directly by the extra enhancement of interest rate. This, of course, is a mistake. The law stands in the way. But there is nothing to prevent an honest cashier from distinguishing between borrowers, and lending open-handed to one, while "regretting the inability" of the bank to assist another. If the borrower happens to make a "turn," and so is able to pass over an envelope to the officer with eight or twelve hundred dollars in greenbacks slipped in for a Christmas present, what clause in the charter forbids it? There is certainly some way of bridging over the chasm between "no loans" at the bank and plenty of loans on "the street," if one be willing to pay for them. At all events there are banking-houses whose capital is limited, but who never appear to be without a free flow of money, just when the bank presidents are assuring brokers that it is impossible to get it.

When a broker agrees to "carry" stock, he says, "Seven per cent, unless the market tightens." There is a world of meaning in those words. The scale of rates slides up, — seven per cent *coin*, seven per cent *plus* commission of 1-16, 3-16, 5-16. Even one per cent will be charged. This is confusion to the uninitiated. It means simply that, besides the legitimate seven per cent, the borrower must sell and then buy back the stock, paying from $\frac{1}{16}$ to $\frac{16}{16}$, or one per cent higher, when delivered the next day. The men who do this call themselves banker brokers, and the excessive interest is readily met by dealer's who have had their securities thrown back upon them by the banks, and are compelled to borrow in other quarters rather than risk the sacrifice of their stock in a falling market. By selling cash and buying back regular, they obtain a day's respite, and in the meanwhile money may become easier. After the famous Black Friday, at which the great gold "corner" culminated, this one per cent commission *plus* seven per cent in coin per annum was paid for a loan from Saturday to Monday, with the highest class of government bonds as collaterals. In many cases, when the security was less satisfactory, a very much higher percentage was charged.

All sorts of causes conspire to bring about this activity of the loan market. Sometimes it is an artificial lock-up in which bank directors form coalitions with great operators, and withhold ten millions from use. A sub-treasury sale of gold may assist. The fact that the New York City chamberlain draws out three or four millions from the Broadway bank, to pay interest and part of the principal of the municipal debt, has increased rates for a day. The mere intensity of speculation, causing a borrowing demand too great for the supply, occasions it. Often no possible explanation appears, and a stringency amounting to twelve, fourteen, or sixteen per cent in a forenoon may suddenly relax by 1 P. M., without warning or excuse. The Stock Board has made vain efforts to protect itself against these changes, and at one time greenbacks were sold in the Long Room, and a Loan Office opened at Regular Sessions; but it was found that this subterfuge only intensified the evil.

So far as the outside customer is affected by a money tightness, the effect is seen either in the drooping value of the stock speculated in, requiring increase of margin proportionate to the decline; or in a heavy addition to the interest charge. Thus, an order may have been given to Money, Bonds, & Co., in 1869, to buy and carry a thousand shares of Rock Island. The middle of November the lending bank refused to continue its loan, owing to the tightness of the market; and the firm, having no other alternative, resort to Smith & Jones, banking brokers. The latter agree to make the accommodation for a month at six per cent *per annum* and two per cent commission. This neat profit is called a "turn." We have already alluded to it. Practically, it is an artifice to avoid the hazards of the usury law, precisely as fashionable pawnbrokers lend a hundred dollars on a diamond breast-pin, and give a paper which stipulates that the holder can buy back the property at one hundred and ten dollars within a month. The borrowing stock firm sells the shares at about ruling rates, cash, and then buys them back at two per cent higher, buyer 30. Supposing the date of the transaction to have been November 15th, they could probably have received a *par* advance, and would have given 102. The subjoined acknowledgment would have been made by the borrowing house.

MONEY, BONDS, & CO.

1,000 *Shares.* 102, *B.* 30.

NEW YORK, *November* 15, 1869.

We have PURCHASED of SMITH & JONES One Thousand (1,000) *Shares of the Capital Stock of the Chicago, Rock Island, & Pacific R. R. Co. at One Hundred and Two* (102) *per cent, payable and deliverable, buyer's option, within Thirty days, with interest at the rate of Six per cent per annum. Either party having the right to call for a deposit of Twenty per cent during the pendency of this contract.*

MONEY, BONDS, & CO.

Smith & Jones, by this transaction, net two thousand dollars, and a more profitable style of operation is not to be found in Wall Street.

Why did not the customer of Money, Bonds, & Co. sell his stock by an option, instead of "carrying" it with the risk of this heavy usury? As in such case there would be no interest to pay, and if the purchase itself had also been made by option, there would have been only six per cent interest, the question is natural. One reason is that a buyer's option is usually much more above the market than it would cost to "carry" stock, while a seller's option compels the purchaser to depend upon the will of another, and the very opportunity of speculation may be lost. *Per contra,* if sold during a tight money market, less would be made than if the high interest were met. Moreover, by carrying his stock, a speculator is enabled to seize upon all sorts of wayside profits, and to meet the fluctuations of the street just at their tidal height. This especially appears in "corners," where a gain of from twenty to fifty per cent will disclose itself one day, and disappear the next. The man who "carries" realizes the profits; the one who has out a buyer's option must give at least twenty-four hours' notice, and so loses the chance.

CHAPTER VI.

THE METHODS OF SPECULATION.

SOMEBODY is always making money in Wall Street. At the Exchange, the moment the ear catches "Take 'em," "Sold," "Done," we may be sure that on one or both sides there has been a profit more or less large. This gain may not always appear, seeing that it possibly covers some loss of the future or the past; but it is pleasant to believe in the certainty of a good bargain either for buyer or seller. Moreover, no one speculates to lose, and in analyzing the modes of stock operations, it is well to look at the sunshine. What are these modes? At bottom, only two. The "street" condenses its whole speculative business into a couple of monosyllables,—"long" and "short."

If you are *long*, you are a "bull"; if *short*, a "bear."

Much nonsense has been written and a vast deal of fanciful etymology wasted over these zoölogical distinctions. Their real origin is, probably, like all other broker metaphors, due to a pungent conception of facts. If a bear finds anything in his rural peregrinations, whether it be a turkey on the roost or a man in a tree, he lifts his paw and pulls it down. The bull, on the contrary, lowers his head only to give men and things a decided upward tendency.

The application of these habits to speculative phenomena is too obvious to need explanation. Bull operators take a stock at its lowest, and attempt to toss it up as high as may be. The bears, on the other hand, prefer to pull values down to the lowest possible figure. Believing that prices are too high, they sell, and are therefore "short," precisely as people who have disposed of their money are "short" of change. The bull buys, confident that stocks will be higher, and is said to be "long," possibly because this word is the opposite of "short," possibly, also, as suggestive of the dimensions of his purse.

Into these two classes all the speculators who are the life of Wall Street, are divided. But the epithets are temporary rather than permanent. There are men, indeed, who are constitutionally hopeful, — always looking for a rise; and others who equally disbelieve everything, and invariably sell down the market. The vast majority, however, alternate from bull to bear and from bear to bull, according to the speculative outlook. Curiously enough, the dialect of "the street" — prolific almost, to distraction in the language of buying and selling, in the nicknames of the various orders of brokers, and in phrases descriptive of pure jobbery — is exceedingly poor in words which tersely define the different methods by which operators make money in stocks. The thing is present, but the name is wanting. There are a hundred different methods of dealing the cards, but the play is either "long" or "short." When there are high stakes, it is "cornering." When one bets on the players, it is a "call" or a "put." Beyond this, for the infinite permutations and combinations which street transactions allow, the imagination and ingenuity of brokers are sadly at fault.

The first element in speculation is the "point." If the operator has a good "point," he has a "sure thing." This valuable acquisition is something like the advantage of placing your opponent with his back to a mirror. You see both hands. In other words, the "point" is a bit of secret information concerning a stock, whether it be that an extra dividend is to be declared, a bull movement is organizing, an emission of new shares is to take place, or some other cause is at work, or likely to be at work, which will seriously affect prices. According to this knowledge you buy or sell, and *if you have not been misled*, you are certain to make in proportion to your venture. Wall Street is full of these "points." The Stock Exchange is paved with them. There is a certain other place floored with good intentions, and where, if one stumbles, he burns his fingers. Points frequently have this quality. To understand this very completely, the reader should comprehend that beautiful problem in stock chess which we will call

THE DREW GAMBIT.

A great man, with vast heaps of money made by gathering bulls and other cattle for the slaughter-house, one day gets possession of nearly the whole of the capital stock of the celebrated E. Rye Railroad. Looking around him he sees a neighbor with a small purse, and whispers "Buy." Straightway this neighbor, whom we may as well name Trustful, does buy, and his thousands become ten thousands. Then after some days the low voice sibillates "sell"; and Trustful's ten thousands turn to hundred thousands. So the neighborly good work continues until the benefactor of mankind has enabled his *protégé* to surround himself with all the glories of sudden wealth, and to proudly read in his bank-book those delightful Arabic signs whose interpretation is half a million. This sum Trustful has acquired, not directly from his patron, but through the losses of other operators.

One day the great man, having tired of E. Rye, determines to shake himself loose from the burden. Trustful comes and asks for a point. With mysterious nods and knowing looks he is told that a broad-gauge road is always a good purchase, — in fact, there never was a time when one could buy at such great advantage as now. Forthwith Trustful goes into the market and spreads his half million in thin margin over the whole street, buying and buying. The more he takes the more is supplied him. Presently he can buy no longer, and the stock strangely falls. His margins are washed away. A sea of debt sweeps over him. The magnificent lord of E. Rye has "sold out" his stock and his neighbor! The world shrugs its shoulders, as it bows to the king of the shorts, whose ways are ways of cleverness, and whose "points" are moral guide-boards.

If rumor be veracious, old Captain Hancock, of the famous Troy line of steamboats, once played out this game so as to checkmate the king. The story is worth telling, as showing that the "gambit" is not always safe. The Captain had a friend named Daniel, who had helped him by various "points," until he was one of the mighty magnates of the money quarter. One day, however, this friend advised him to buy all the stock of the great Blank Railroad he could possibly carry. Hancock did buy in blocks of five thousand, risking about all the wealth he was master of. A lucky accident revealed to him that Daniel, through his brokers, Largebeak & Co., had been selling the stock upon him. When the clerk of the firm brought the shares and asked for payment, Hancock gave a check for the full amount, but notified his bank not to cash it. Presently back comes the clerk, full of indignation, declaring that the check is worthless, and demanding the return of the shares.

The Captain, however, in the mean time had walked over to Largebeak & Co.'s, and, entering the private office, found Daniel comfortably seated at a desk. After a very brief preliminary, Hancock went straight to his work. He had been persuaded to buy a big load of this infernal Blank Railroad. He had bought of several parties; among them, it appeared, of Largebeak. Blank had gone down. Daniel had deceived him, and tried to "wipe him out." "Now, then, I have this lot of Largebeak's, and will keep it, if I have to spend every dollar left in the courts, unless you agree to take back all you sold on me." Having said this, he turns upon his heel and retires. Then the brokers and their client contemplate the situation. Largebeak & Co. naturally object to the loss of some ten thousand shares, and call Daniel's attention to the awkwardness of litigation. The sequel of the whole matter is that Hancock gets rid of all his Blank, saves his fortune, and thenceafter seeks his points in other quarters.

It should not be inferred, however, that there is always an intention to lead astray, even when a speculation, founded on hints of this nature, results badly. In fact, half the failures of the street are due to points which brokers believe in, not only to their customers' but their own ruin. Apart from the operations based upon secret intelligence, there are a variety of combinations that are certain of profit if well managed. Of these, the prettiest is

THE TURN.

In a previous chapter we illustrated this as applied to loans. Its application is similar in regular transactions. Thus, occasionally, during a day's fluctuations, an operator can buy a stock at 90, buyer 30, and sell it off at 92, seller 30. But these opportunities, however sure when the chances allow it, are apt to be, like white blackbirds, not over common. One modification of this is the *Spread Eagle*, formerly a highly popular style of speculation with capitalists who had plenty of money and a wide-awake broker. Its method was delightfully simple.

An operator, A, buys 5,000 Northwestern of B at 84, seller 30, and sells it to C at 85, buyer 30.

The fluctuations and rivalry of the market continually afford opportunities for combinations of this kind, and brokers can frequently close with simultaneous offers and bids answering to all the conditions of this speculation. The *gist* of the transaction is apparent on the face. A sells higher than he buys, and is enabled to do this readily by making the options to the advantage of both parties with which he deals. His profit in every case will be the difference between buying and selling price; and the premium on options, as well as the variations in all stock, would not seldom permit of a larger margin of gain in the sale. He must be prepared to take the stock when it is delivered, and provide the stock when demanded. At the end of the thirty days, supposing both the contracts fulfilled, A will have made one per cent, or $ 5,000.

The danger of this operation is in a sharp upward and then a downward turn in the market. If the stock should rise to 100, C would at once make a demand for the stock, and A must buy again at the high rates in order to keep to his contract. Should the stock fall immediately after to 69, B would come forward and propose settlement. In that case A will have lost by both C and B $ 30 on each share. Were the market to permanently rise or fall there would be no loss in the end, but in the ordinary conditions of the present market this form of speculation is perilous. We are informed, however, that years ago it was quite frequently practised. Its real enemy is

THE CORNER.

This device is tolerably understood through the events of the great gold panic of September, 1869. It requires large masses of capital, great shrewdness, a happy combination of circumstances, and adroitness in turning even ill fortune to advantage. Its effect upon speculation is very much like trolling in the fishing-business. Its definition is simple, but its applications are full of variety. When more of a stock has been bought than the market can furnish, the corner is inevitable. The conditions of the problem may take two forms: —

I. Twice or thrice the whole capital stock of a railroad or other corporation may be bought through time purchases. If, simultaneously, sufficient stock be sold for delivery after the period that the purchases fall due to cover the sum total of actual shares in the market, the scheme becomes perfect and the profits are immense. It was in this way that the Morris Canal corner and the corners in Harlem, Prairie du Chien, and Michigan Southern, were engineered.

II. Again, the amount of stock of a given corporation that is in the street may be accurately ascertained. A further estimate may be made of the proportion of stock held for investment which is likely to come upon the market during the crisis. The speculators then purchase largely in excess of both these amounts, although not up to the total of the capital stock. Here, also, time sales must be made enough to unload the full bulk of deliveries accruing from the purchases.

It is clear that this style of corner is surrounded with difficulties. There may be an underestimate of the resources of the street. The outside holders may crowd into the market beyond the speculative calculation. The Erie corner in November, 1868, and the famous gold combination of September, 1869, both failed from inadequate preparations for overcoming these suddenly disclosed obstacles.

Problem No. I. may be thus illustrated: —

Capital stock, 50,000. Current street sales of shares at 40.

Through a dozen or more brokers 150,000 shares are bought on buyer 30. The Long Room is the battle-ground, as there no registry is made of transactions. Coincidently other brokers sell freely for the combination at seller 60, 30, 15, 10, and 3, the latter class of sales being made as the corner matures. Cash stock is made plentiful. Large quantities are lent on call at low rates to give the market an appearance of natural ebb and flow. In three weeks' time some 100,000 shares have been contracted for at an average of 55, and 50,000 at 70. Sales of 50,000 had been effected at the same time for an average of 50.

The purchases, all at buyer's option, are at once called in. The street is in dismay. The clique owns all the stock. It has matured contracts for nearly three times the whole capital stock. Men who held the shares which they had agreed to deliver whenever the buyers presented themselves had sold them under the seduction of the upward tide of the market. They now find themselves in the same condition as others who had sold what they did not possess. As the shares rose, the clique had rapidly absorbed all floating stock, supplementing the accumulation in their tin boxes by putting forth fresh contracts. Locked up behind the bars of Trust

Companies, and in innumerable bank and private safes, at the order of the combination, are the very shares which the street had reckoned upon for satisfying their bargains. Deliveries must be made. Stock for delivery can only be secured through the clique agents. A month before it was waveless as a stagnant pool in the dead quietude of 40. Now it rises and falls in fierce but swollen fluctuations, — to-day 150, yesterday 160, to-morrow at 200, — as the ring changes its tactics or indulges its enmities. Some settle at once; others borrow of the combination from day to day, paying fearful usury and hoping against hope. At the end, however, all contracts must be settled, and the average compromise is at 165. Supposing that the shrewder portion of the street had long before settled at 90, and that the proportion stood 100,000 at 90, 50,000 at 165; then the clique's account would stand: —

DR.

To 100,000 shares bought at 55	$ 5,500,000
" 50,000 " " " 70	3,500,000
" net profit	6,250,000
	$ 15,250,000

CR.

By 50,000 shares sold at 90	$ 4,500,000
" 50,000 " " " 165	8,250,000
" 50,000 " contracted to be delivered at 50	2,500,000
	$ 15,250,000

This statement of profits is, of course, incomplete. It does not include the money accruing from loans of stock, nor is the percentage of brokerage deducted. But the gain of over six and a quarter millions would necessarily result from the speculation. Of course, such a corner could only be engineered with vast capital and under powerful interests. Some two millions would be required for margins. A considerable portion of the *bona fide* stock would probably be bought out and out, or previously held by the speculators. But the character of an operation like this is such that the money could mainly be borrowed on easy terms.

In the famous Morris Canal corner of '35, a clique in New York and Newark quietly bought up all the stock at thirty or forty per cent below par. They then went into the street and made enormous time purchases. On settling-day the pool unloaded at 150, clearing nearly three hundred per cent.

A still more audacious corner was effected the same year in Harlem. The stock consisted of 7,000 shares. 64,000 shares were bought by the ring within a period of seven weeks. Settlement-day was in September. Stock bought in July at 123, buyer 60, paid a difference of seventy-two per cent to the pool who held the market at 195. On two days of the middle of September four thousand shares came due with differences mounting up to $ 100,000 in favor of the pool. The short interest was frantic. A meeting of the Board was called, and the discussion was fierce and protracted. The final vote decreed that contracts must be satisfied. But the shorts were determined, and the ring foolishly gave a fresh twist to the stock, running it up to 200. The Board was convened anew, and the brokers elected a committee of four, to whom differences should be paid, and who should arbitrate between the parties. The New York *Advertiser*, in its comments, intimated that the street was ready to settle at 160 or 170 for corner stock, and the clique subsequently consented to the compromise.

In November, 1865, the clever Prairie du Chien corner was sprung upon Wall Street. This then obscure Western road had a capital stock of $2,900,000, and the shares, when the speculation started, were selling for 60. The clique lent out thousands of shares, and created an enormous short interest. On the last Monday of the month Prairie du Chien had been forced up to 250. Settlements were made from 110 to 210, and one banking-house paid $125,000 to escape. Wm. H. Marston, once cashier of an Illinois bank, was the leading spirit of this ring.

Two years before, John M. Tobin undertook his corner in Harlem. The stock was selling at 40. Commodore Vanderbilt was interested in the Broadway Railroad grant, and the Common Council of New York had thrown its influence against it, many individual members at the same time going short on Harlem. As Tobin owned, or had privately purchased the entire capital stock of the road, it was easy to run the price up to 164. This was in September, and as soon as settlements were made the shares dropped to 80. Early the next year the Legislature of the State repealed the grant, and half the Assembly entered on a bear raid against Harlem. The stock began to fall. The shorts increased. Then Tobin sought the assistance of the Commodore, and together they run the shares up to 285, at which point many contracts came due. Several houses failed, and not less than three million dollars were taken from the street by Tobin and his colleague. Individual operators who had agreed to deliver from 1,000 to 1,200 shares, were glad to compromise by paying some one hundred and eighty thousand dollars.

The extreme prices in corners are to be explained simply from the fact that the cliques hold all the stock, and can therefore exact whatever rates they please. Nevertheless, apart from the power of a monopoly, there is a subtle force which in all scarcity raises the selling rates of an article out of all proportion to the actual deficiency. Gregory King, in a series of studies upon the prices of the food market in Europe, generalizes from the statistics at his command the following conclusion:—

A deficiency	of	1 tenth	raises	the	price	3	tenths.
"	"	" 2 tenths	"	"	"	8	"
"	"	" 3	"	"	"	" 16	"
"	"	" 4	"	"	"	" 28	"
"	"	" 5	"	"	"	" 45	"

In shares, however, it is probable that the earlier deficit produces less effect, while great scarcity tells in even more rapidly ascending ratios.

Problem No. II. may be thus exemplified —

Capital stock, 50,000

10,000 held at London and Amsterdam.

20,000 held by farmers, local tradesmen, professional men, etc., in the section where the property lies.

20,000 in the street, selling at 40.

The clique quietly buys 40,000 shares at an average of 60, seller 10, and buyer 30. The movement is concealed by cash sales and free loans for a week, and then the deliveries are demanded. In its efforts to cover its shorts (*argot* for purchasing sufficient stock to fulfil contract), the share rate is run up to 120. The ten-day men are forced to settle at this figure; the thirty-day men are equally embarrassed. There has been no time for the unspeculative holders of shares remote from the market to bring any large portion forward. The foreign holders cannot make a delivery by cable, and, before telegraphic intercourse, they could not be advised of the combination. The ring's account would stand as follows:—

Dr.

To 40,000 shares bought at average of 60 .	$2,400,000
" 2,000 shares, bought to steady market at 120,	240,000
" net profit	860,000
	$3,500,000

Cr.

By 20,000 shares compromised for at 120 .	$2,400,000
" 22,000 shares worth at cash sale 50 . .	1,100,000
	$3,500,000

The 2,000 shares represent the portion thrown in by outside holders eager to profit by the rise. They inevitably gain, as the clique is compelled to pay the high price in order to make a basis for the settlement of differences. As the combination must take all the stock offered for delivery, it comes out with 22,000 shares in hand. It might have sold this before the culmination of the corner, at seller's option, — the only safe and quickly profitable procedure, as the street can now heavily bear the market, running the stock down to 25. But it is evident that the ring can afford to throw the whole mass of shares into the East River, and still come out with two millions in hand. Furthermore, the short interest developed by the desire for revenge may immediately be caught in a second corner far more disastrous than the first. In effect this last strategy was put into practice by Leonard Jerome, and a few of his friends, in the Hudson corner of '63. This scheme was the impulse of the moment. The bears had hammered the stock down to 112 and below. Jerome was a large holder, and, irritated at the decline in price, sent orders to several brokers to take all that was offered at seller's option. This continued for several days, till the market began to fail. Then the ring began to buy cash stock until nearly the whole of the capital stock, except some held as investment, had been secured. At this stage applications were made to bear houses to "turn" the stock. They bought it cash of the clique, and sold it back at an advance, upon ten, twenty, or thirty days' options. This apparent weakness so far persuaded the street that the ring was in sore need of money, that a short interest again developed, and cash stock was sold for future delivery freely, — the clique quietly absorbing it.

When the options, given in the turns, matured, the bears found themselves in "a corner." There was no stock to be had. Hudson mounted to 180. Then the lending houses began to implore and bewail. They had made "the turn" simply as an accommodation, and it was exceedingly unfair that they should now have to lose five or six thousand dollars on every hundred shares. The clique, however, was inexorable, but condescended to lend the stock at five per cent a day. There were 50,000 shares due, and on a large proportion this extreme interest was paid for several days. At last, in despair, the bears bought the stock. What little remained was disposed of at private sale. The profits of the ring can only be estimated by millions.

The risk, in this species of corner, lies in a miscalculation of the amount really held by the street, and in an underestimate of the number of outside holders ready to avail themselves of the rising prices. Thus, the actual state of the stock just used for illustration might have been as subjoined:—

Capital stock, 50,000

5,000 held in Amsterdam.
5,000 recently held in London, but already in Cunard steamer, due at New York in two days.
5,000 held in Philadelphia.
3,000 held in Boston.
2,000 held in Providence, in hands of large capitalists.
10,000 held by small capitalists at a distance.
20,000 in the street, selling at 50.

The clique buys 20,000 at 60, seller 10, and 20,000, buyer 30, for same average. It then runs the price up to 120, at which rate it had secretly determined to settle. Up to this moment it had absorbed the recent invoice from London, the Philadelphia supply, and the 20,000 block held in New York. But as no contract had matured, it could not be conscious of the situation. The ring could buy 3,000 at 120, to hold the market, but there its resources ended. Boston sells at once, and the stock recoils to 80. Providence sells, and the shares slide down to 50. From all quarters come telegrams from the minor holders with orders of "Sell" and no limit, seeing that at 120 their hopes have become illimitable, and in a drooping market 2,000 more shares are thrown in, leaving the stock flat at 30, with no buyers, and at that point the sellers at seller 10 deliver. The account would stand:—

Dr.

To 40,000 shares bought at average of 60 . .	$2,400,000
" 2,000 " " " " 120 .	240,000
" 1,000 " " " " 110 . .	110,000
	$2,750,000

Cr.

By 43,000, market value 30	$1,290,000
" net loss	1,460,000
	$2,750,000

The clique might, perhaps, have sold their 40,000 at 60, sellers 30, before the real shaping of the market was known. That would have placed the credit statement thus:—

By 40,000	@ 60 . .	$2,400,000
" 3,000 . . .	@ 30 . . .	90,000
" net loss		. 260,000
		$2,750,000

In this case their loss would be moderate, and would yet remain a quarter of a million. It will be observed that in this aspect of the corner the small outsiders are proportionately the heavier losers. They sold at 30, and will ever after regard Wall Street as the treasure-house of thieves.

One hazard overhanging all corners has yet to be noted. Our previous suppositions have implied the integrity of capital stock. But in pursuance of modern ideas, the directors of great corporations sometimes hold that their affairs should be managed with an eye to the street. The single eye is full of light, and the more light reserved for the Stock Exchange the less of it that remains for a disagreeable illumination of the ways and sinuosities of the management. Accordingly, money is borrowed for dividends in order to keep the stock high in the register, or the earnings which should have been distributed among shareholders are transferred to construction account lest dividend day might affect the stock market by an unhealthy appreciation of shares. Nearly all our great railroads have charters in which a high-priced New York lawyer can detect an obscure and inferential permission to enlarge the capital under certain conditions. Bonds also are frequently possessed of the privilege of conversion into stock without very definite details regarding time or manner. Judging by not infrequent occurrences it may not be far wrong to suppose that the sufficing motive for a fresh emission of shares or conversion of bonds is to be found in the appearance of a corner, or of a movement partaking in some degree of the nature of this phase of speculation. Perhaps, indeed, a more accurate definition would be that railway companies are empowered to add unexpectedly to their capital stock whenever controlling directors are not members of a cornering combination, and are so far operators in the street as to be affected disastrously by the success of such combination.

Railway directors are the heavy artillery of the stock market, and no corner can attain Napoleonic victories without them. An important feature in this speculation is to know who are the real holders of stock. This can be discovered most expeditiously by an examination of the transfer books; and, of these, the directors hold the key. They also can alone check the influx of newly rustling shares. This was the secret of Tobin and Vanderbilt's "Harlem Squeeze" of 1865. They owned the property and knew all its points.

It was this satisfactory reliance which upheld famous Jacob Little when in a great strait. He had been selling Erie for future delivery. He was no one knows how many hundred thousand dollars short in the stock. Every broker in the Board combined against him. On settlement day, as the story goes, he walked up Wall Street with serene countenance, while the joy of expectant disaster gleamed darkly and scornfully at him from a hundred eyes. He had been long known as the Napoleon of the Exchange, and all the brokers said that two o'clock would be his Waterloo. At one P. M. he stepped into the Erie offices, presented a block of convertible bonds, and demanded instantaneous surrender of equivalent shares. Then he rode round to his office, and the startled Stock Board found that Blucher and night had come! Daniel Drew in similar extremity has mounted the Erie stairway time and again on the same errand, and with like success.

The celebrated corner in Milwaukee and St. Paul was undertaken without the safeguard of a co-operating direction. The feature of this speculation was the employment of calls instead of buyer's options. Its master-mind was Garner. The stock was selling at 47 in January, and the operator bought calls at twelve months, covering the whole capital stock, — paying $800,000 in premiums. He then put his broker into the Boards with orders to bid it up, and by October it was quoted at 111. At this point the direction voted an immediate issue of shares upon a "construction" pretext, and the market at once broke to 61.

It is evident that the essential principle of the corner is simply the aggravation of ordinary stock speculation. A man who sells seller 30 hopes that his commodity will decline in value. If it rises, he suffers, and expects to suffer. But in ordinary cases the exact limit of suffering is known. In a perfect corner there is no limit, or rather the limit is the extreme verge of price at which it is prudent to force a stock. It is clearly better to settle with a man at 150 than compel settlement at 200, thereby breaking him and receiving only fifty cents on a dollar.

A peculiar danger to which corners are incident is the perfidy of a portion of the clique. There is scarcely a single great operator that has not been charged with this weakness. It consists in quietly selling the stock which has been pledged to the pool, the clique buying it at high rates in order to keep up the price, and without suspecting the source of the supply. The Rock Island corner of '63 – '64 partly split upon this snag. It had been engineered by Morse of Fort Wayne fame and Dr. Durant, the hero of the Union Pacific Railroad. In December large quantities of the stock was hypothecated on a sixty days' loan. Then heavy purchases were made. More than 56,500 shares, constituting the whole capital stock, was held or purchased at short options. Indeed, it is asserted that 20,000 shares in excess of capital were bought. The price started at 107, and went rapidly up to 149. At that point it was discovered that the pool was being betrayed. The detection arose from the sale of certain certificates whose numbers were known as belonging to a member of the clique. The compromise with the shorts was at once effected at 140 – 143. This was on February 10. The next day a broker sold 10,000 shares, buyer 10, immediately upon the close of second session, and the corner subsided directly after.

An absolute equivalent to gambling is not to be found in any phase of speculation, but what are sometimes called "privileges" approach very nearly to the nature of a bet.

Privileges are either *puts* or *calls*.

A *put* is where a certain sum is paid for the privilege of delivering a given amount of stock, within a stipulated time, at a definite price. Suppose an operator, A, on

March 20, 1868, paid John Jones $200 for a *put* on two hundred shares of Hudson at 135 any time within twenty days. The contract of the giver of the *put* would read as follows:—

NEW YORK, *March* 20, 1868.

For Value Received, the Bearer may DELIVER ME Two Hundred Shares of the Stock of the Hudson River Railroad Company, at One Hundred and Thirty-five per cent, any time in Twenty days from date. The undersigned is entitled to all the dividends or extra dividends declared during the time.

JOHN JONES.

The stock sold at 138 on the day of the bargain. It is evident that a fall of one per cent on "put" price would be necessary for the recovery of the whole premium. After that every fractional decline would be a gain. Hudson was 123 on April 9. A then presented the above slip of paper, and received the difference between the price contracted for and the street rate. His profit stood thus:—

Received $ 12 a share on 200 shares . .	$2,400
Paid for privilege one per cent . . .	200
Net gain	$2,200

A *call* is simply the reverse of a *put.* A sum is paid as premium for the privilege of demanding within a designated date a given amount of stock for a certain stipulated price. In April, 1868, Rock Island sold low. It had been ranging for some months previously from par far down into the nineties. On April 15 a broker in the bear interest sold five hundred shares at 85. Suppose on that day a speculator, C, had offered $100, or half of one per cent, for the right of demanding two hundred shares within twenty days at 89. The market was unstrung. Various rumors were afloat to the detriment of the company, and the *call* sought for was readily sold. The blank agreement, when properly filled in, read in this wise: * —

NEW YORK, *April* 15, 1868.

For Value Received, the Bearer may CALL ON ME for Two Hundred Shares of the Stock of the Chicago and Rock Island Railroad Company, at Eighty-nine per cent, any time in Twenty days from date. The bearer is entitled to all the dividends or extra dividends declared during the time.

BELDEN FISK, JR.

The aspects of the speculation may be thus stated: If, up to May 4, Rock Island had remained constantly below 89, C would of course have waived his right. The premium would in that case be a dead loss, but that would be his whole loss. At 89¼ he could make his *call*

* This agreement is not perfectly explicit. In the Vanderbilt Harlem corner, an old operator unsuspectingly sold a number of "calls" at about 130. When Harlem had reached 250, a demand for the stock was made. He fell back on the ambiguous wording of the paper, declaring he was the victim of a conspiracy. The agreement which he had signed was, as he claimed, a permission on parties to call for the stock without a word requiring his delivery of it. As a criticism the excuse would seem valid; but usage and the operator's own intent when he made the sales were both against this absurd subterfuge.

and recover half his premium; at 89½ the entire bonus would be recovered. In other words, the transaction, to be profitable, presupposed a rise of more than half of one per cent.

Actually, however, on May 4 the lowest quotation of Rock Island was 98, and C *call*ed upon Richard Roe to keep to his contract. The speculation, when Roe settled, was in this shape: —

Roe paid C in differences $9 a share on 200 shares .	$1,800
C had previously paid as premium for call . .	100
C's net profit	$1,700

It is apparent that no one would wish to deliver stock at less than the market price, or demand it on terms above ruling rates. The person who purchases a *put*, therefore, anticipates a decline below the percentage fixed in the contract. The holder of a *call*, on the other hand, buys it in hope of a rise.

The scientific operator varies these simple forms by several classes of artifices.

1. He buys a few *puts* and covers with purchases of as many *calls* as the market will accept. The former transaction deludes the street. The business is done through different brokers, and it is clear that the steadier the price of one class of privilege, the cheaper and more plentiful will be the market of the others. For example: —

On a certain October 11th, D buys five 30-days' Erie *puts* amounting in all to 600 shares, the delivery price being 40, and the premium four per cent. The next day or the same day he buys thirty days' *calls* for 10,000 shares of Erie at 40, paying half of. one per cent premium. He looks to a rise, and on October 31 finds his foresight confirmed, and Erie stiff at 50. Settlements are demanded, and the speculation in *calls* closes with the subjoined result:—

Ten per cent in differences on 10,000 shares of Erie .	$100,000
Deduct premiums, one half of one per cent on 10,000 shares of Erie	5,000
Balance of profit	$95,000

Erie failed to fall below 40 till after November 10. The *puts* were therefore a clear loss. Deduct four per cent, = $2,400, and the final result of the venture stands $92,600.

2. Another method is one which the great "speculative director" of Erie had the credit, a few years ago, of putting into practice. It consists in secretly buying up the great bulk of a particular stock, and then selling some fifty or a hundred thousand dollars' worth of *puts* for thirty, sixty, or ninety days. The stock must be one of seeming weakness, and 69 or 70 are good figures on which to base a contract. As soon as the *puts* are sold, the operator has only to keep the market above 70 till the ninety days are past, which is easy, because the previous purchases naturally render the shares buoyant precisely as in a corner. The operator pockets his premium, and also sells off the stock he had accumulated at probably a handsome advance. In August, 1865, if current rumor is to be credited, a trap to catch green-

5*

backs after this beautiful system was set by the munificent founder of the Drew Theological Seminary. On the last week of that month Erie sold for 82, and *puts* were freely offered at one per cent for thirty or sixty days, at 80 or 81. The street caught at the prize, purchasing *puts* in blocks of 500, 1,000, 5,000 shares,—in any shape and to any amount offered. Something like $300,000 were quietly absorbed in five or six days. Then Erie began to rise: one day it was 84, the next, 87. Shrewd speculators, with their pockets crammed with privileges, thought they understood the game, and at once thronged to the Long Room and bought heavily. No blunder could have been more absurd. The man who sold the *puts* held Erie in the palm of his hand. He could depress it to 80, he could raise it to 90; but the price rested with himself. When they bought, it fell; when they sold, it rose. By the time the privileges had expired, these vibrations of the market had enabled the king operator to add to his gains in premiums two fresh profits from bull and bear. It is a curious incident of this bit of strategy, that the stock had really been accumulated for the purpose of controlling the annual October election of directors, the rich harvest from the street being a mere episode in a great campaign.

3. There is a yet further and, under certain conditions, an absolutely secure method. This consists in buying a *call*, and immediately selling one half the purchase at buyer's option; *videlicet*,—

B on November 20, 1868, buys a *call* for 200 shares

of New York Central at 30 days; delivery rate, 126; price of *call,* $200. The same day he sells 100 shares, seller 30, at 125. Supposing stock falls to 115 and keeps there, the account would then be:—

	100 shares New York Central, delivered at 125	$12,500
Deduct	" " " " at ruling rate 115	11,500
	Difference in B's favor	1,000
	Loss of premiums on *calls*	200
	Net profit	$800

Suppose, however, the stock had risen to 136, the result would then read:—

10 per cent profit by call on 200 shares New York Central	$2,000
11 " lost on 100 shares sold at 125	1,100
Take out premium of *call*	200
B's net gain	$700

B would have been saved from loss in the first case, even if Central had fallen but two per cent, viz. 123; and in the second case if it had risen to only 127. Had the speculation really taken place at the time stated, and under the designated conditions, the record of the share list shows that B could have bought in at 115, seller 20, the 100 shares sold at 125, seller 30, thus realizing $1,000. At the same time he would have been able to make his *call* when the stock was at 159, clearing thereby $6,600, or making in the whole, with premium deducted, the neat sum of $7,400 on a risk of $200. For it was in December, 1868, that the celebrated scrip dividend of Commodore Vanderbilt was declared, and the street startled by one of the most audacious strategetic movements of the year.

Brokers, who are fond of metaphysics, prefer to consider "privileges" as in the nature of an insurance. The claim has plausibility, and undoubtedly the underlying principle of not a few of these transactions is one of protection against changes in the market. An operator may be long in a certain stock. The price begins to falter. The indications of a fall accumulate. If at this point he can buy a *put* for an amount covering his venture, he is safe against all hazards. A short interest, of course, would be protected by a *call*. A year or two since, within the writer's knowledge, a gentleman bought 1,000 shares of a certain stock at 65, and sold it at 69, clearing $4,000. He bought again at 67½ and sold at 71½, making $4,000 more. He then bought 1,000 at 60. The stock dropped to 59. He grew timid. The street was full of rumors, and he determined to hedge. He found a broker who agreed to sell a *put* for 1,000 shares at 55 on payment of $10,000. The money was given, when the market suddenly veered round and the stock went flying up to 71. There he sold, gaining $11,000, or, deducting the exorbitant premium of the *put*, $1,000. He had previously cleared $8,000, and was wise enough to stop. In the Erie speculation alluded to in a previous page the *puts* were largely bought as a safeguard against a possible break in the market, and to that extent the purchases were wise.

CHAPTER VII.

CONCERNING STOCK-BROKERS.

MEMBERSHIP of the New York Stock Exchange is the equivalent of a liberal education. It costs quite as much in hard cash and brain wear, and is worth neither more nor less when acquired. There are brokers, as there are lawyers and doctors, who lay up no treasures on earth, yet manage to slide up and down between debits and credits with average comfort and some felicity. There are brokers whose candle of fortune has been snuffed out in a day, and who wander about the scene of their financial demise with the tenacity of spectres. There are others still, whose hands have the Midas touch, — men of large ideas and generous luck, keen, versatile, coining advantage out of misfortune, — the stamp of humanity which, in the sarcastic *mot* of Napoleon, wins a fortune as one gains a battle.

In the good old times (nobody knows the date, and it was probably in dream-land), brokers throve mightily, and grew passing rich simply upon their commissions. There is a tradition of this in the manual of the Stock Board, and no one, from reading that terse but over-dry code, would suspect that brokers ever did aught beyond buying or selling for other men in consideration of due percentage. In fact, were these commissions always equal to the lawful *maximum*, and the volume of actual business really dependent upon outside orders, there would be, as we have seen, the neat average income of about $109,000. Before the war, when the bulk of securities was not half that of the present, legitimate brokerage was a profitable profession, and the pressure of rivals did not seriously affect the old houses. But with the great national debt, the fluctuations in gold, and the rise in shares, a crowd of new men came pouring into the street. The Stock Exchange shut its doors against this influx. New members were elected with exceeding reluctance, and under constant peril of blackball. Unquestionably one motive for this exclusiveness was the honorable desire to preserve the integrity of their business. Dealing in values whereof much is unsubstantial, and in a class of trade where, in the opinion of a prejudiced public, a narrow margin of fact skirts a boundless space of fiction, they were justly urgent that the margin itself — the *terra firma* of capital and credit — should be as solid as practicable. High above the instinct of safety, however, was the instinct of profit.

Of course, the attempt to monopolize proved nugatory. The Stock Exchange maintained its respectability, but it could not prevent men hungry for wealth, determined, full of eagerness and *élan*, from crowding the pavement, extemporizing a market, and finally establishing organizations of their own. Hence rose the Open Board and the Gold Room.

The members of these competing associations called themselves operators, and preferred the ten and twenty per cents of speculation to the driblet earnings of commissions. They all had customers. They took orders even more freely than their neighbors of the old school. They would work on lower margins and smaller percentages; but it was because their speculations covered wider ground, and their customers' capital helped to strengthen their own position. Naturally, in the demoralization of all values by the greenback era, — fortunes rolling up between sunrise and sunset, a furnace heat of speculation glowing all around them, — even the most conservative brokers of the "close" Board yielded to the fascinations of the period, and ventured into extensive operations. Probably there cannot be found a single house in Wall Street, no matter how wealthy or bound up in traditions, which could show books clean of stock speculations made in the firm interest. In many cases these operations may be hid under a thin veil of personal accounts, — Smith being in stocks; Jones being in gold; but Smith & Jones claiming to do nothing except a commission business. Even this pretence, however, is seldom kept up when broker talks with broker. When the Open and the "close" Boards so far coalesced as to meet in one Long Room, old notions had become so thoroughly rubbed away that members spoke frankly of their "neat turns" and "flyers"; and the great majority were quite ready to allow that, although *they* never speculated, they really could not name another house of which so much could be affirmed. To-day the street has made such progress in conforming language to facts that the *habitués* of the Stock Exchange are classified into bankers, brokers, and operators. By going one step further, and defining operators as men who speculate generally for themselves, sometimes for others; brokers, as persons who buy or sell for outsiders *and* themselves; and bankers, as a combination of the operator, the broker, and the money-lender, the conclusion of the whole matter would be reached. For of such, and only of such, is the present kingdom of the stock market.

But while it is highly essential that the speculative aptitudes of Wall Street should be kept steadily in view, it is not less important to guard against exaggerated conceptions. Taking the houses connected with the Exchange as a class, there is probably a greater average conservatism in their transactions than in those of many leading departments of trade. The high rates of commercial paper, compared with the low percentages of even time loans, which the city banks freely make to the really first-class bankers and brokers, is strong testimony in favor of this position. And this will further appear in the fact that a very considerable portion of the securities dealt in by the great establishments are governments and the class of State bonds which in *ante-bellum* times furnished the groundwork of our entire banking system. There are dozens of houses in the financial quarter whose footing is as stable, and whose method of business is as guarded as that of the private banks of London and the English provincial cities. They take money on deposit, negotiate loans for the chief railroads, simply as agents purchase and sell for customers, and in case of speculation operate in descriptions of securities which even in adverse fluctuations will not endanger their solvency. Their connection with the Stock Board is mainly indirect, and their profits are quite as much by lending money as by stock transactions. They are represented at the Exchange by the second partner, by that indefinite human quantity known as "the Co.," by an *attaché* of the office, or through any one of a score of brokers who take orders at second hand.

Enter their offices, and you discover all the appointments of a great bank; every department having its appropriate desk and officer, a score of clerks working behind the elaborately carved railings, whole suites of carpeted apartments, with rooms within rooms, — a vast, silent, but ever active financial machine, which can cash a check for ten dollars or certify another for a hundred thousand, sell fifty government bonds or buy fifty thousand over the counter, negotiate a railroad loan of ten millions, and exchange fractional currency for one gold dollar. Such a house is that of Jay Cooke & Co., whose connection with the government during the war is historic. Its annual dealings are estimated only in hundred millions. It receives orders from every State, buys, sells, loans, to amounts that would startle the public, if accurate figures were procurable. Henry Clews & Co. are of the same class. They are agents of a dozen railroads, and receive orders daily from all points of the compass. Fisk & Hatch, another firm, are notable as negotiators of the famous Central Pacific Railroad bonds and other securities. These three houses, with the addition of Vermilye & Co., absorb within themselves nearly the whole of Wall Street dealings in governments. Among the other first-class bankers are Babcock Brothers & Co., Baltzer & Taaks, Richard Bell & Co., August Belmont & Co. (agent of the Rothschilds), Brown Brothers & Co. (connected with Brown, Shepley, & Co. of Liverpool, London, and Rio Janeiro), John J. Cisco & Son, Dabney, Morgan, & Co. (J. S. Morgan & Co., London), Drexel, Winthrop, & Co. (with houses in Paris and Philadelphia), Duncan, Sherman, & Co., Eugene Kelley & Co. (branch house in San Francisco), James G. King's Sons, Howes & Macy, Maitland, Phelps, & Co., W. C. Pickersgill & Co. (agents Glyn, Mills, Currey, & Co., London and New Orleans), James Robb, King, & Co., Winslow Lanier & Co., S. G. & G. C. Ward (agents Barings), Frederick Schuchardt & Sons.

The influence of houses of this character upon the Stock Exchange, and especially its Government and Bond department, cannot be overestimated. They constitute the great centripetal force of the street. Many of them owe the bulk of their vast wealth to the war. Growing up with the National debt, and extending their sphere of action in exact proportion with the increase of our legitimate speculative arena, they afford the best possible guaranty of the future. Every step toward the development of New York as a world-mart must be an advancement of themselves, and self-interest alone is sufficient to make them guardians of the integrity of the Stock Board.

Besides these great establishments, whose really

special feature is that they are agents and dealers in the heavier and more substantial classes of securities, and sell or buy in great quantities "over counters," i. e. directly in their offices, there are several firms of commanding influence who deal mainly through the Boards, but have extensive offices and a half-dozen active and silent partners. Among these are John Bloodgood & Co., J. L. Brownell & Co., Camman & Co., Clark, Dodge, & Co., Thomas Denny & Co. (agents for many New England and New York banks), Fearing & Campbell, Fitch & Bowen, David Groesbeck & Co., Hallgarten & Co., Durant & Earle, Kidd, Pierce, & Co., Kissam & Co., Lawrence Brothers & Co., Lees & Waller, Lockwood & Co., Marvin Brothers & Co., H. T. Morgan & Co., William and John O'Brien, George Opdyke & Co., William M. Parks & Co., Riggs & Co., Robinson, Cox, & Co. (brokers for Daniel Drew), Stone, Nichols, & Co., Smith, Gould, Martin, & Co. (agents for Jay Gould and James Fisk, Jr.), Ward & Co., Trevor & Colgate (brokers for Dr. Shelton), Wood, Campbell, & Co., Whitehouse & Co., Smith, Randolph, & Co., George B. Grinnell, Frank Work & Co. (the two last-named houses are special brokers for Vanderbilt), M. Morgan's Sons. Many of these houses are connected with the Gold Board as well as the Stock Exchange. Several will carry a line of stocks from five millions upwards. The commissions of leading houses on outside orders alone are oftentimes enormous.

The location of these firms is in Broad Street, Exchange Place, New Streets. Some also are still to be found in William and Wall Streets. But the application of Wall Street as a name for the seat of speculation is now to a large extent a reminiscence. Some of these offices are on ground floors; others, one flight up stairs. Many of them rival the government brokers in the magnificence of their furniture. Not a few have counters, but, in addition, there are always to be found high screens not unlike Exchange shops, with private doors opening on inner rooms, and one or more windows looking out upon the narrow vestibule where one enters, at which clerks sit on guard. A small aperture, large enough for the thrust of both hands, is cut through the lower portion of each window, and a stranger peering up from under this outlook can hold parley with those inside. If all is satisfactory, he is admitted at the side-door; otherwise he departs less evenly tempered than he came. At these little trap-holes brokers' clerks are perpetually presenting themselves, with budgets of stocks or checks. If the latter, the outsider holds it firmly with one hand, while with the other he seizes the parcel of shares extended to him from within. The clerk at the desk has his grasp likewise upon both check and stock. Then each simultaneously relinquishes the hold of one hand. The shares go out, and the representative of bank deposit goes in. And so the final part of one transaction is completed.

The full number of these broker offices is between four and five hundred. Some of the smaller firms have lodgement several flights up, and the region between Williams and New Streets is literally honeycombed with them. They differ in amount of capital, credit, capacity; but otherwise are very nearly of a kin. The theory of the street is that there should be at least two partners, one for the office and one for the Board. Where one man carries on a business he is invariably known as an operator, buying and selling almost entirely for himself. Many of the operators, as well as the smaller brokers who act principally for other houses, and are styled 1-32 and 1-64 men, have simply desk-room. They number in all some two or three hundred, and include a not inconsiderable proportion of capitalists.

The effect of speculative concentration is more and more apparent in the money quarter. The great broker and banker firms gain every year in power. The lesser houses are becoming dependent. The number of individual small operators and brokers is diminishing. The Bankers and Brokers' telegraph has largely assisted this revolution. Dating its practical acceptance by the financial community only two years back, this strange automatic messenger now finds its way into more than four hundred offices, printing and rolling off, with wonderful accuracy and in the full legibility of type, the exact history of the stock and gold market, second by second, and almost instantaneous with the actual bidding. Customers may enter behind the black-walnut or other screens which shut out the profane public from the mysteries and secrets of brokerage, and read the execution of their orders within a half-hour of their delivery, and the brokers themselves are enabled by this unique contrivance to manipulate the market with an ease and certainty before impossible. Not only does this expedient place the less wealthy broker at a disadvantage, it also renders the duty of buying and selling at the Board more mechanical. The work can be delegated to clerks by power of attorney, or to operators who will divide up commissions with the large houses. Habitually in firms composed of two members, the abler and older partner remains in the office, while the younger representative of the house is constantly at the Exchange, executing the orders with which the day starts, and receiving fresh messages from head-quarters as new commissions flow in, or the opportunity of a happy turn presents itself. Establishments like Jay Cooke & Co., Henry Clews & Co., Vermilye, Lockwood, and Trevor & Colgate, sometimes employ a dozen operators acting at the instance of the managing head of the house.

The problems before a thoroughly wide-awake broker, who has his future to make, are something beyond a parallel with any other profession. He cannot scheme out a single movement without first taking in at a glance the entire field. There are the banks and brokers,— the question of an easy or stringent market compelling to a wide knowledge of trade influences, exports and imports, cotton, wheat, whether the Secretary of the Treasury will buy bonds or sell gold,— a mass of facts which must be comprehended as fully whether the speculation involves five hundred shares or a block of ten thousand.

Then the great operators must be watched. Is there a clique movement developing? Every broker must be

THE REGULAR BOARD.

taken up in detail. Are or are not Robinson, Cox, & Co. selling for Drew? Is Lockwood buying for Vanderbilt or on private account? Such scrutiny is no holiday task. The kings of the stock market are not prone to let the street understand their tactics. If a large operation is to be made, *Ursa Major* gives the word to some special agent, who distributes the order to A, B, and C; A whispers to D, C instructs F, B commissions G, and so the complication extends. This *finesse* is one of the difficulties of the game which perpetually confront the player. Brokers, however, have eyes like ferrets and the instincts of a Fouché. They detect the instruments of a clique leader almost from their first bids. Sometimes they go wrong, but averagely their suspicions are infallible. It will be apparent, therefore, that the duties incident to attendance at the Exchange are anything but light. Indeed, there is no limit to the shrewdness, coolness, mental alacrity, and aptitudes of all sorts which are developed and strengthened by the ever-fresh conditions of their profession! They go to the Boards as athletes enter the ring. They scan the offers and bids, and detect each incipient indication of unusual movements, of a "weakness" in this stock and a forced market in that. The whole luck of a customer's order or personal ventures may depend in shouting a half-second earlier or longer, or an octave higher, than one's neighbor. Half the small fortunes of speculation are made in the snap of the fingers, in lightning-like zigzags of buying here and selling there, both in the same breath, and over the heads of a hundred rivals. A stranger may visit the Exchange every day for a month, and learn something fresh each hour. There is no end to the humor, the quick expedients, the volatility of these men. A well-perfected combination in some particular stock has been upset for the day by the ready-wittedness of one or two brokers eager to foil the game. The manual of the Stock Exchange is plentifully besprinkled with by-laws enforcing special fines for special offences. They indicate an absurdly frolicsome spirit in members. But half the foolery has a meaning. The plan may be to run up Michigan Southern. The Vice-President calls off the stock, and a burly broker starts it off at an advance of a quarter. A neighbor tickles his ear, and in a flash down goes the offender's hat over his eyes. All around the table the brokers are in a sudden ferment. The hammer rattles at the desk. "Fine Peters, —fine, fine, fine Peters. Fine Henderson, Henderson, Henderson"; the mob cheers and shouts, and rolls hither and thither. When quiet returns, Michigan Southern has disappeared and the call of a dozen stocks has intervened. The broker who caused the tumult has gained his point, and is quite willing to pay his fifty or sixty dollars of fines.

Still further, the operator must not only anticipate the loan market and clique schemes, he must equally carry in his head the transactions of every member of the Board. He must know what stocks Vermilye & Co., Henry Clews & Co., Smith, Gould & Martin, D. Groesbeck & Co., etc., are carrying, what houses are dealing heavily in options, who are holding off, who are entering the field in force,— in a word, he must know all the cards and every man's style of play, before he can confidently set forth privateering. There are brokers, according to rumor, who from time to time fee half the clerks of Wall Street, in order to hold every "point" which a knowledge of office books would afford,— who favor club men with choice opportunities for speculation, and then use them for extracting information such as can be gleaned in the open talk of the up-town club palaces.

Even with all these precautions, the risks are enormous; for just as Robinson is going to sail down upon Fort Wayne, with cannon all mounted and with confidence that so over-weighted is the street with this stock, and so active is the money market likely to be, that a sharp sale of five hundred or two or three thousand shares will knock down everything, it may happen that Messrs. Roe & Doe have just received a Western order to buy eight thousand, and instead of a falling market, the stock rises perhaps two per cent. Robinson's "short" sale proves, therefore, ruinous.

Naturally, the operator likes to be on the side of the heavy artillery. To be "in with" a great speculative leader, to buy and sell with him, to take his points and hold the same line of stock, are prudential measures which Wall Street thoroughly understands. It is not always safe, as the Drew Gambit shows; but it is another element of power which is worth all the more if not too confidingly relied upon. Old members of the Board have an inveterate dislike for cliques. What the sportsman feels in regard to a Jersey decoy-hunter, or your genuine Down-East fisherman thinks of the trolling butchery, the thoroughbred stock-broker of the bygone school holds respecting these immense combinations which take more money out of stocks in a day than individual operators would absorb in a year. The gold corner of September, by the reaction which it caused in every class of speculation, had a disastrous effect upon the great mass of brokers' business, which was felt for three months after. The outsiders were frightened off. They no longer consented to feed the street with fresh funds when every calculation, however accurate on general grounds, was liable to be upset by a sudden inroad of from five to twenty millions of dollars, sweeping down or up the stock gamut with no regard whatsoever to the natural laws of the market. Of course in time this timidity disappears. The birds return to the plucking, and all is once more merry. But to brokers the sense of insecurity is constant; and houses which have no connection with the great rings look in vain for the same success in their business which was possible when such influences were exceptional.

The customer is an important integer in brokerage. The most speculative house in the street has an ambition for a good line of outside commissions. In fact, average experience proves that this is the sheet-anchor of brokers. Few houses or individuals get rich and keep rich by speculation alone. We shall revert to this phase of the business in another chapter. But there are one or two points which more properly belong to the present page. Brokers are very careful of new men. No respectable firm will take a commission from any one who has not been properly introduced. They want to know all about his means, whether he be slippery in his dealings; in fact, everything bearing upon his business peculiarities. This scrutiny is an absolute prerequisite. Scarcely any broker who disregards this safeguard but fails to pay dearly for his folly. And the reason of the caution will be readily apparent. Customers invariably buy or sell on margins. If the former, they are quite apt to desire to have their stock "carried." Hence it is necessary to be assured that when further margin is required the money will be forthcoming, and in case the loan market is exceedingly tight the additional interest will be paid without murmur. Above seven per cent is usury under the law, and there are not a few individuals of the "shyster" class who are ready to break their word, when they can shield themselves from prosecution under the pretence of illegal rates. Recent decisions of the courts have made it obligatory to serve a notice personally upon customers when a fresh instalment of margin is called for. This rendering of the law has an element of justice, and is a healthy check upon sharp practice on the part of brokers; but it furnishes a loophole for a great deal of outside trickery. Men give orders, leave deposits, and then retire. If the stock falls, they have hasty business out of town. The broker's messengers look for them in vain. Every moment, however, the shares are declining in value. The law forbids their sale, although the descent of prices may cause a loss to dealers of five or ten thousand dollars. Some sell at once. A few days after, the stock jumps up in flying leaps of twenty or thirty per cent. The John Smiths suddenly reappear, rubbing their hands gleefully. "That is a neat figure for Northwest. You 'd better sell." "Not by an acre. You did n't put up the margin, and we dumped the stock into the market." "The de'il you did. Now that won't do. I never got any notice. If you don't compromise in forty-eight hours, paying up the difference to full rates of to-day, I 'll see what the judges have to say about it." Most brokers reply that he may go to law as soon as he pleases. An energetic expletive is apt to couple itself with this permission. Possibly a suit follows, and the affair is prolonged for years in the court by sharp lawyers. But a settlement is usually cheaper in the end, and the wiser brokers content themselves with simply branding their customer in such a way that he finds it henceforth no easy matter to speculate. It may have happened that the shares in question were only sold after the reaction, and therefore with great profit. Ought the customer to participate in this gain, when he failed to maintain his portion of the contract? These are subtleties of conscience and logic which confront brokers every day, and make them more apt to conciliate their patrons than to indulge in the folly of anger.

Indeed, one of the wonderful things in brokerage is its development of philosophy. This wholesome rule of guidance displays itself, not merely in the serenity with which reverses of fortune are met, but in a certain beautiful instinct of forgiveness. "Street" quarrels are quick mended. The man who is denounced as an infamous swindler to-day is accepted as a confederate in some fresh transaction to-morrow. Some feuds last a year; the majority, a week; not a few, from ten hours to ten minutes.

The happy Chinese principle of compromise with that large class which is apt to be oblivious of the eighth clause of the Mosaic by-laws was first made fashionable among Anglo-Saxons by Wall Street. When Jerome was robbed of his bonds, he offered to share with the appropriators, and no questions asked, if the deficit should be promptly made up. Bank directors learn their lessons in this school of the brokers. There is an amusing story of this description afloat. X, the cashier of a certain bank, had "appropriated" a hundred thousand dollars, and lost it in speculation. The day for the examination of the books was at hand. In great fear X called in his lawyer, and asked advice. "I have a reputation to sustain. My wife, children, the church,—it would be a horrible scandal. What can be done?"

"You can't raise the money?"

"No."

"Well, there *is* an easy way out of it."

"Eh!" gasps the cashier.

"Why, you should simply absorb two hundred thousand more, and the day before the scrutiny call together the directors, and make a frank confession."

X grew interested, asked more questions, and then decided to follow up the suggestion.

When the outraged officers met, X was overwhelmed with mortification. He was a defaulter for $300,000.

It had all gone in that infernal Harlem. He was exceedingly sorry. "Of course, gentlemen, there is the law. You can expose me. You can throw me into Sing-Sing, shock the community, and hurt the bank's credit. It ought to be done. I have not twenty dollars. But then my friends are exceedingly concerned. They agree — if you will keep the whole affair silent, give me a letter regretting that I am compelled from my health to resign, and duly testifying to my integrity — to privately collect one third of the amount and place it to your credit. You can figure to yourself the pain such a proposition causes me. But then there is the family, *and* the bank."

The directors reflected for thirty-six hours. Then they called X in, and asked if the money was certain to be paid over. He referred them to a "friend." All was satisfactorily arranged. The bank got back its one hundred thousand, the cashier retired on a hundred thousand, and the letter of regret and admiration remains in the family archives as evidence of the incorruptibility of its worthy but invalid member.

Among brokers this exquisite anecdote has a certain lack of freshness. It is what the street has been doing for years. Half the time, indeed, the cashier is not even suspended, provided he guarantees that the deficiency shall be made good. Four years ago a firm, now dissolved, had a clerk named Jackson, who was simply invaluable. He never made mistakes, — could figure up the most complicated transaction with a rapidity and cleverness that invariably redounded to the profit of the brokers, however it might be with the customers. One day the house had five hundred shares of Fort Wayne to deliver. Jackson sent the boy out with three hundred, intending to take in the remaining two hundred during the morning, and so make the balance good. Back comes the office lad with a check for an amount covering five hundred shares. The blunder was clear, but the clerk held his peace, and before night distributed the missing shares so completely, by sales here and there, that it was quite impossible to trace them.

Smith, Jones, & Co., who had unwittingly checked for more than they got, soon came round to the firm for an explanation. The boy swore he had delivered five hundred. He had caught the cue at once and would have taken his oath in court. Jackson was innocent. *He* certainly sent over the whole lot. The injured brokers were in an unhappy plight. Their check was equivalent to a legal receipt. They were *short* with a vengeance, and with no redress.

The members of the house in which Jackson was employed were of keen honor. Nothing was left undone to get at the facts. In two or three days some of the Fort Wayne was traced. Everything pointed to the clerk.

One evening they called him into the inner office. "Now, Jackson, we understand how that matter occurred. It was a natural temptation. You have been speculating, and you wanted to do better. Of course you would never steal from anybody. If those shares are produced by noon to-morrow, there will be no trouble. Otherwise — "

Jackson was not a character for a novel. He neither turned pale nor bit his lip. They might do their worst, but he was not in the conspiracy. Next morning, however, a package carefully tied and containing the equivalent of the missing shares was found by the office-boy when he came down town and unlocked the door. The partner sent it over to Smith, Jones, & Co., and Jackson kept at his desk without being troubled with further annoyance. Two years after, when the house broke up, the clerk was provided with flattering testimonials, and to-day is one of the smartest men in the street.

Every day clerks are discharged for dishonesty. There is hardly a house in the whole money-quarter that has not suffered from peculation; but it never goes so far as the police court. The defaulter is advised to resign, receives a great deal of sound counsel, couched in tolerably strong Saxon, and walks forth to fields and pastures new, with no fear of further harm, save through whispers and the shrugging of shoulders. Even that degree of punishment is seldom inflicted, and the secret is locked up forever. Unquestionably a generous unwillingness to destroy a reputation beyond all future retrieval is the cause of most of these evasions of justice; but there are men understanding stock-jobbing thoroughly who explain the habitual lenity on other grounds.

Brokers have a certain phrase implying a peculiar injustice to which customers are frequently subject. "Speculating upon orders" is the technical wording. A man wishes a lot of stock bought. His broker executes the order at 69. In half an hour the shares rise to $69\frac{3}{4}$. He charges his customer for the stock at $69\frac{1}{2}$, and so clears half of one per cent, besides his commissions. Or he agrees to sell at seller 30, and, believing, from the fact that this stock is very active, that his customer will probably close up the transaction in four or five days, he sells at a lower figure, seller 10, and charges an average of the day's bids at thirty days. This may afford a difference of two per cent in favor of the broker. Perhaps in eight days, if not before, the whole business is completed, as anticipated. Technically, the customer has not suffered injury; but it is not thought advisable to spread abroad the fame of this astuteness. There are hundreds of ways to speculate upon orders without much risk of discovery, and with a thin gauze of justification for every infraction of theoretic honor. The purchases or sales are always charged down within market rates; if usury is paid, it is never put in the bill above the quoted terms, and the broker's conscience is readily quieted by the fact that he might have been compelled to pay all that he asserts that he paid, the difference being due to his superior cleverness. As the customer does not attempt to remunerate him for that, he ought not to have the profit of it. All these neat side-transactions are known to the employees. Frequently they are demoralized by them. And if the human nature of a broker's clerk grows weak, and he occasionally makes slips of the pen whereby his pocket is benefited, it is human nature in the broker to condone, lest his speculations on orders should be brought to light in unpleasant ways.

It is asserted that this is one of the most forcible motives for abstention from criminal procedure. Some outsiders, who have lost money, go so far as to insist that even the most respectable houses have secrets that are all the better for remaining secrets. This is probably pure prejudice. At all events, with the better class of brokers, there is probably not so much trickery as in other leading pursuits. Between themselves members of the Stock Exchange are peculiarly honorable. Up to 1865 only three brokers had been expelled from the Boards, one for misstating the price of Hudson to a customer, another for giving checks on a bank where he had no deposit, and the last for forgery. Indeed, the whole influence of the government of the Exchange is thrown against the least indications of financial irregularity, and, under President Neilson, the lines have been drawn with far greater rigidity than at any previous period.

Thus far we have omitted mention of a very important feature of the street. During the old days of the war a casual visitor in Broad Street at the twilight hour would have observed outside of the Stock Exchange, upon the pavement, a crowd almost as large as that within, bidding with even fiercer emphasis and with less decorum, — cigar-smoke mingling freely with the shouting, — queer habiliments, queer faces, the Jew physiognomy predominating over the Gentile. That was the once powerful, the obstreperous, burly, ancient "outside" Board, whose roof was the sky, whose offices were in their pockets, whose aspirations were boundless, and whose lives were an incessant romance. One reason for their decadence is to be found in the Brokers' telegraph and the monopolizing tendencies of speculation. Another cause of their recent disappearance was undoubtedly the establishment of the National Stock Exchange, whose room is on the opposite side of Broad Street. This organization, the outgrowth of the temporary exclusion of Erie from the call at the Regular Board, has acquired a definite position since the old Open Board ceased to exist.* Solid brokers are wont to scoffingly declare that it represents some hundred millions of defunct capital, its members being mainly street bankrupts who have lost credit and standing by unfortunate speculations. In street *argot*, they are "snipes" and "lame ducks." But this view is not destitute of prejudice. In fact, the new Exchange is a composite body with its future before it, and a modest judgment will not overlook the truth that Fortune in our great money-mart is a very fickle goddess, and that the most successful men in all new countries are those who have known failure and risen superior to it. Their greatest obstacle, however, is to be found in causes which we have already noted, and which have proved signally efficient in clearing the pavement of its former *habitués*.

* The organization of this Board dates with February 7, 1869. The dealings are in railroad stocks and a few of the more active mining and petroleum shares. The admission fee is $500. The President is A. L. Mowry. The second Vice-President calls the stocks, and receives $5,000 a year. Many members of the Gold Board are on the roll-call of this Exchange. The total of members is about three hundred.

The story of "outside" brokerage cannot be written in these pages, but it would be found full of thrilling and amusing chapters. Every great stock market has had this fringe of speculation clinging to its surface like barnacles. It has been the school of many famous operators. Its wit is pungent, its schemes wild in daring, its courage and tenacity wonderful. Whatever is piquant and coarsely racy in street *argot* had its birth here.

What is broker *argot?* It is half technicalities, half slang. Brokers have this in common with the liberal professions, — they deal in a dialect which is caviare to the multitude. Nobody buys coffee or copper, teak-wood or tea-chests, for purposes of profit, without a tolerable insight into trade-marks, ways of sale, and ordinary merchant "shop" talk. But mankind goes to its doctors, lawyers, architects, chemists, stock-brokers, with a distinct feeling of ignorance, and a consciousness that an assumption of knowledge would be extra-hazardous under the circumstances. Very clever money men, unless they have taken lessons in the school, will find themselves beyond their depth in attempting fluency in Wall Street jargon. Ordinary amateur speculators are as amusing as Mrs. Malaprops. For although constant iteration has made certain phrases familiar, yet there is a subtle something in the intercourse of habitual dealers in stock which renders a counterfeit distinctly recognizable.

Street *argot* is like other *argot.* It is mainly the outgrowth of necessity. In sale or purchase, such abbreviations as "Cash," "Regular," "Buyer 30," "At the Opening," "About," "Sold," "Ten up," with their endless variations, are phrases without which, or without some similar abbreviations of speech, a large stock market would be impossible. Values change with such rapidity, new tactics and strategy must be assumed so suddenly, that a systematized and routine vocabulary is as essential as the keys of a piano to the musician. Many of the sale phrases of the Boards have already been incidentally given; others will presently be explained. But there is a great mass of jargon which does not strictly belong to this specific field. Every style and manner of brokerage has its name. Every shade and flavor of speculation — the artifices, frauds, deceptions, of the business — are generally nicknamed and gibbeted with an epithet. Some of this jargon owes its origin to 'Change Alley and the Paris Bourse. Much is essentially American. Always more piquant than select, racy, rank with a certain street flavor like the perfume of hostelries, sometimes cruel, gross, harsh, — it presents a strong fusion of the coarseness of money-getting with the *élan* and vivaciousness of successful speculation. It would be useless to attempt a complete glossary. There are words of a day, as well as the picked phrases of centuries. For stock-dealers are the keenest men in the civilized hemispheres, and no possible variation or new shuffle of cards but finds some one witty enough to pinion it with an appropriate epithet. Many of the phrases which we subjoin have already been explained in connection with the machinery of speculation.

A "break" in the market. Where stock is kept up by artificial means, and a money stringency, or similar cause, makes it difficult to carry the load, the attack of a bear clique or the actual inability of holders will produce a decline in value. The market "breaks" down.

Ballooning. To work up a stock far beyond its intrinsic worth, by favorable stories, fictitious sales, or other cognate means.

Block. A number of shares, say 5,000 or 10,000, massed together, and sold or bought in a lump.

To "buy in." The act of purchasing stock in order to meet a "short" contract, or to enable one to return stock which has been borrowed.

"Carrying" stock. To hold stock with the expectation of selling it at an advance.

Clique. A combination of operators, controlling vast capital, in order to unduly expand or break down the market.

Conversions. Bonds are frequently issued with a provision whereby they can at any moment be exchanged for equivalent stock. Such securities are called "convertible," and the act of substitution is styled "conversion."

Corners. When the market is over sold, the shorts, if compelled to deliver, find themselves in a "corner." The *modus operandi* is detailed in Chapter VI.

Collaterals. Any kind of Wall Street values given in pawn, when money is borrowed.

"Cover," to "cover one's shorts." Where stock has been sold and the market rises, the seller buys where he

can, in order to protect himself on the day of delivery. This is "covering short sales."

"Curbstone" brokers. Men who are not members of any regular organization, and do business mainly upon the sidewalk.

Delivery. When stock is brought to the buyer in exact accordance with the rules of the Stock Exchange, it is called a "good delivery." When there are irregularities, — the shares being of unacceptable issues, the power of attorney not being satisfactory, or in some way the rules of the Exchange are contravened, — the delivery is pronounced bad, and the buyer can appeal to the Board.

Differences. The price at which a stock is bargained for and the rate on day of delivery are usually not the same. The variation is known as the "difference," and occasionally brokers pay over this money balance instead of furnishing the stock. Such cases are exceedingly rare, notwithstanding public opinion to the contrary.

A "drop" in a stock is equivalent to a "break," except that it may possibly be due to wholly natural causes.

Duck; Dead Duck; Lame Duck. Phrases as old as the London Stock Exchange. The "Lame Duck" is a broker who has failed to meet his engagements; and a "Dead Duck" is one who is absolutely bankrupt past all recovery. If he haunts the street, it is as a "curbstone" broker.

Forcing Quotations, is where brokers wish to keep up the price of a stock, and to prevent its falling out of sight.

This is generally accomplished by a small sale, or by "washing."

Flat. This term is used where money or stocks are lent without interest.

A "flyer," is a small side operation, not employing one's whole capital. It is nearly equivalent to what is ordinarily known as a venture.

Gosling. A Lame Goose.

Gunning a stock, is to use every art to produce a "break," when it is known that a certain house is heavily supplied, and would be unable to resist an attack.

Gutter Snipes. Curbstone brokers.

Holding the market, is to buy sufficient stock at the Boards to keep the price from declining.

Hypothecating. Putting up "collaterals."

Jobbers. Used only conventionally in Wall Street. In London it is the equivalent of an operator.

Josh. A word shouted at the Exchange in order to wake up a sleepy member.

Kite-Flying. Expanding one's credit beyond wholesome limits.

A "let up." Employed when an artificial pressure upon money or any other cause leading to a stringency in the loan market suddenly disappears. When the high prices of a corner cease on account of the clique's withdrawing, the same phrase is used.

Load. To "load" one's self with stock is to buy heavily.

Long in stocks. When a man is carrying a stock for a rise.

Milking the street. The act of cliques or great operators who hold certain stocks so well in hand that they cause any fluctuations they please. By alternately lifting and depressing shares, they take all the floating money in the market.

An "off" market, is where prices have fallen either in a week, a day, or even an afternoon.

"Out," got "out" of stock. When an operator has rid himself of a certain line of stock.

To "pass" a dividend, is a euphemism adopted by directors of corporations to express an act which in ordinary English would be called *not* passing a dividend. In other words, a dividend is said to be *passed* when the directors vote against declaring it.

A Point. A theory or a fact regarding stocks on which one bases a speculation.

Pool. The stock and money contributed by a clique to carry through a corner.

Saddling the market, is to foist a certain stock on the street.

Salt down stock, is to buy and hold for a long period. It is nearly the equivalent of investment.

To "sell out" a man, is to sell down a stock, which another is carrying, so low that he is compelled to quit his hold, and perhaps to fail.

A Sick market; the market is Ill. When brokers very generally hesitate to buy. Generally the consequent of previous over-speculation.

Short. When one has sold stock.

Spilling stock. When great quantities of a stock are

thrown upon the market, sometimes from necessity, often in order to "break" the price.

Swimming market. The opposite of a sick market. Everything is buoyant.

"*Ten up*," the phrase used at the Boards when a broker's ability to keep his contracts is questioned. It means that a deposit of ten per cent on the selling value of the stock bid for must be put up before the contract can hold good.

Traps. An almost obsolete phrase for broken fancy stocks, depreciated railroad securities, etc.

Twist on the shorts. A clique phrase used where the shorts have undersold heavily, and the market has been artificially raised, compelling them to settle at ruinous rates.

To Unload, is to sell out a stock which has been carried for some time.

Washing, is where one broker arranges with another to buy a certain stock when he offers it for sale. The bargain is fictitious, and the effect, when not detected, is to keep it quoted, and, if the plotters buy and sell the stock to a high figure, to afford a basis for *bona fide* sales.

Watering a stock, is the hydraulic artifice employed by modern managers to double the quantity of a stock without improving its quality.

To wipe out an operator, is to entangle him in transactions until he loses his footing and fails utterly. It is one of the malignancies and cruelties of the street.

CHAPTER VIII.

HABITS AND HUMORS OF "THE STREET."

ONE of the finest characteristics of brokers is their generosity. There are few mean men in and around Broad and Wall Streets. The miser instinct is impossible. Dealing with money values constantly, they attach to them more accurate ideas than is the wont of portions of the outside world. They *know* that greenbacks are for use, and although in no region are there such opportunities for making the most of every dollar, there is probably not a community so liberal and free-handed, so considerate and kindly, in the employment of its surplus resources. They lend to friends with a superb carelessness for receipts or times of payment. They give largely to charities. Churches in need of funds, colleges seeking new endowments, benevolent institutions that do not care to imitate Müller's "Life of Trust," send their broadcloth beggars into the down-town offices by swarms. Every great banking-house has a host of such applicants. Sometimes brokers will mass their benefactions in one great gift, like Messrs. Trevor and Colgate, who placed two hundred and eighty thousand dollars to the credit of a Baptist church at Yonkers not many months ago. Others distribute their largesses more evenly, and the number of those who have bought certificates of life-membership in Bible and Missionary societies is simply legion. They take the certificates at par, and neither sell nor employ them as collaterals. But it is not merely in what we may perhaps call routine charities that brokers evince their munificence. The instances are common of young men, just breasting the tide of luck or loss as operators, who support mothers or invalid fathers in elegance, send their brothers to college and their sisters to the musical conservatories of Germany. A painful phase of brokerage is that final winding-up of a hard-fought career by an unexpected inability to meet one's contracts. "Jones *busted*" passes from mouth to mouth. The Vice-President hammers the tumult around the table into silence. "Gentlemen, Mr. Paul Jones is unable to fulfil his contract with Make & Mendum, and I have, therefore, to buy 10,000 shares of Erie under the rule." Then the auctioneer biddings follow in swift succession from the rostrum. When all is bought, the difference between the rate of bargain and the purchase price is charged to the defaulting member, and until he satisfies this debt he is "suspended." Very possibly it may amount to a sum beyond his crippled resources, and the broker may not only be irrevocably ruined, but the anxieties to which it gives birth may bring on nervous prostration and disease. Such calamities frequently come even without failure, when dealers, by the chances of the market, have lost their last margin of capital. In such an event the impecunious or broken brokers receive assistance in misfortune from the Society of Mutual Relief, which has long been an institution of the Stock Exchange. Thoroughly independent of the business organization in its officers and government, this association includes in itself almost every member of the Board. The yearly assessment is twelve dollars, but one can commute for a life-membership by payment of two hundred dollars. Although comparatively few brokers have availed themselves of the privileges of the association, yet necessarily not a little of quiet benevolence has resulted from this thoughtful scheme. The sick are cared for; the dying father feels that in his burial no pauper reminiscences will cling around his memory,—that the widow will be watched over and the orphan protected. The merchants of New York who call stock operations gambling would do well to take a lesson from this association, instead of allowing some of the men once leaders in their ranks to fall from bankruptcy into pinched distress, with Blackwell's Island as a not infrequent sequel.

There are two ways of construing the golden rule, and the street adopts both renderings. It looks after its neighbors, and it cares not less for itself. Broadway tailors glorify their craft by regal achievements in the furnishing forth of their broker customers. Their bills are long, but they never encounter long faces on presenting them for payment. Some of the Broad Street operators are unique in the elegance of their attire. John Bloodgood, one of the most dashing, incisive, and brilliantly successful of speculative brokers, bears the just appellation of the Beau Brummel of Wall Street, on account of his superiority in this not ignoble rivalry. Good lunches as well as good dinners are thoroughly appreciated at the Stock Exchange. Delmonico caters in Broad Street. Occasionally a party of brokers will open a lunch account, investing a few hundred dollars in stocks, and charging the gain or loss to wine, cigars, and oysters. When men speculate for their stomachs, they are apt to win; and the balances of this curious account are often large enough to allow of an intermittent "spread" up town. About nightfall the Nicholson pavement fronting the Sub-Treasury and flanked by the Regular and National Exchanges is lined by hacks. A few are private, but the larger proportion wait for chance patronage. Brokers who have made lucky strokes during the day, and are in good humor with the world at large, button their coats gayly, pick out their carriage, step in with a nod to the Jehu, and bowl away up Broadway and the Avenue to Vanity Fair. Some find an excuse for the extravagance in desperation itself; holding that if they have just lost nine thousand nine hundred and ninety dollars, they cannot do better than toss the driver an X. and so even the deficit up to ten thousand. There are a great number of speculative hack "pools." One firm, in recently taking annual account of stock, found itself *minus* five thousand dollars through transactions looking to a constant supply of funds for carriage hire. This was not as profitable as the lunch ventures.

It is impossible to treat of all the peculiarities of the Stock Board without becoming inconsecutive. There are not a few independent operators who are what may be styled "free lances." They have abundant capital, and watch the chance turns of the daily market for large

BROAD STREET FROM WALL STREET.

profits. They buy or sell at one session, and cover either at the next call or in the Long Room. A gain of one quarter or one half per cent on the sale price of shares satisfies them; and the opportunities for a tolerably safe speculation are extremely frequent. Any financial report in the commercial column of the daily papers will show variations between morning and afternoon. Thus, on the 29th of November, 1869, New York Central and Hudson Consolidated Stock sold at eleven A. M. for 78. By three P. M. it was quoted at 76. Had a block of 10,000 shares been sold in the early part of the day and bought in later, $20,000 would have been cleared. Of course, so large an operation would have been apt to miscarry, unless the market was very firm at first, and correspondingly weak at the close. But transactions of a lighter calibre are by no means unsafe. December 1 we find that 400 shares of Toledo and Wabash sold for 60 at first call, and that at the second board 100 were bought at 58 and 300 at 57⅞. If this was the manipulation of the same operator, he must have made $837.50. December 27, 30,000 New York Central and Hudson River Consol. sold at early board for 81⅞, and 1,400 were bought back at one P. M. for 81¼. Out of this change of five-eighth per cent $875 was the profit. The next day Pacific Mail sold for 47½ and 46⅛; New Jersey Central for 92½–90½. These vibrations, perpetually recurring, are the source of hundreds upon hundreds of lucky hits. Naturally there are numerous workers in this rich mine, some with far less capital than assurance. These latter form an outlying fringe, to which the slang of the street has given the expressive term, borrowed from the army, of "bummers." An eighth or a quarter satisfies them. If they make a fortunate stroke, they rest upon their laurels, loitering about the Long Room or before the Vice-President's pulpit for days after, ready to try another "flyer" if the chance comes, or to indulge in every description of tomfoolery, if the bidding is dull. They are the *bêtes noires* of more sober brokers, and the additions their wild exploits make to the semiannual balauces of the Roll-Keeper average tens of thousands of dollars.

An exceedingly ingenious device of some of the younger men of this class consists in having a minute automatic syringe filled with perfumed water and concealed behind a large signet-ring. Armed with this amiable weapon, the broker leans carelessly on the shoulder of an acquaintance, and dexterously sends an imperceptible streamlet of Lubin just on the edge of the ear. Off goes his hat, and down goes the Vice-President's mallet. The real criminal escapes, and the luckless member who has ventured to take the law in his own hands is amerced sundry dollars. The old Open Board has witnessed hundreds of such scenes. No one knows how much of Billy H——'s income for the past half-dozen years has been swallowed by fines, into which his unbounded humor has involved him. One day he stood up some six minutes behind his brother, then Vice-President, holding an umbrella wide open like an immense canopy over the official head. Suddenly the latter turned round, and the click of the gavel kept company with "fine, fine, fine, fine, fine, fine," the routine penalty going down every time the word was uttered, until the fraternal offender had subsided in his seat. Another time a broker-member of a young banking-house, on a certain blue Monday, had invited a customer just in from the country to go over with him to the Board. This customer had lost fifteen thousand dollars in speculations, and was meditating the wisdom of plunging still farther into the whirlpool,—a tall, dreary-looking person, with a down-drooping, long, melancholy face, as woe-begone a spectacle as one might see in a lifetime. The Open Board in Broad Street was provided with a broad aisle, on either side of which were dense rows of arm-chairs which members took by allotment, and were compelled to remain seated in during sessions. Down this aisle went the broker and his sad-visaged friend. The market was spiritless, and over the thin murmur of offers and bids, Billy H——'s voice was heard screaming out, "There goes one of Granger's victims!" The aspect of the man, so unexpectedly become the centre of all eyes, corresponded so remarkably with the jest that the whole assembly went wild with merriment.

How much may be written of these daily escapades, of these absurdities, this overflowing humor, shot like silver threads through the dull and exhausting routine of the market! A member drops asleep; worn out, it may be, by long nights over ledgers and feverish daily wrestlings with bull or bear. "Josh," "Josh," "Josh," comes roaring up from a dozen leathern lungs, and the broker lifts his head, and rubs his eyes, startled from slumber by the traditional rallying-cry. A rural stranger stands within the railing, invited by one of the Board to see the sights. "Hats off," somebody shouts. The visitor doffs his fresh-brushed beaver in decorous submission to what he takes for an official order to the whole assembly, and discovers when too late that he is the victim of metropolitan sportiveness. To an outsider this lack of dignity is confusing and inscrutable. That men whose fortunes or whose customers' fortunes depend upon an earnest attention to every phase of shares should break out into the effervescence of a school-boy recess, tossing "paper darts," jerking off hats, singing "So say we all of us," "Shoo, Fly," Opéra Bouffe, "John Brown"; extemporizing mock markets; forsaking the regular call in order to be onlookers in a fracas between two irate brokers, who commence their "mill" at the Board, and adjourn to an up-stair committee-room, where the fight is carried to the bitter end amid the cheers of a hundred friendly bystanders; — that such scenes should be so frequent as to be an admitted feature of broker life is a puzzle that we will not venture to solve. It is one of the mysteries of Providence, and, like other mysteries, has, perhaps, a wholesome and saving element behind it. In an insane asylum, dancing and theatrical exhibitions are sanitary measures. And the tense brain fibres of these soldiers of finance would paralyze under the incessant strain of business, were it not for these occasional outbursts.

Through all this spontaneity and effervescence of animal spirits there runs a vein of genuine manliness and nobleness. The death of a member throws a gloom over the Board.. The Stock Exchange flag runs up to half-mast, and an adjournment is voted at the end of the first call, or at the beginning of the second session. Even the obscurest member cannot die without some official mention ; and although the buying and selling may precede or follow the announcement, there is a moment of breathless silence in which every hat is decorously raised from head. The stock-brokers were the first to initiate the general closing of all business, on news of the assassination of President Lincoln. The decease of Ex-Secretary of War Stanton caused an immediate adjournment, with appropriate resolutions. During the years of the war the brokers were loyal to the core. Men suspected of hostility to the government found it impossible to gain admission to either Board, no matter how well indorsed. The black-ball was as relentless as the bullet. As soon as gold appeared likely to be a perplexing financial element, and a barometer of the waning or rising faith in the nation, it was stricken from the call.

In their intercourse with strangers, the brokers are exceptionally courteous, and cases where the boorish instinct discloses itself are extremely rare. If Mr. Johnson introduces you to Mr. Smith, the latter is at once at your service, and to every apology for encroaching on your time replies that he is only too happy to be of use to any acquaintance of his friend Johnson.

The genuinely beautiful feature of this affability is, that Smith really means all that he says, and is prepared to prove his earnestness by long-suffering of even the most pertinacious bores. As time is peculiarly money in New York, and as in the street five minutes are more precious than half an hour in any other part of the town, all the more praise is due to these amenities of brokerage.

The Stock Board appreciates talent, and stands by its favorite officers. Mr. Wheelock, the first Vice-President, has been connected with the Exchange for more than a dozen years. Occupying the most important of positions, and constantly compelled to interfere in disputes and to fine disorderly members, he rarely gives offence, and has no permanent enemies. His conduct on stormy days, and in great panics, is masterly, and he rules the turbulent masses around the table with a generalship and tact that partakes of the marvellous. Mr. Broadhead, the Secretary, has had an even longer connection with the Board, and is universally popular. Under the new *régime*, far greater authority now rests with the official staff than previously; and the arbitration committee, in particular, has frequently very delicate work on its hands. To decide irrevocably upon cases involving large sums of money must inevitably produce dissatisfaction on the part of the losing side; and it is remarkable, in view of the absolutism displayed, that there should be so general an assent to the acts of this department of government. There has, thus far, been but one revolt. Randal H. Foote had a transaction in gold with Alexander T. Compton. The latter, acting under the direction of his partner, a Mr. Pardee, refused to abide by the contract. The case was brought before the committee of arbitration, and decision made in favor of Foote. As Mr. Pardee was not a member of the Exchange, he carried the question to the courts, and Judge Cardozo instantly issued an injunction upon the committee. An appeal to Judge Barnard resulted in reaffirming the position taken by his colleague on the bench. A court of equity, outside of the tribunals selected and solely authorized by the State, was declared to be an anomaly demanding the interposition of the legislative arm. Of course there can exist no doubt of the justice of this verdict from the stand-point of ordinary jurisprudence; but the members of the Board are unanimous in their disapprobation of the rebellion against the committee. It is a denial of prerogative, and a departure from the code of honor, on which, indeed, the whole business of the Stock Exchange rests. As a consequence, the by-laws have since been so amended that a member appealing from the decision of the committee to the courts forfeits membership by the act.

There are many stray shreds of facts regarding brokers and brokerage that can only be alluded to or lightly touched upon. When a dealer becomes a father, he is extremely solicitous to keep the news from the street. No sooner is the fortunate *accouchement* exploited, than a superserviceable friend hurries to the Board, communicates the intelligence in a mock-heroic speech, and immediately offers his hat for the pennies of sympathetic members. A few dollars are quickly collected, and a gold or silver trinket is purchased as a testimonial of affection from the numerous admirers of his or her infantile highness, according to the sex of the new-comer. One modest broker, in terror of ridicule, sent his wife to Paris; but his brethren of the Long Room soon penetrated into the secret, and added to the usual gift a sum sufficient to cover the expense of a cable telegram announcing the happiness of the Stock Board over the auspicious event.

The afternoon before a holiday is sometimes marked by special excitement. Speculation often runs high. The Exchange is crowded till dusk, every broker being eager to make a lucky turn, and so go home to his Fourth of July, Thanksgiving, Christmas, or New Year's festivities in a jubilant frame of mind.

It is astonishing with what rapidity the shares of active stocks circulate from broker to broker. There is a perpetual round of lending and borrowing. In sales, 600 shares will frequently do the work of 2,400, and give commissions on twice that amount. Brokers will send out 300 shares from their offices at ten minutes of eleven, and receive the same lot back from third hands in an hour. Here is, of course, the secret of occasional sales of the whole capital stock of a railroad in one day, when not a quarter is in street hands. All the great corners turn upon this celerity in the interchange of shares.

Just before 4 P. M. strangers in Broad Street will notice a great number of nattily dressed men, hurrying toward the Exchange with heavy tin boxes in hand. They are the confidential clerks or junior partners of broker firms, and their goal is the Stock Exchange vault. This vault is reputed to be the largest in the world, with massive sides and heavy granite foundation. The interior room, reached by passing through iron gratings behind which officers detailed from the police staff are always stationed, is one hundred and six feet deep, and about twenty feet broad. Two hundred and four safes, each a foot and a half square, face either side. In these narrow receptacles a large proportion of the securities of the street is daily placed. Frequently one of the boxes will contain collaterals or governments, held for speculation, to the value of a million, and the lowest estimate of the securities nightly stored here for safe-keeping is over two hundred million dollars.

CHAPTER IX.

THE GREAT OPERATORS.

THE grand old captains of other days were wont to lead in the onset and bare their own breasts to the foe. That was the way of Richard Cœur de Lion and Jacob Little; of Nelson at Trafalgar and Nelson Robinson in the stock-slaughter times of '45· Fashions change, but sometimes almost repeat themselves; and on the great Gold Friday of September, when the head of one of the most famous of the ring firms went down into the whirl of battle "round the fountain," and both Clews and Colgate led the fierce bear attack, it seemed as if the years which were gone were returning to us. That spectacle, however, was a mirage. The genuine modern general remains prudently in the background. Napoleon stops at Hougemont. Fisk watches from the glades of the Opera House. Vanderbilt haunts the recesses of the Bank of New York. Drew closets himself in a broker's office. The combat rages from without; the telegraph clicks within. At the Boards messages come and go, but none know whence or whither. Bids and offers boom in the poisonous air. Surging masses of attack and defence, rumors which spread panic, stratagems and strategy, — all the forces of speculative warfare in fullest play; while the great captain sits quietly in his arm-chair and reads off the history of his own achievements, as it flows down along the paper tape from the automatic machine at his elbow.

There are operators and operators. There are men who move noiselessly, spread their nets, gather in a great harvest, retire, reappear, but love not the glory of notoriety nor the *éclat* of a large clientage. Observers note a tidal rise or fall, and ascribe it to bad crops, diminished earnings, to stringency of money, or again to those incidental forces which tend to appreciate securities. The master-spirit which has controlled the destiny of the market is content to leave the world to its surmises. Of this class was Henry Keep. Tradition affirms that he was born in a poorhouse, and worked for some years as an apprentice to the selectmen of the town. The American who can boast of a similar career with Keep's might well be proud of a like nativity. To begin without a mill, and to sleep the final sleep of the prosperous under a mausoleum costing a hundred thousand,—that is what Wall Street did for him whom it habitually named Henry the Silent. Seldom is a man so happily characterized in a word. He dealt in monosyllables. Whatever is known of his stock operations comes from his friends, not himself.

At nineteen he tired of his rural apprenticeship, and ran away to Rochester. There he secured the position of boot-black and porter of a hotel. Saving his wages and carefully watching his chances, he saw an opportunity for making something by buying uncurrent money between the United States and Canada. After accumulating a few thousands, he opened what was known as Keep's Bank. By 1854 he was worth $ 60,000. That year he came to New York. By '59 his capital was so far augmented that he was ready to enter into that lucrative and passionate pursuit of wealth which attaches to speculations of comprehensive grasp and upon the grand scale. He purchased great quantities of Michigan Southern when it was selling at five dollars a share. He also profited largely in Chicago and Alton, and his operations in Cleveland and Toledo, during '61, were very extensive. His great achievement was in Chicago and Northwestern. A "pool" was formed in October, '67. More than twenty-five thousand shares in addition to the whole capital stock were purchased. Rufus Hatch, a well-known broker, was very prominent in this corner. Through his manipulations the realizations netted $ 2,185,000 in eight months. Keep's share alone was a million and a half. He died in the summer of '69, leaving four and a half millions to his family. William H. Webb belongs to the same quiet order, although his operations have been mainly limited to a single stock. Everybody has some recollection of the opposition line to California. Fares were put down almost to zero. Pacific Mail felt the competition very seriously. The explanation of the fight has been variously stated. But if the great New York ship-builder were disposed to tell all that he knows, the public might learn that the opposition steamers paid handsomely, seeing that their owner had an immense short interest in Pacific Mail, and the thousands lost in one direction were made up by tens of thousands in speculative street profits.

There are other operators who hunger for sensations, who are perpetually attitudinizing, and plotting, and making their *coups financés.* Even the leader of leaders cannot escape this fascination. All Vanderbilt's victories are dramatic. If he invents a corner, the stock flies up from 20 to 200, and for seven days the torturing screws are turned down tighter and tighter, till the Stock Exchange rings with the clamor of his victims. If he deals in privileges, it is to sell a "call" for 50,000 shares of Erie any time within four months at seventy per cent, taking a million dollars as premium. When summoned before court, his memory of this large transaction, which would test the sanity of an average man, fades out so completely that he forgets dates, and men, and even his own signature. There is something so magnificent in a career in which a million dollars is like a ten-cent piece taken by a shoe-blacking *gamin,* — not to be thought of after, in the great influx of other ten-cent pieces, the product of industry and perseverance! He buys or holds on December 19, 1868, some 130,000 shares of New York Central at 120, and in a night session of a handful of directors declares an eighty per cent dividend, which tosses the shares to 165 within forty-eight hours; — stripping the street of five millions and a half with the same *nonchalance* as he would win a hundred dollars of Ben Wood at "Boston." A rumor that he has fallen from his Portland clipper, while out on the Bloomingdale road, sends down the whole market five per cent.

The news of his visit at the Bank of New York on the day succeeding Black Friday checked a stock panic which would have been a whirlwind in an hour. The surface biography of this man has been told a thousand times, and with scarcely one fresh item; but the genuine personal history, the record of secret schemes, the hidden plots and counterplots, are exceedingly difficult to reach. The real fact that he is probably worth some fifty millions in property carried almost in hand is, after all, the great thing. What possible limit is there to the power of so much money? Putting aside the opportunities of generosity and philanthropy, the speculative energies involved in the ownership of half a hundred million are simply incalculable. Commodore Vanderbilt is constitutionally a bull. He likes to survey a rising market. He is so far a good citizen that he takes pride in making enterprises "pay" through large economies and skilful management. The spendthrift tendencies of too many of our representative corporations find a wholesome corrective in the examples which his career affords of how a watchful regard for small things will bring up dividends to the ten per cent ideal. Sometimes this saving habit unites with foibles. He strips the brass from the Hudson River locomotives, and erects a brazen monument of his grandeur upon the flat ugliness of a freight depot. But nothing should make one forget the genuine respect due to the ingrained disposition for appreciating the value of whatever property is intrusted to him.

There is no bound to the evil which might be wrought by such a man, if the Napoleonic instinct were associated with an undue dominance of the destructive faculties. The New York *Tribune*, in an editorial, meant for the loftiest eulogy, recently described the conduct of Vanderbilt when at sea during a perilous storm. All around were fishing-smacks, schooners, brigs, — half seen in the mist and darkness, — which to strike was to destroy, and to avoid called for a humanity and dexterity which unnerved the captain of the ocean packet. The Commodore, according to the story, seized the helm and kept the prow remorselessly upon a straight and cleaving course, discounting in a second the number of lives that would probably be sacrificed, and of ships that would go down under the terrible momentum with which his vessel was sweeping on.

Suppose, from some far-reaching purpose, the man whose determination has the hard, pitiless daring depicted by the *Tribune* editor should see fit to put his total wealth into greenbacks, and initiate a fierce bear campaign. It might be simply for speculative profit, or in order to gain control of all the great trunk lines in the country. No power in the market could withstand him. He could sell down every railway stock on the share list into the abysses of panic. He could coin wealth out of each daily fall, and on ten per cent margins hold majorities of capital stock of all the speculative lines from New York to Omaha, and, if the Pacific Railroad shares were on the call of the Exchange, straight through to San Francisco. By combinations of men and means, such as would be easy to a mind of such magnetism and fertility of invention, the pallor of a great despair could be thrown over the face of the whole country, and the imagination itself becomes impotent in the attempt to compass the infinitude of evil which would inevitably result.

The full power of our imperial capitalists has never yet been fairly felt by the public. Such occasional diversions as corners, money lock-ups, wholesale stock-watering, and kindred devices, are the indications of forces with large reserves of strength. They illustrate, but do not measure. Their influence upon legitimate speculation has been ruinous, as being an incalculable as well as an immense element. A certain railroad stock is selling for 40. Its par value is 50; but it earns no dividends. If foreclosed and sold under the hammer, it would be worth in real estate, rolling-stock, right of way, just ten per cent discount, neither more nor less. By influences not clearly seen the stock rises to 60. It has no real addition of value. There is no legislative gift. There is no improvement in travel, freighting, or in any of the causes which produce dividends. It is just the same stock. The brokers and small operators know this, and consequently sell for future delivery. They sell and sell, until they have agreed to deliver the whole capital stock, say 70,000 shares. It ought now to fall back to 40. It ought to go even below that figure, because these sales indicate want of confidence, and in a rebound all securities go beyond or below their real worth. Instead of falling, however, it rises. Long before the options on which sales were made have expired it is at 130. The street agreed to furnish 70,000 shares for $ 2,800,000; to do it, there is a necessity to buy the stock at $ 12,600,000. Some one has gained, therefore, $ 9,800,000. That was very much the manner in which the last Harlem corner was manipulated. It required only about three million and a half of money to strip the lesser operators and outsiders of nearly three times the sum. Very properly, the moralist, taking the side of the strong, thinks that they were "served right." But this is not the point of discussion. What can be done in Harlem can be done in anything, — in fact, is done in greater or less degree, every month of the year. One man, or a body of men, by buying or selling in vast bulks, and concealing the movement until all the necessary safeguards have been used, may practically control the Stock Exchange. The only danger lies in the appearance of a still greater leader, and a more powerful clique. The mere guerilla force of ordinary speculators is of no efficacy whatever. That the brokers of New York feel this is shown in their strong dislike for all the king operators. Drew, Vanderbilt, Fisk, Jerome, Jacob Little, all the heroes who still breathe vital breath, or have already gone down to the under-world, have never failed to be unpopular on "the street."

One consequence of this pervading ill-feeling is that the stories of the great speculators, current in and around the Stock Exchange, must be accepted with caution. The newspaper belief that Vanderbilt never "goes back on" his friends is not generally assumed as truthful by brokers.

There is a tradition that in years gone by, when the Commodore used to ride down to the old homestead on

Staten Island, he would now and then meet a man who courteously offered to hold his horse. Something in the appearance of the stranger struck Vanderbilt, and he inquired into his history. He had been, it seemed, a broker in "the street" and, having failed badly, had decided to follow Horace Greeley's recommendation, and take to country life.

"If you will come to the city, I will start you again," said the king of Central.

Nobody could be more grateful than the Staten Islander. He returned to Broad Street, acted upon the Commodore's hints, and in due time began to prosper. Brokers soon had faith in this *protégé* of the great man. They watched his movements at the Board, and bought or sold in accordance.

One day the Commodore was planning a large operation. In came Blank, seeking for a point. "*I*'m buying," said the railway lord.

Blank buys bravely, — the street follows. Presently down slips the stock, and the Staten Islander is henceforth a "lame duck." "One of the Commodore's stool-pigeons," is what the irate brokers chose to name him.

Similar incidents, trustworthy or otherwise, are narrated by the dozen.

Horace Clark, Vanderbilt's son-in-law, was always a favorite with the stately old gentleman. The current gossip about his marriage is not lacking in amusement.

Clark was high-spirited even when poor. Having decided to wed the young lady, he called upon his future father-in-law, and, without preliminary, began: —

"Commodore, I wish your daughter in marriage."

"Hey?" quoth the money-king.

Clark repeated his words.

"You mean, you want my money," growled Vanderbilt, from his chair.

"You and your daughter be d—d," flamed out the young lawyer, as he clenched his hat in his hand, and turned to leave the room.

"Hold on, young man," said Vanderbilt, straightening himself on his feet, and looking wonderfully suave and paternal,—"hold on. I rather *like* you. I did n't say you should not have my daughter. You may *have* her. I rather LIKE you, young man."

Clark never did get much of the Commodore's money, except in indirect ways. He had shares in speculations, and was always well supplied with points. Once Vanderbilt determined to "use" him. Clark lost hundreds of thousands of dollars. He boldly told his father-in-law what he thought of it, and after a time the losses were made good. This habit of utilizing everybody has been exercised, if we may trust rumor, on nearly every member of the family. William Vanderbilt is credited with having been favored this way. One day his father came to him and suggested that he had better sell Hudson; 110 was too high for it.

"Thank you," said the son.

Nevertheless, William concluded to look about him first. The stock kept steady, with ups and downs of fractions of one per cent. By peculiar ways it was discovered that the elder Vanderbilt was buying quietly.

William determined to follow suit. Up jumped the stock to 137. It was a clear twenty-six per cent in pocket.

When the operation was concluded, the Commodore rode round to the son's office.

"Well, William, how much did you lose?"

"I went in at 110 on 10,000 shares. That ought to make me two hundred and sixty thousand dollars —"

"Very bad luck, William," quoth the father, trying to look extremely troubled, — "very bad luck, this time."

"But then I bought, and so made."

"Hey? What sent you doing that, sir?"

"O, I heard that was your line, and so concluded that you meant long instead of short."

"Ahem!" croaked Vanderbilt *père*, as he buttoned up his fur overcoat, and stalked out of the open door. He has always had a high opinion of William since that event!

It is hard to put faith in the Staten Island story, in view of some unquestioned facts. That Vanderbilt should occasionally mislead here and there a member of his patriarchal household seems not at all improbable, as in such cases he can always make amends, and the policy may be very naturally a *sine qua non* in the success of his schemes. But there are not a few examples of his steadfast and undeviating friendship toward men who in some way have happened to attract him. John M. Tobin belongs to this class. He was a curbstone operator before 1862; rather unlucky in speculations, and with only two or three thousand dollars capital. Taking the Commodore as a guiding-star, he began to purchase heavily immediately upon the first greenback issue. Stocks went up. He cleared $ 300,000. Then he began to extend himself. His favorite style was to bid seller 3 or seller 30. His imitators followed in the same line. The bears grew dubious and began to cover. If he changed his mind about the prospects of the stock, the rise thus effected by his tactics enabled him to sell to advantage. He foresaw the crash of '64, and unloaded the last of March. He habitually "bulled" stocks and "beared" gold. He shone in the Harlem corners and cannot have made much less than three millions. In the first corner he was cunning as a fox. He wandered through Wall Street looking pale and thin and weary. His friends whispered that he was broken down by anxiety on account of the immense amount of the stock he was carrying. The Street was deluded, and sold short. In faro he is reported to have won sixty thousand dollars of Morrisey in one night. The game continued, and the gladiatorial member of Congress soon recovered all his losses and much more besides. Tobin refused to pay the balance, and Morrisey never alludes to the circumstance without finding the English language unequal to his indignation.

Morrisey himself is one of the Commodore's favorites. He was unlucky enough to have imitated the Albany legislature when it went short in Harlem. The corner nearly ruined him. One day he was driving out on the road at Saratoga; his horse was known far and wide among turf-men,—a magnificent pacer. Vanderbilt saw the animal at full speed, and could not well help expressing his admiration. "So you like his gait?" "Yes; do you want to sell?" "No, but I will give him to you!" The king of Central accepted the present, and has paid for it a thousand times over in the opportune suggestions and happy points with which Morrisey has been guided into return of fortune. In the September gold corner he was one of the outsiders who had sold to Fisk through their brokers. While other men had the folly to enter the courts and wager hopeless warfare with that redoubtable legal limb of the Erie Railroad, David Dudley Field, — Morrisey quietly put his muscles in prime working order, and then repaired to the Grand Opera House. With some difficulty he penetrated into the inner sanctum. The prince of Erie was alone.

"Well, Morrisey, what is it?"

"Simply your check for $ 50,000 in that little matter of ——." The name of the broker was given, but, as it is no part of the story, we suppress it.

"I never bought that gold. It's only a lawsuit, any way."

"Bah! we are not going to law. I've evidence enough, and you may as well pay without more bother." The hand of the ex-champion of the P. R. was tightening, and his attitude became menacing.

"See my lawyer," whispered the prince, moving uneasily in his chair.

"Not at all. Your signature is sufficient."

"This interview had better be ended. If you can't

find the door, I will ring for somebody to show it to you." As the hero of the broad gauge spoke, he sprang to the bell-cord. When the Ramsey deputy-sheriffs called at the Erie Opera House, they had a feeling sense of what the tinkle of a bell means. Morrisey, however, had no disposition to look in the faces of a dozen roughs. Intercepting the movement, and lightly brushing back the irritated prince, he broadened his shoulders, threw back his arms in position and significantly said, —

"You will not ring, and you *must* pay."

A muscular Christian with a right arm that could stun an ox with one blow, and who has decided upon a *rôle* that he would play out to the bitter end, has a certain coercive force which wise men recognize. The check was drawn out, signed and passed over. What further happened is not known; but Morrisey, if we may trust the story, got his money back, and as yet has not been called upon in the courts to explain his process of obtaining it.

Wall Street men are without equals in prodigal supply of anecdote, if not in fecundity of invention. The story which we have just related has been told in twenty ways, and may, after all, be pure fiction. In these pages we vouch for nothing, but at the same time state nothing that has not come from sources supposed to be "reliable." Who knows the real history of James Fisk, Jr.? The biography which appeared in the Springfield *Republican* has been pronounced inaccurate by a very high authority. If the subject of that sketch denies its truth, it would certainly seem that no person whatever could be in a better position to know whereof he affirms. Fortunately, the childhood and early career of the great are not so important as the events of maturity. Mr. Fisk's maturity dates with his entrance as partner in a well-known Boston jobbing-house. Here his felicity in schemes, magnificent combinations, and general speculative activity became so out of proportion to the routine business of the firm that he was finally persuaded to sell out his interest, a large bonus being paid to expedite the affair. Having become once more his own master, Mr. Fisk now wended his way to New York. His first experience with bull and bear was not gratifying. Two or three large transactions in which he had boldly entered resulted so fatally that he soon had not margin enough to float a 1-62 curbstone broker. Then, according to veracious rumor, occurred one of those dramatic passages which lend grandeur to human existence. Seating himself upon a stoop overlooking the Stock Exchange, and surveying the eager sea of faces which on that day heaved and billowed upon the Broad Street pavement, Mr. Fisk swore a mighty oath, that since Wall Street had ruined him "Wall Street should pay for it." Shortly after he took the Shore Line route for the metropolis of New England. Destiny threw him in conversation with a young man who, as it proved, was on the point of despair from difficulties connected with a valuable patent belonging to himself and his father as partners. It was an invention of the utmost importance to a vast manufacturing interest. The mill-owners were using it, and resisting the patent in the courts. His money was gone. So was his father's. Nobody would lend capital, and the lawyers refused to push the case further. Mr. Fisk's curiosity grew with each new revelation. Finally he proposed to his companion to accompany him to Boston. The sequel of the acquaintance was the purchase of the right for a song by Fisk and one or two friends, and a succession of litigations which ended in a sweeping victory over the manufacturers. Congress renewed the patent, and the profit of the second owners was immense.

The money-centre of America soon became aware of the opening of a new office, with "Fisk and Belden, brokers" in flaming gilt over the doorway. The era of Erie was at hand. To detail subsequent events would be absurd. They are part of the national history. In injunctions and counter-injunctions, in issues of stock by millions, in steamboat speculations, theatrical and operatic magnificences, in ferry-boats and transfer-coaches, in lock-ups of money, and lock-outs of sheriffs, Mr. Fisk has obtained a splendor of reputation which will make him forever memorable. His threat of vengeance upon the street has been realized in a way that is comparable only to the exploits of Hyder Aly. More brokers have been ruined by the two *coups financés* of 1868, and the upheaval of the gold market in '69, than by even the great panic of '57. Readers, desirous of informing themselves more particularly regarding Mr. Fisk's stock manipulations, should purchase Charles Francis Adams's "Chapter of Erie." It tells the story with admirable lucidity and piquancy. There is one unpardonable omission, however. Nothing is said of the United States Express Company speculation. This corporation had a contract with the Erie Railway. The clique went short in the stock, and then suddenly annulled the agreement. Down went the shares and the ring covered, at the same time buying heavily for a fresh operation. Then the contract was renewed. Of course the profit by the rise was as handsome as the previous one by the fall. Fisk created this scheme. Indeed, he is the great originating mind of all the genuinely sensational measures of the Erie party. He outlines them rapidly while retiring for the night, sleeps upon them soundly, scrutinizes every point anew on waking, and then launches the thunderbolt. Authentic facts of this nature are never without interest to those who respect true greatness.

Daniel Drew holds a high rank among the king operators. Of late he has allowed the laurels of Erie to grace younger brows, but his early successes with that wayward divinity are not likely to fall into oblivion. He fills the gap left by the death of Jacob Little, and until recently had an office with Daniel Groesbeck, who once was clerk on a small salary under the Napoleonic Jacob. Mr. Drew was a large dealer in gold during the war, and has at times extended his sphere of operations over a very wide field. He is instinctively a bear, and has seldom "gone long" without regretting it. On two separate occasions, once in Michigan Southern and again in Harlem, he extricated himself from serious difficulties by resorting to what is known in street *argot* as "squatting." In other words, he dishonored his own contracts and entered upon a lawsuit to cover his duplicity. More than once since he has employed the very artifices in Erie against which in the case of others he had appealed to the law. There are few jewels of consistency in Wall Street!

Mr. Drew is singularly lacking in popularity. The belief that he never hesitates to sacrifice his friends, if the necessities of speculation require it, is entertained with such unanimity in the money-quarter, and is illustrated by so many anecdotes, that one is compelled to acquiesce in it. This foible is the more salient on account of the genuine piety of the man. All who have heard him speak at Methodist Conferences are struck by the fine religious fervor and earnestness of his demeanor. In austere ways, he is superbly generous. He has built churches, founded a Theological Seminary, and given away prodigally to individual charities. Yet he has the reputation of being close in the extreme. Probably the secret of this amazing contradiction between facts and opinion is to be found in the enmities which his daring, subtle, and obscure speculations have excited. He is the sphinx of the Stock Market.

The annals of the Exchange are rich in reminiscences of men who, for short periods, have filled the city with the rumor of their speculative achievements.

Sam Hallet is a notable representative of this, class. A school-teacher in Western New York, next a lumberman, floating rafts of timber down the Coshocton and Susquehanna rivers, subsequently a book-keeper to

Mr. Mitchell, famous for his land operations, and presently a banker in Hornellsville, N. Y., he finally entered the city of New York about his thirty-first year, and opened a banker and broker's office. His initiative step was to draw up a circular which soon caught the eye of brokers on account of its valuable tabular statement regarding stocks. He saw the inevitable rise in gold very early in the war, and bought largely. His prestige soon became great. Customers flowed in rapidly. Long before his own capital began to accumulate, he had vast sums at his command from outside margins. With a remarkable financial grasp, and singular power in arithmetical combinations, he united a certain persuasiveness of manner which fascinated all who approached him. His office was crowded with a retinue of followers. A mere hint would make men buy or sell by the fifty thousand. Speculators often paid very high commissions to induce him to go to the Boards and buy in person. The street would suppose that Hallet was operating for himself, and the stock would rise proportionately. A respectable company holding property of unimpeachable value gave him $165,000 for the privilege of opening their books at his office and placing his name among the directors. James McHenry credits him with having originated the Atlantic and Great Western Railroad. His operations in the Kansas Branch of the Union Pacific Railroad were a magnificent series of audacities and headlong violence. The old board of directors were ousted, and the contractors, who had been at great expense in gathering men and material from

Canada and Europe, were driven from their work at the point of the bayonet.

In stocks he speculated in the same bold, uncompromising, and sledge-hammer manner. Though a bull to the tips of his fingers, he would sell a million in a day in order to break the market. 1863 was his gala year. In '64 he attempted to control several lines of stocks at a time. Boards of railroad managers changed their policies to suit his strategy. The vision of a fortune that might rank with Vanderbilt's began to rise from out the future, when Chase and the April panic swept over the street, breaking him in forty-eight hours, and dragging down dozens of his friends in the ruin.

Hallet's supposed connection with an over-issue of Indiana bonds had previously shattered his credit. The Kansas and Pacific Railroad imbroglio added a fresh blow to his reputation. One day, after his failure as a broker, he found himself at Washington, full of schemes and eager for Congressional help. On applying to the President, Mr. Lincoln passed him a letter, written by an engineer on the road named Talcott, in which Hallet's private and public character was the subject of sarcastic comment. When the latter reached his rooms, he telegraphed his brother, then in the West, to seek out the engineer, place him over his knee, and summarily chastise him. Hallet went to Kansas himself a month or two later, and found that his order had been obeyed to the letter. The joke, however, had a sequel. Goaded by the insult, and irritated by the loss of his situation, Talcott grew moody. Accident or intention brought victor and victim face to face. The engineer drew a pistol, and Hallet fell dead. Sixty years would have been a brief term for a life of such wide vicissitudes, of high excitements, of narrow poverty and extreme wealth, of commanding influence and illimitable schemes; yet he was only thirty-seven when assassinated!

The career of the brothers Jerome has been marked by a boldness, *verve*, and large magnificence of view and action which perpetually suggest a parallel with the lives of the more noted speculators of the Paris Bourse. Jerome *père* was a farmer in Onondaga County, one of the lake districts of New York State. Addison G., the eldest son, came up to the city when quite a lad, with very little other capital than that which belongs to a brave heart and a keen brain. Strolling about town with eyes open and superabundant provincial hopefulness, he chanced to see the sign of John Stewart, an eminent dry-goods merchant. Walking straight up to the head of the establishment, he told his story in a few nervous words. Mr. Stewart received him kindly, but had no vacancy. "But you *must* try me. Give me anything, no matter how slight, and I'll write my name in your check-book before I get through." The answer struck the great dealer, and after a moment's thought he made a proposition which Jerome instantly accepted. In three years he made his pledge good, by entering as a partner in the firm. Subsequently he withdrew, and joined forces with two well-known dry-goods men; the new house calling itself Fitch, McNeal, & Jerome. They soon had a large connection with the Southern trade.

About 1850 their affairs, however, took an unfavorable turn, and the firm was forced to suspend. Addison lost everything. Hard pressed, and with no very clear future, he leased an out-of-the-way office in Wall Street and began life anew as a broker, with his sum-total of capital consisting of three chairs and a table, worth perhaps five dollars at the most. Thirteen years after, his books showed a daily business of five millions, while his commissions on outside orders frequently netted ten thousand dollars a week!

There was a curious episode connected with this failure. As soon as Addison had met with some success in his early dry-goods' venture, he sent his favorite brother, Leonard W., to Princeton College. When Leonard was graduated, he went to Rochester and edited the *American* in that city. The journal was of uncompromising and lively Whig politics. Millard Fillmore, then President, took a liking to the young editor, and the result was a consular appointment to a small Italian port. Leonard had been in Europe a year or more, when he received a letter from New York, in which Addison spoke enthusiastically of his prospects, and proposed that the two should enter into partnership. The idea fell in with Leonard's fancy, and in a very brief time he resigned his office and started for Paris. There a letter reached him, announcing the failure of Fitch McNeal, & Jerome! His consulship was irrevocably gone; his vision of a partnership and prosperity had vanished; the outlook was of the bluest. Nevertheless, Leonard W. was not easily discomfited. He took the steamer for New York, and on reaching the city decided to adopt the new line just selected by his brother. After the usual ups and downs, he finally entered into partnership with William R. Travers, under the firm name of Travers & Jerome. This event dates with '56. The new house operated in Michigan Southern rather extensively. One day they took sides against the Litchfields, who then had a large influence over the stock. Jerome went in as a bear, and threatened to break Michigan Southern, even if it carried down the whole market. As the shares of no road stood firmer, or were better regarded, the menace was laughed at. Had it been only an affair of stock manipulation, the vaunt would have been idle enough. But Leonard W., however meagre his bank account, was fertile in expedients. He had learned the value of printer's ink at Rochester. It now occurred to him to put this immense force at work in New York. The *Herald* opened its columns to him. He influenced other journals. Every day appeared articles predicting a crash. The country was overtrading. Credit was so extended that it would snap into ribbons at the first gale. Stocks were exorbitantly high. Wall Street was a gigantic bubble. Half the shares on the lists had nothing but rottenness to sustain them. Michigan Southern was a fair sample of the bubble prosperity of the street. Repeating these views in a hundred new shapes, always striking at the road with which he was at deadly feud, disentombing old reports of the Company, analyzing the figures relentlessly, and with a clearness hitherto unknown in

New York finance, he soon began to affect public confidence. His articles were copied from newspaper to newspaper all over the country. Holders began to sell their stock. The terror spread. The Litchfields struggled, but the weight was too great. Michigan Southern fell sharply. It was impossible to check the decline. Victorious at this point, Jerome still stood by his bear *rôle*. On the street and in the daily papers he steadily persisted as an alarmist. One day he was on the pavement near the old Stock Exchange talking down everything, predicting universal failure, denouncing almost every security quoted on 'Change. A broker stepped up to him. "Say what you please, the Ohio Life and Trust Company is a good stock at all events." The dealer, as he spoke, pointed to the edifice of the company near by, and his gesture was such as a traveller in Egypt might employ in asserting the solidity of the pyramids. "What *is* Life and Trust?" asked Jerome. "103," was responded. "I'll sell a thousand at 50, seller one year," quoth Leonard. "Take 'em," shouted the broker. Sixty days after the Life and Trust Company failed for sundry millions, and dragged, not only Wall Street, but the entire commerce of the country with it. The purchaser of the thousand shares of Life and Trust compromised at a handsome figure. With the money coming from this lucky hit, and by other realizations upon short sales, Jerome felt rich enough to dissolve partnership, and shortly after sailed for Europe on a two years' vacation.

Meanwhile Addison G. had been making his own fight; was a bull through '56 and '57, and came out of the panic with health and capital shattered. He used his experience to advantage, and by 1860 had laid the foundation for a splendid future. He was one of the few men who bought largely at that period when the share market was at its lowest ebb. By '62 and '63 the result of his prescience disclosed itself. His realizations were enormous. He was loyal to the core and found his profit in it. Dealers noticed that the moment stocks broke upon the news of a defeat of the Union forces, Jerome was always in the market as a buyer. The policy was subtle, and not readily followed. It was based upon a theory, borne out by facts, that with every disaster came a new emission of greenbacks. The more greenbacks the higher prices. Addison coined money by the hundred thousand through these tactics. His office swarmed with eager speculators. He was now worth millions. He had been the leading spirit in the organization of the Open Board, and was looked up to as one of the longest heads in the street. At this juncture he formed a tacit alliance with Vanderbilt. The latter had acquired the control of the route from New York to Buffalo. Jerome already held a portion of the connecting roads beyond, and now determined to buy up Michigan Southern, and thus complete a through line to Chicago. While occupied in absorbing the majority of the shares, he was struck by the abundance of cash stock, and by the fact that he had options out for nearly the entire capital of the road. The opportunity for a corner was too tempting to be put aside. He concerted his measures, bought quietly thirty thousand more shares than the whole capital stock, and soon had the street in his toils. The shares went up by flying leaps. He was upon the edge of untold opulence. Just as he was beginning to bring the corner to an issue, however, he suddenly observed a weakness in the stock. Contracts were met promptly. Although he owned the whole railroad, everybody appeared to be supplied with certificates. The secret was not long in transpiring. The directors of Michigan Southern, with Henry Keep at their head, fearful of losing their ascendency, had availed themselves of a clause in an old charter of one of the roads of which it was a consolidation, by which they were authorized to issue stock at par for construction purposes. This new emission they had been furnishing Jerome at corner rates! The latter at once appealed to the law, but in the meanwhile his affairs were inextricably entangled. Stock that he had himself bought at from 100 to 112, he was forced to sell off at 75 and 70. He lost a million by the blow. Shortly after, he died from a heart trouble, superinduced by excitement, bestowing a considerable fortune and the Michigan Southern lawsuit as a legacy to his family. He left a rare name in Wall Street. His friends affirm of him that he was never known to allow an oath, a lie, or a vulgar jest to pass his lips. As the money-quarter goes, this is immortal eulogy.

Some time in '60 or '61, Leonard W. Jerome returned from abroad, and opened a new office in the street, with the firm name of Jerome & Riggs. Operating very generally along the whole line of stocks, his interest soon centred upon the Pacific Mail Steamship Company. He took the stock when its selling rate was about 62, and carried it up by 1865 to 329. His realizations even at the earlier stages of the rise were enormous. He spent his money as freely as he made it. Fifth Avenue was in a whirl of amazement at his social audacities. He bought a magnificent steam-yacht. He dashed through Central Park in his four-in-hand. He gave dinner-parties of the most sumptuous character. At one of these feasts every lady guest received a bracelet with some rare jewel pendant. He created the Jockey Club, and established a private theatre of his own. One day he was at Newport chatting with Mrs.——, then a leader of fashion. "Why don't you give a party?" inquired Jerome. "Because my husband can't afford it." "Pshaw! what will it cost?" An estimate was made. "That is easily done. I have a capital point in Hudson River. Deposit a few hundred dollars with my firm, and we will see what will come of it." The margin was put up. In a few days Jerome sent back the money increased beyond the wildest dreams of Wall Street speculation. Of course the party was an immediate sequence.

It was impossible that such a man should not provoke enmities as well as make friends. He was exceedingly disliked by a large proportion of brokers. Sometimes they united and struck him hard. But Jerome could bear a square blow without flinching better than any one. His *sang-froid* was inimitable. After a hard day of ill luck at every point, he would sit down with his friends at supper, brimming over with animal spirits, telling a story or singing a song with the gusto of one who had just made half a million. He never acknowledged a moment of despondency, except in reference to one occasion. This happened in connection with the corner in Hudson in '63, the main features of which have been described in a previous page. Jerome had made all his combinations, and, satisfied with the outlook, took his yacht and set out on a pleasure-trip up the river to West Point. Beginning to have misgivings, he steamed back to the city, and, reaching the pier, found bad news awaiting him. The scheme did not work. Everything was at a dead stop. For a half-hour he was unmanned. Nevertheless, he kept his own counsels and revolved the problem over and over till daybreak. By that time he had laid out a fresh line of strategy, and canvassed it point by point. Satisfied with the plan, he gave his orders, and went up to West Point again. The result of that night shortly showed itself in the rapid culmination of one of the most brilliant corners ever known in stock speculation.

There are a host of stories afloat about Jerome, illustrating his ready wit. One of them, which will lose none of its piquancy by suppressing the real name of the party most interested, is told in this wise. He had been carrying a heavy load of Michigan Southern at one time, in anticipation of a rise; but somehow the stock remained quiet. The way of throwing it off without a loss was not very apparent. At this juncture he happened to be walking along Broad Street, when some one tapped him on the shoulder. Looking round, he saw an old Rochester acquaintance.

"Why, Kelley, what brings you here?"

"Business. We have just opened an office,—Kelley & Cutter. We want you to give us some orders."

Jerome shrugged his shoulders. "I'd like to do it, Kelley; but it would n't work."

"Why not, Mr. Jerome?"

"O, you'll never make money in the street. You can't keep a secret. If I gave you an order you would run off and tell everybody. All the brokers hereabouts would know what I am doing."

"I pledge you my word that we will keep your orders sacred," said Kelley, warmly.

"Then there's another thing," continued Jerome. "If you take a commission from me, you will think you've got a good point. Next you will speculate. Then we shall hear that you've 'busted.' No, no, Kelley, it won't do."

The representative of the new firm declared that his house was resolved to do a purely commission business,—would never speculate,—was the house of all others that Jerome ought to patronize.

"Well, Kelley," said the other, after a moment of deep reflection, "I'll give you a trial. Go and buy five thousand of Michigan Southern."

Kelley went off elated, bought the stock, and whispered into everybody's ear that Michigan Southern was "a mighty good thing to hold. Jerome was buying by the block. There was a big rise in prospect."

Pretty soon the market began to falter. Jerome & Riggs had seized upon their opportunity and quietly sold. The stock plunged down.

Some days later Kelley met his new patron.

"Well," said Jerome, "how do you get on?"

"Have n't you heard?"

"Eh, what 's up?"

"Why," responded Kelley, with a woful expression of countenance, "our house is 'busted.' We bought some of that confounded Michigan Southern on our own account, and it swamped us!"

"*Speculated*, hey?" quoth Jerome, with great concern. "Now, Kelley, my boy, next time *do* remember my advice!"

There is an anecdote about Addison G. that may not inappropriately be told in this connection.

A well-known quiet operator had invested largely in a certain stock,—that of the Reading Railroad, if we are not mistaken. Not liking the look of the market, he determined to sell; but as he was carrying ten or fifteen thousand shares, he was afraid to resort to the Exchange for fear of breaking the price. He knew that the elder Jerome was weighted down by the same stock, and was also working to get rid of it. Here was a loophole for escape. Going into the office of ——, the principal broker agent of Addison, he whispered, "I say, come along with me." As soon as they were on the street, the wary speculator instructed —— to accompany him over to Williams Street, and if they happened to meet Jerome, and if also the latter offered to buy

Reading within certain figures, he should sell him all he wanted. The two sauntered along, and presently met Jerome, evidently in a brown study. Greetings were exchanged.

"Michigan Southern is looking well," begins the plotting operator.

"Yes, very well. Cleveland and Toledo sold handsomely to-day. Then there 's Reading."

"A good stock, that. I 'll give '14½ for five thousand!"

"As you say, a capital stock. Going higher too! I 'll buy any part of ten thousand Reading at 115, buyer 30.

"*Sold*," screamed the broker, taking out his book.

"How 's that?" inquired Addison, with admirably assumed carelessness.

"Simply that I have sold you ten thousand Reading at 115, buyer 30," said the broker, pencilling off the item as he spoke.

"All right," replied Jerome, quite aware that he had been trapped, but recognizing the force of the street rule which makes a bargain sacred wherever and however made. How Addison G. extricated himself from his double load of the stock we do not know; but as Reading sold up to 128 in the course of the year, it is pleasant to believe that he finally lost nothing by his unexpected purchase.

The Fordham Race-course owes its origin to one of the outside speculations of Jerome. The trains of the New York and New Haven Railroad enter the metropolis upon the Harlem track. Justified by highly satisfactory reasons, the management of the company decided to secure a different means of ingress to the city, and a tacit agreement was made with Leonard W. Jerome to the effect that if he would secure the right of way from the proper terminus of the New Haven Road clear through to New York, they would change their route. The firm at once bought all the land they could find along a strip of nine miles through Westchester County, up what is known as the Saw-Mill River Valley. Some portion of their purchase cost them at the rate of $ 300 an acre. Meanwhile Commodore Vanderbilt got news of the movement, bought largely of the New Haven stock, and at the succeeding election of directors was able to make such changes in the board as effectually estopped the change of base from the Harlem Line. The contract on which Jerome had acted was not in such a form as admitted of litigation. He had acquired an immense amount of real estate with no prospect of immediate realizations. Then came the idea of the race-course. Not less than $ 100,000 was cleared as net profit from that expedient. Another portion of the land was sold as a cemetery. But Jerome has the greater part of the property still on his hands.

It was in the month of February, 1867, that Jerome met with his great disaster. Pacific Mail was always his favorite. He had made it one of the most popular stocks at the Exchange. During the year just named Leonard was so thoroughly preoccupied by up-town amusements, the Jockey Club, his steam-yacht, dinners, and every description of social extravagance, that he neglected his affairs in the street. He controlled a majority of the shares of Pacific Mail; the directors, though nearly evenly balanced, stood one in his favor, and although the annual meeting of the board to decide upon a dividend was at hand, Jerome gave himself no anxiety. At this juncture a rapid combination was effected between certain capitalists who were largely interested in the stock, for a purpose which can be best understood by results. Men who were in the secrets of the movement affirm that it embodied some of the most startling and romantic phases of stock brokerage ever known in the street. Brown Brothers & Co. are credited with being especially prominent in the scheme. An essential part of the Jerome programme was the declaration of a large dividend and the issue of a favorable report. When the board came together, however, the director upon whom Leonard relied threw his vote on the adverse side. The dividend was cut down to three per cent, and the newly formed clique sent forth whispers to the effect that the affairs of the company were anything but in a satisfactory condition. The news of the action of the directors spread like a prairie-fire. Pacific Mail dropped thirty per cent. Leonard Jerome was carrying the main part of his stock on borrowed margins, and was wholly unprepared for the blow. Between Monday and Saturday he fought against the market with untiring pluck and pertinacity, raising $ 800,000 by sacrificing all his other ventures, and not giving up the battle until every dollar of this large sum was melted away by the continuous decline of the stock. Then he sold. The previous loans, however, together with the persistent depression of the shares, prevented any considerable realizations from the sales. Jerome was now hopelessly crippled. Nothing was left but to extricate himself from the ruins; and the fact that by the vicissitudes of the fight he had become largely indebted to certain leaders of the opposition party afforded a means of escape from what now constituted his main embarrassment. This was the contract, still in force, by which he had bound himself to take $5,000,000 of a new issue of the company's stock. The responsibility had been assumed in the heyday of his power, and the corporation held his note for the shares, which had been sold to him at twenty-five per cent below the then market price of Pacific Mail. He now compelled the directors to resume the stock at thirty per cent above the depreciated rates of the street. Since this event, Jerome has had very little to do with Wall Street operations, preferring the excitement of Paris to the troubled waters of speculation.

Anthony Wellman Morse made a brilliant reputation in Wall Street, during his brief career. He came from a good family. His grandfather, Major Anthony Morse, fought at the battle of Bennington, and witnessed the surrender of Burgoyne. On his mother's side he was related to the Rev. James Wellman, who holds an eminent place in the annals of New Hampshire; to the Pattersons of New England and Maryland; and to Dr. Russell, one of whose kin protected the regicide judges Goffe and Whalley, — the latter being related to the family by blood. Young Morse was born at Hanover, New Hampshire, March 8, 1834. In his seventeenth year he entered the treasury office of the New York and New Haven Railroad, under the patronage of Morris Ketcham. Here he was brought much in contact with iron men, and kept the books for two large houses concerned in this trade. This led to his accepting a position under Balch & Zimmerman, contractors for building the Great Western Railroad in Canada. Thence he went to Savannah, Georgia, as book-keeper to the Marine Bank, and on the breaking out of the yellow-fever in that city he returned to New York, entering the banking-house of Corning & Co. The crash of '57 carried away this firm. Morse now joined in partnership with Edward Wolf; and the new house, under the name of Morse & Wolf, started a bankers and broker' office at 60 Wall Street. Speculating largely and not too cautiously, the young brokers failed to a heavy amount in '61. Anthony next went in with his brother, L. W. Morse; and the two opened up a flourishing business until the Trent difficulty, when their affairs became seriously entangled. Soon after A. W. retired from the firm and formed a copartnership with Isaac Kip, Jr., under the style of Morse & Co., 24 Williams Street.

He at once took hold of Fort Wayne, and Cleveland and Pittsburg, buying always for a rise and making handsome realizations. After accumulating something like half a million dollars, he purchased the yacht "Gipsey," and in the spring of '63 sailed for Europe. The ocean voyage in so small a craft was then a novelty. His reception, therefore, was in the nature of an ovation. For six months he was surrounded by the fastest set of London and Paris fashionable yacht and turf men,—the keenest stock-gamblers in the Old World. The whole talk of the Continent was against the North. Everybody predicted failure, the repudiation of greenbacks, and the general ruin of the country. When Morse came back to the city in December, these ideas had burnt into his brain. Believing that almost any description of security was better than the national currency, he soon became one of the most conspicuous bulls in the street. His first operation was in Rock Island. T. C. Durant was also in this pool, but Morse was the directing and creative spirit. During its manipulation the street suffered by a sharp "squeeze" in the money-market, and the ease with which Morse pushed aside this obstacle gave him an immense reputation. Although but thirty years old, his office was daily crowded by eager throngs, anxious to get points. He would buy five thousand shares of Chicago and Northwestern. Men would ask what stock was likely to rise. "Northwestern" would be the answer. Off went the speculators and distributed their orders. Naturally the stock mounted rapidly at the boards, and Morse made ready realizations of the shares he was carrying. An illustration of his popularity was afforded by the quickness with which the stock of a coal-mining company organized by him was absorbed. The day the subscription-book was opened, outsiders fought with each other for the privilege of signing their names. One man who took a large amount, after having pushed his way forward with great violence, presently returned, and, walking up to Mr. Morse inquired, " I say, Mr. Morse, was that gold or coal stock that I just subscribed for ? " The high fever of speculation made rapid fortunes. Morse was now worth nigh three millions, and determined to do in Fort Wayne what he had previously accomplished in Rock Island. The stock started at about 60, and was most admirably manipulated, until it finally touched 152. Although the corner was but half completed, Morse was carried away by his success. Upon the rumor that government was at the point of selling gold, he sent a despatch to Washington, offering to buy whatever the Secretary of the Treasury might put in the market. This was April, '64· Mr. Chase came to the city, sold nine millions of bullion, and withheld from circulation the thirteen or fourteen millions of greenbacks with which it was purchased. The sale, and the accompanying lock-up of money shook the street, and Morse & Co. were the first to fail! Their losses were immense. Morse never recovered from the blow. His death occurred in New York some four years after.

William H. Marston has had a remarkable career as a leading speculator. He made his first money as a broker, having an office at 17 Wall Street, and doing a heavy and legitimate commission business. There is a tradition that on the day of his admission to the New York Stock Exchange he gave a great dinner to the members, at Delmonico's, spending no one knows how much money, and literally floating his guests in champagne. The next morning, as gossip affirms, he " broke " for half a million. Although the story is sacredly believed upon "the street," it is a trifle too dramatic. The lunch was given, and the failure took place, but the two events were months apart.

Subsequently, Marston paid up every dollar of his indebtedness, entering the market as an outside bull operator, and invariably "carrying" whatever stock he touched, until it reached a figure admitting of superb realizations. In the summer of '65 he initiated the first of a series of magnificent operations, by a transaction in Michigan Southern in conjunction with Henry Keep. From this he cleared $ 90,000. The fall of the same year he engineered to a brilliant conclusion the great Prairie du Chien corner. In a previous chapter we have described the main features of this celebrated strategic movement, but we omitted to say that the original intention of its promoter was simply to place the stock at par. "The street" entered into a combination to thwart the scheme, and began to bear the market mercilessly. Marston, irritated and indignant, at once extended his programme, set a hundred secret agents at work, encouraged the short interest, and in forty days succeeeded in so manipulating the stock that it rose to 250. His profits could not have been less than a million and a half dollars. One man who was in the secret made sixty thousand dollars on three hundred shares. The stock in hand when the corner culminated was exchanged at the rate of 100 shares of Prairie du Chien for 100 shares of Milwaukee and St. Paul common and 50 shares of the preferred. The two roads were then consolidated. The act of "unloading" was therefore quite as unique and satisfactory as the previous operation.

The next spring Marston formed a pool and bought five millions of Cleveland and Pittsburg at 83. The final realizations were at from 95 to 105. The net profits were enormous. In June, Erie was bulled by the same skilful hand. Shares to the extent of 70,000 were bought at 57 and 62, and afterward sold for from 73 to 77. Daniel Drew was entangled in this speculation, and is credited with a loss of $ 1,700,000. This operation in the broad gauge shares proved so flattering that in the fall of '66 a party was formed, under the inspiration of Marston, to purchase 130,000 shares of Erie. The stock was bought at from 65 to 80, and the realizations were at 97. On thirty thousand shares the originator of the pool made $ 900,000. Later in the same year Marston entered into a combination to bull Northwestern common, buying 60,000 shares at 47, and carrying the stock easily up to 60 and 63. His gains were immense.

Fortune is a fickle goddess. The winter of '67 Marston entered upon transactions on an enormous scale, bought heavily in the stock of two or three railroads, and handled his cards deftly for a stupendous rise. The luck of the market, however, now turned against him. He lost all his previous accumulations and failed for $ 600,000. Some forty brokers were swept out of "the street" by this collapse, which is still known as "the Marston Panic." The hero of Prairie du Chien bore his losses bravely, and may be seen almost every day on

Broad Street, — one of the most wide-awake men in the money-quarter; fertile in schemes, and likely at any moment to reappear in some gigantic combination.

Thomas C. Durant has an enviable reputation for financial boldness, quickness of insight, and Dantonian audacity in execution. He practised medicine for a brief time in the South; and, although he abandoned his profession at an early period, his friends always speak of him as the Doctor. Like Vanderbilt and Drew, he acquired his primary education in speculative finance as a shareholder and manager of Hudson River boats. Afterward he became contractor for building the Chicago and Rock Island Railroad. He completed this line six months before he had agreed to deliver it over to the directors; and, with his usual dash, placed cars and locomotives on the track, and made a neat fortune in working the road, during the *interim*, upon his own responsibility. His next achievement was upon the Mississippi and Missouri Railroad, receiving his pay for the contract in land-grants and bonds. Returning to the city, he soon made his influence felt in the street. His most brilliant exploit was the Rock Island corner; but his strategetic combinations in gold, and some of the favorite railway fancies gave him large reputation. He was the leader of the Pacific Railroad movement; and that mine of wealth, the Credit Mobilier, owed all its glory to his fine executive ability. No one knows how much he is worth. The Doctor himself could not tell. He has given his wife a magnificent estate on the Isle of Wight. He has a house in Brooklyn, a house in New York, apartments at the Fifth Avenue, at the Hoffman House, and at the Westminster. He owns a steam-yacht and a private clipper. At present he keeps a sharp eye upon the opportunities of the Stock Exchange and the Gold Room, while pushing with great energy his last pet scheme, the completion of the Adirondack Railroad.

Another operator of note is Dr. Shelton. He lives at Newburg, remaining in the country all the summer and beginning his annual speculations in October. His career covers the space of twenty years. He was carrying a heavy line of stocks in '62, and made a vast amount in the subsequent rise. At the close of the war he was short 75,000 shares in different railroads, and at the same time was bearing gold. The surrender of Lee proved a very profitable event, therefore. He almost invariably sells, and not seldom gives his broker the order to go short 500 shares on every stock called. Recently his visits to the Exchange have been infrequent.

William S. Woodward has the credit of experiencing great financial vicissitudes. He is bull or bear alternately, and operates both in stocks and gold. His speculations in Chicago and Northwest have generally been profitable, as also have those in Rock Island. He led the rise in the latter stock in May, 1869, when the shares reached 139⅞. He was prominent in the gold corner, and used his utmost efforts to persuade the clique to retire when gold had reached 145. He is said to be now worth about $3,000,000.

Vanderbilt, Drew, Horace F. Clark, William H. Marston, Woodward, Fisk, Jay Gould, Dr. Shelton, Dr. Durant, David Dowes, John F. Tracy, Russell Sage (said to have a cash balance of six or eight millions constantly on hand), Amasa Stone of Cleveland, John Steward, James H. Banker, and Alexander Mitchell, President of the Chicago and Northwestern and of the Milwaukee and St. Paul Railroads, now constitute the leading operators in the New York Stock Market.

CHAPTER X.

THE OUTSIDERS.

TAKING x as the unknown quantity which embraces that portion of the universe given to speculation in stocks or gold, and calling the brokers a, and the recognized heavy operators b, we have in $x - (a + b)$ an algebraic definition of what are known as outsiders. The term includes, not merely the promiscuous and intermittent body of individuals with small purses and large desires, but also merchants, manufacturing capitalists, bank officers, and citizens who have retired upon their fortunes. Every owner of governments, from the sixteen hundred and odd National banks, and the multitudinous Savings-banks of the United States, down to the possessor of a single fifty-dollar bond, in some way or other, at some time or other, comes in contact with the market, and affects, or is affected by, its prices.

All along the lines of our railroads are men who hold shares or bonds. In Ohio it is estimated that more than half the capital stock is in the hands of local holders, although many of the roads are of the speculative class. Illinois Central is extensively distributed among the small capitalists of the State through which it passes. The people of Pennsylvania and New Jersey are large owners of stock, daily quoted on the Exchange; and, although very much of the one billion dollars which are said to be annually saved for investment in the United States disappears either in private channels, or is locked up in close corporations and securities, circulating in circumscribed limits, yet in no inconsiderable degree these representations of value are employed to feed the fever of speculation. Stock-brokers are always ready to take city bonds or manufacturing shares of good character, as a basis of margins. The outsider may hesitate to buy out and out the favorite shares of the Board, but he is only too eager to have his surplus in the more stable classes of securities, and to use them as collaterals for obtaining money to operate with in the street. The wide variations in the prices of the market have, therefore, had a double effect. They have penetrated the public with a desire for investment in stocks not quoted on share lists, and stimulated it into constant ventures of purchase or sale in the very arena which it otherwise shuns.

Some idea is furnished of the area of outside speculation by the testimony of telegraph operators. The exact average of daily orders from different sections, which reach the New York Stock Exchange by this channel, including not only the offices of the Western Union and the Bankers and Brokers' Telegraph Company, but also the Atlantic and Pacific and the Franklin, varies from 2300 in lively periods to 850 in dull times. The National Stock Board, in addition, receive about 300 a week. By the English cables some 150 messages come to New York brokers every day, and half that number arrive *via* the French wires. Not less than $1,200,000 is paid yearly by members of the Stock and Gold Exchanges for oceanic despatches! Omitting the foreign business in the present view, and confining our attention solely to domestic localities, we find that Philadelphia exceeds all other cities in its orders. Boston and Baltimore follow next. Hartford, Providence, St. Louis, San Francisco, and Chicago use the wires very freely. But the most significant illustration of the deep-seated and widely ramified tendency toward speculation is found in the occasional commissions which trickle in from strange and wayside places. Villages whose names are scarcely known beyond the boundary of their counties have their rustic Fisks and Vanderbilts. Sparks of electricity fly up from the marshes of the Mississippi Valley, from the golden desolation of Nevada, from factory hamlets in Connecticut, from the pastoral seclusions of Vermont; bearing emergent orders to sell Hudson short, to buy 500 Fort Wayne, to take a put on Rock Island, or a call on Tennessee 6s.

In the flush days, between '63 and '67, the sum total of these outside speculators reached enormous figures. New York City, and the population included in a radius of a hundred miles of that centre, furnished its thousands. Women pawned their jewels for margins. Clergymen staked their salaries. One man sent his horse to his broker, and realized in the end $300,000 from this small beginning. Brokers cleared from three hundred to three thousand dollars a week in commissions alone. The unlucky never tell their misfortunes.

An author in two months lost the profits of three books. A bank clerk, in one of that chain of towns between Albany and the city, on the Hudson railway, made thirty thousand dollars, in successive strokes. Then he offered himself to a fair young girl, and put the whole of his gains into the street, promising his affianced the rarest of bridal gifts. Three days after he received a despatch with the warning word, "Ten per cent more margin." His resources were exhausted. He hurried to New York, begged, implored, labored with his brokers for hours, to induce them to have pity on his situation. But the stock was plunging downward, and they were "carrying" more than their capital would allow. They gave one day's grace, and then sold their customer out. He returned to his home a broken man, with all his old shrewdness and self-confidence gone forever. There are hundreds upon hundreds of such human wrecks scattered through towns and cities, some shut up in asylums, others living out aimless lives, — mental paralytics, dazed or crazed by the swift shock of ruin. Those who escaped simply with the annihilation of their wealth or competence might be deemed happy, compared with others whose ventures left heavy debts of honor, which absorbed the surplus of future years. Men in positions of trust, who in some ill-starred moment had taken the funds of which they were sworn guardians, in order to cover unexpected losses, were frequently at the mercy of brokers as unscrupulous as cruel. The fate of Jenkins, the cashier of the Phœnix Bank, who defaulted for $ 300,000, the large proportion of which had been paid over for hush money, is but a single instance out of scores of cases, very few of which have come to public notice. It was asserted in a New York paper of February 2, 1869, that Mr. Webster, then Assessor of the Wall Street Internal Revenue district, had discovered that two millions were employed in stock transactions by metropolitan church trustees, out of the ecclesiastical revenues under their control. Church edifices were mortgaged in order to preserve margins. Prominent pastors were said to be heavy speculators, and their frequent presence in brokers' offices was a matter of scandal. An eminent Episcopalian divine is reputed to have made over fifty thousand dollars. Where the shepherd wanders wool-hunting, the sheep are apt to go astray. Probably if the facts regarding the use of fiduciary securities as a means of speculation were fully known, it would be a revelation as fatal to credit as the revulsion of '57. Veteran brokers, prone to cautiousness in speech, declare that breaches of trust are far more common in wardships, and those other guardian offices which are a part of purely private life, than in the more public departments of commerce. The trustee perceives an opportunity for rich profit. His first step is the one that does not cost. He wins and wins, always employing his private capital, and staking each new accumulation for a larger gain. Presently the tide changes. He touches the sacred legacy. Another turn of the die restores all that was taken, and the secret rests in his own bosom. If he be still unfortunate, it is not difficult to entangle his wards in the net, and persuade them that it was their folly which has wrought destruction. Even at the worst, a frank confession, with the honest remorse that the hardest natures must at such a crisis feel, will coerce the victims into the forgiveness which robs the law of a criminal.

The story of financial "irregularities," caused by unsuccessful stock speculations, is one of the sombrest chapters in our recent history. The moral censor who should undertake the thankless task of gathering the hard, painful, romantic facts of bank, railroad, insurance-company, and mercantile defaulters, and weave them together in a volume, could have at his command material that Juvenal might well have envied. Until society gives the lie to that obsolete truism which declares poverty to be no disgrace, such labor would be only a fresh injustice. To penetrate the walls of state prisons, and the veiled secrets of the cemetery, in order to unearth the misdeeds of forgers, the malefeasances of bank presidents, at whose funerals clergymen by the dozen lent the testimony of their presence, and the unsuspecting frankincense of impassioned eulogy, — of men who committed the suicide of the body rather than endure the penalty of social suicide which their foolishness had wrought, — of individuals dead, or dying under feigned names in foreign lands with the misery of a blighted past haunting them to the last breath, — this is to add crime to crime as long as the public insists upon the worship of success, and measures its honors by length of purse. The glory of Wall Street lies in its magnificent opportunities for satisfying in a few months the demands of civilization. It is the greatest money-making and money-losing spot on the globe. Pio Nino never asks how his Peter's pence are gathered together, nor do brokers feel bound to enter into all the interior history of the margins which come to their hands. Their office is to make ten dollars out of one. It is a mission quite as distinct as that of the reformers, and a thousand-fold more appreciated. The fallacies of a few individuals who are weak enough to put themselves under the ban of law and society without enough reserved strength to ultimately break through the meshes, ought not to abate our admiration of that gigantic speculative machinery which most exactly answers the requirements of the age.

Most of the outsiders who have lost money through the Stock Exchange have themselves to thank for it. Some are careless in their choice of brokers, and where there are three or four hundred houses of thorough integrity which they can employ, they evince preternatural alertness in selecting the genuine vampires of the street. Others put all their savings into one throw, and in the natural oscillations of stock their margins need strengthening just at the moment when they cannot lay their hands on additional funds. Many are eager to appear learned in broker's slang, and so give orders the reverse of what they mean. Not a few besiege their friends for points, and when they have elicited some vague reply, such as "Fort Wayne is a good stock to hold," "Erie must fall under the pressure of the new issues," they plunge in, are entangled in some unexpected clique movement, and come forth *minus* their shekels and full of wrath against the unoffending individual who had unwittingly given the hint which betrayed them. Occasionally these victims of their own imbecility seek redress in the courts. A late lawsuit, in which Colonel Hawkins figured as plaintiff, illustrates a phase of this subject, although in the particular instance to be cited it was not at all clear that the defendant did not pass the boundary of prudence. During the session of the great Sanitary Fair of New York, George Bliss, Jr. and Colonel Hawkins were active members of the sub-committee of arms and trophies. The latter was somewhat "in stocks," and alleged at the trial that Mr. Bliss called his attention to the Wyoming Valley Coal Company as affording peculiar opportunities for investment, especially intimating that he was in with the ring and knew the stock would rise. Mr. Bliss, it should be noted, gave testimony to the contrary, and insisted that, so far as he eulogized the stock, he was justified, inasmuch as Leonard W. Jerome, then in the flower of his career, had purchased a call for a large amount, and this single fact ought, as speculation goes, to have enhanced the market value of the property.

Whether the victim of self-deception or of over-confidence in his Sanitary Fair colleague, the Colonel decided to make a venture in Wyoming Valley, buying 1,000 shares and paying $ 52,500. This was in April, 1864. All through the summer he waited patiently, but the stock either kept steadily at the sale figure or vibrated in slight degrees downward. Early in the fall it dropped sharply down, and by November the speculation had so untoward an aspect that Hawkins decided to sell five hundred shares. In March of the next year he threw the remaining instalment into the market.

The profit and loss account run as follows:—

To 1,000 shares Wyoming Valley Coal @		$ 52½		$ 52,500.00
By 500 shares		$ 25.75	$ 12,875	
" 400 "	"	27.50	11,000	
" 100 "	"	27.75	2,775	26,650.00
				$ 25,850.00
In addition, the Colonel's brokers brought in a bill for interest and commissions of				2,926.61
Giving a net loss of				$ 28,776.61

These figures need no comment. Yet in one respect the operation conformed to one of the most important laws of speculation. The stock was bought and carried for from six to eleven months. Had there been as much wisdom in selecting as there was tenacity in holding, the balance-sheet would probably have been very different. Either by selling when the market is unduly high, or buying when it is unquestionably low, and then carrying the venture for a year if necessary, an outsider has at all events *equal* chances of gain or loss. This balancing of risks is in itself an advantage which veteran operators can best appreciate. The difficulty with the Wyoming Coal was that it was emphatically a "fancy" stock. There were twenty good railroad properties on the share list which, with fifty thousand dollars of capital, would have insured a safe profit either in a "long" or "short" operation.

It is partly for want of courage to endure an occasional "break" in stocks, and partly from lack of common-sense in the choice of time and of securities, that those outsiders who are free from the other weakness to which we have alluded so frequently meet with misfortune. Brokers are fond of telling their customers, jocosely, that the true way to speculate is to buy when stocks are low and sell when they are high. As a matter of fact, the advice is not more sound than feasible, and the few who act upon it invariably become rich. There are scores on scores of capitalists in New York City, Providence, Hartford, Philadelphia, and other places, who have always adopted this policy. They watch the market, study the earnings of companies, look into the character and bent of mind of directors, and when certain stocks fall to a reasonable figure they buy, generally upon wide margins. Any yearly chart of prices will show the safety of such procedure and the frequency of opportunities for acting upon it. The following chapter will be found full of illustrations touching upon this subject. The great operators do not care to employ this method, as they find quicker profits in corners; the brokers cannot, as their capital is limited and they are compelled to turn it constantly,— their separate speculations seldom lasting more than a month or two. Meanwhile, the great proportion of outsiders, new in the field, impulsive, easily influenced, are captivated by some active stock, buy it when the market is booming, and sell upon the first decline. Where there is not timidity, there is very apt to be obstinacy. It is one of the most harassing functions of brokerage to convince a customer that the fact a security is quoted at 150 is an argument in favor of letting it alone. One class has implicit faith that it will rise to 200, and at 175 refuses to sell. Of course a reaction sets in. Possibly a defalcation is announced, or the capital stock has been watered into twice its former bulk. The tumble downward commences, now 140, next 120, 110, 90, 85, 70. The fresher the men the greater the bulldog spirit, until when the shares reach 60, a panic seizes them.* They sell peremptorily, only to find, a week or two after, that the stock has recovered to 85. Nothing could be more absurd than this, and nothing more habitual. To buy at the crest wave of extreme advance and to sell at the lowest ebb of the tide, are what brokers assure us to be the judicious customs of ninety out of a hundred of the people who bewail their inexplicable misadventures in stocks!

* We trust the reader will not infer that because a too quick abandonment of a speculation is unwise, it is therefore necessary to cling with undue pertinacity to property which has lost value. Every broker has his anecdote of customers who have been caught by "traps" (*argot* for worthless "fancy" shares), and have kept them for years in hope of a change in the market. The most remarkable instance, however, of infatuated obstinacy in this regard is to be found outside of stocks. In 1825 there was a great speculative mania in cotton, followed by a short decline. A Liverpool merchant that year had sold most of his consignment at the top prices of the time, but still had on hand some 2,000 pounds, which had cost about 43 cents a pound. When rates lowered, he stored the bales away, determined not to sell until the market recovered. The lot was finally sold in 1849. By that date it had cost in storage, interest, etc., $ 2.60½ a pound, or a total of $ 5,210. It brought 15¼ cents, giving a net loss of $ 4,905!

"Short" transactions are apt to be a stumbling-block to beginners. The first speculations of outsiders are always for a rise. To sell what you have not got, and yet make money by it, is a species of metaphysics that comes only by education. One reason for its unpopularity is that the new men are thorough bulls. They have money. Their feelings are buoyant. The stock market is *couleur de rose.* It is the melting down of margins and a few sharp losses which develop the bear.

Among city clerks and men about town with small means, a common habit is to give a broker acquaintance an order to buy on a ten per cent margin, with the provision that if the price drops down to the point covered by the advance, it shall be sold without recourse; if it rises five per cent, the broker is to realize. Not unfrequently five or ten persons club together, putting in $ 200 each. This allows of a purchase of $ 1,000 in stocks, which, if the quotation be 50, would give two hundred shares. At 55 they would double their money. Occasionally a complaisant operator will agree to take two per cent margin, buying or selling short in the morning, and reversing the course in the afternoon. Ten per cent has been made by this process in a day, a thousand dollars admitting of a transaction in 500 shares, giving five thousand dollars clear in the fall or rise between 100 and 110. Generally, however, one, two, or three per cent is all that can be obtained. Even a fluctuation of $\frac{5}{8}$ would thus make more than half the money risked in margin.

A very considerable share of commissions comes to New York indirectly. Banks all over the country form little centres around which local speculation collects. The advice of cashiers or presidents is taken. Tradesmen with a surplus balance of five or twelve hundred dollars look into the financial columns of the city daily or weekly, compare rumors, make partial decisions, and then go to the bank and ask if Milwaukee and St. Paul would n't be safe now; or whether New Jersey Central is not likely to react. After due hesitation they finally conclude to try Cleveland and Pittsburg, or possibly one of the other stocks just mentioned. The cashier telegraphs or writes to his usual broker, transmits the money, and in a day or more receives the stock. His action is unofficial, and very commonly he derives no profit from the service. The people who purchase in this manner always buy out and out, although with the purpose of realizing in an early future. Even heavy capitalists employ the same agency, operating both on margins and by solid purchases or sales.

CHAPTER XI.

MOBILITY OF STOCK.

AT various times ingenious accountants have sought to devise a system of weights and measures for the Stock Market. Sometimes the basis of these calculations has been the average rental rate of real estate; at others, the annual worth of money lent freely upon unimpeachable security. The method is not difficult in its arithmetic, and has doubtless a certain use, as illustrating the difference between the selling rate of stocks and their theoretical value. Thus, where money brings easily seven per cent a year, it is clear that a stock with guaranteed interest of seven per cent ought to have par value, provided the company which it represents is managed with such care as to insure the property from future injury in its earning power. In other words, stock costing one hundred dollars, and paying seven dollars yearly in dividends, if the precedent conditions were complied with, ought to be exactly as safe and profitable an investment as the same amount of money out at loan. Now, if the same stock should permanently pay eight per cent, its true value in the market would be the equivalent of that sum, which at seven per cent would give eight dollars in interest. Were a capitalist to buy the stock at $114\frac{2}{7}$, his annual dividend would be precisely what the same money would be worth at .07 per year. Thus $ $114\frac{2}{7} \times .07 = \$ 8$. What is true for eight per cent will of course hold in due proportion either for six, ten, or twenty per cent dividends. On this reasoning the subjoined table is based: —

Par of Stock.	Guarantee Interest.	True Value.
100	.07	100.
100	.08	$114\frac{2}{7}$
100	.09	$128\frac{4}{7}$
100	.10	$142\frac{6}{7}$
100	.15	$214\frac{2}{7}$
100	.20	$285\frac{5}{7}$
100	.25	$357\frac{1}{7}$
100	.06	$85\frac{5}{7}$
100	.05	$71\frac{3}{7}$
100	.04	$57\frac{1}{7}$
100	.01	$14\frac{2}{7}$

Any school-boy can see that seven per cent upon $ $357\frac{1}{7}$ would give the same annual sum as that of a twenty-five per cent dividend upon a $ 100 stock. As long, therefore, as it is certain that the high dividend will be permanent, this stock at any point below $ 357 is a cheap purchase.

With gold at 120, the coupon of a $ 100 government bond is worth $ 7.20. The sale value of the bond itself by the above table should have equalled, at that rate of interest, $102\frac{6}{7}$.* While, in fact, 5-20s, when gold is at

* In order to prevent any misapprehension, we may as well repeat what has already been said in a different place, that all fractional prices of stocks are in eighths. When, therefore, fractions *in sevenths* occur in this chapter, it should be understood that reference is made to the table above.

the figure cited, are marketed at 115. Fort Wayne stock is guaranteed at seven per cent by the Pennsylvania Central, the wealthiest railway corporation in the State whose name it bears. The shares ought to sell, *per* table, for 100. They could be bought in December, 1869, at 85. Why will men give twelve per cent above the legitimate value of one security, and hesitate at the apparently great profit of twelve per cent discount in another?

Seventy years ago a chart classifying the great British funds, according to ratios similar to the tables just presented, was published in London, and the subsequent fluctuations of the English stock market must have enabled all who acted upon this guide to make very considerable additions to their wealth. How many men, however, would have the courage to employ such a system, even if convinced that the groundwork were thoroughly sound? Let any reader, fortunate in having money to invest, look into his own heart for an answer. He will find there suspicion, over-confidence, timidity, vacillation, — each and every element which has made the prices of all financial centres through early and latter days fluctuating, unstable, hazardous. Examine any yearly record of sales in the New York Stock Market, and then go back to the emotions of January and compare them with the fact of December. You will find confidence where the registry shows there should have been distrust, hesitation which ought to have been daring, doubts where faith would have been wealth. This weakness of humanity is the life of speculation.

This uncertainty of the future, this susceptibility to momentary influences, affecting the coollest and shrewdest heads, gives even to irrefragable values the quality of quicksilver.

Government bonds, during the last year or two, have maintained great evenness of rates, yet twenty-four sales and purchases either in '68 or '69 would have given fifty per cent profit, apart from the coupons, and in the dark days of the war forty gold dollars would have secured a hundred-dollar bond. Look at the Panama Railway stock when paying, as now, twenty-four per cent dividends, but before the Pacific Railway had materially diminished its earnings. In two years, closing with December, '68, the fluctuations ranged in figures like the following, — 260, 254, 270, 261, 300, 311, 295, 300. Illinois Central is not a speculative stock. It is held at home, in England, in Germany, for its annual fruitage; yet the tidal movements of the Exchange were for the same period, $117\frac{1}{3}$, 111, 129, 122, 135, 147, 137, 159, 144. The Delaware and Hudson Canal is a substantial property, managed in the interests of its owners. During the past three years its shares exhibit an ebb and flow of 133, 150, 145, 155, 152, 160, 139, 163, $119\frac{1}{2}$, 131. Such examples are only too numerous. They are part of the scrutable and inscrutable features of every money mart.

The primary cause of mobility of stock is, and must always be, excess or want of confidence. The artificial unquestionably mingles with the natural class of influences, and there are not a few operators whose style of navigation is to beat up against the wind. But there is not a speculator in or out of Wall Street who is not subject to subtle undercurrents blinding the judgment, coloring all views, depressing or exhilarating, making him bull or bear. The world does not contain a more thorough materialist than the genuine stock-broker. And yet if there be spiritual forces anywhere at play, it is around the temples of the money-changers. Sombre spirits foreboding war in peace, and defeat in battle, failure of crops, a drooping trade, a dying commerce, usury in the money-market, glimmerings of repudiation round the whole sky, dishonesty in directions, peculation, defalcations, all the evils of humanity which in reaction destroy security and strike down the prices of stock. Again, bright spirits bringing the hope of sunny harvests, of peace among the nations, or victory beneath war's whirlwind, of abounding activity in manufacture and trade, of flush money days, and fever for investment and speculation. Spirits who haunt the street for an hour, and others that abide for months,—guardian spirits who make every venture successful, and malignant spirits like Atê or Nemesis driving their victims from failure to failure till the end is reached. We have yet to hear of a genuine stock-jobber who does not believe in chance even against his will. The atmosphere is so fickle, there are such swarms of rumors, the whole market is so subject to evanescent unreasonable transitions that a man who buys or sells, unless on accidental certainties, uses such prevision as is granted him, and trusts to luck for the sequel.

The tendencies of the times are toward instability.

An age of steam and telegraph is necessarily disquiet, impatient, eager to gain opulence by express-trains. Engineers tell us that after a certain point each increase of speed is at double cost in wear and tear. It is so in money-getting. The immense friction rubs away a vast deal of fribbling honesty, small prejudices, super-niceties of conscience. Hard pan is soon reached, and both old world and new are full of hard-pan capitalists. Before 1825 people sought competence. Up to 1837 the end was wealth. Since then our rich men are only content with being king merchants and king speculators, — to have power to rule, to be invincible. If Vanderbilt loses five dollars in early evening at the Manhattan, he will play till midnight in order to win it back. That is the character of the man in a nutshell. And finance is full either of men of that stamp who simply want surplusage of power, or of others who are eager to attain to the plane already arrived at by the others. As a consequence, we have corruption in railway management, *finesse* in telegraph and steamship lines, stock watering by the hundred millions, legislative jobbery, "passing" of dividends, — every artifice of capital, working under high pressure. All the antiquated influences affecting securities, — anticipation of political complications, fears of agricultural, manufacturing, or mercantile depression, foreboding of panics, and the like, are now multiplied indefinitely by fresh expedients — purely artificial — but far more fatal to the equilibrium of values.

Uncertainty, however, is not a disadvantage in speculation. The class of bonds or stocks about which an investor can safely reason, and cipher out profits — which might be taken as a basis for charts like that of Fortune's of London — are not popular with outsiders or operators. The street rallies round the stocks which are most under suspicion; the draggled skirts of Erie have always had a fascination. When Western Union Telegraph stock was on the edge of its present low estate, it was the pet of the street. Enter the Stock Exchange at any morning call, and, apart from mining shares, one might shrewdly select the class of security which will justify investment by the rapidity with which the Vice-President slurs it over. Northwestern, Fort Wayne, Lake Shore, Michigan Southern, Pacific Mail, the Express stocks, the Vanderbilt stocks, Atlantic Mail, Tennessee Sixes, North Carolina Sixes, rise and fall as favorites according as they are doubtful or steady values. The whole life and zest of the market lie in incessant undulations. Take up any annual registry of the Stock Exchange, and you can check off in a moment the temporary "fancies" of the year by selecting such as show the widest vibrations. The serious thing of existence is to buy New York Central at 124 and sell it at 180, leaving the new purchaser to find his profit where he can. Illinois Central in 1862 sold for 60, and was exceedingly popular. Six years later it was almost out of the market, and the few buyers paid from 145 to 159 for their shares. Investment ruined it for Wall Street.

Not only is uncertainty an immense force, but its power is doubled by that strange perplexity of the market, arising from the great difference in the effects of the same laws. The influences which one day will produce a sharp rise or fall, at another time may cause only the feeblest ripples. Thus a number of dealers may be short of shares or gold. They may be very short, anticipating a heavy decline. Presently comes a panic. Everybody perceives that the market has been oversold. The bears turn and buy in order to cover their shorts. The bulls are also purchasing.

On January 23, 1869, the Gold Board had this complexion. Yet the effect was seen only in a rise from 135$\frac{7}{8}$ to 136$\frac{3}{8}$. Eight months later a similar complexity carried gold up to 160, with consequences sufficiently known. Stocks under such contingencies will rise some three or four per cent, and again, as was the case with Erie on November 14, 1868, shares that sell in the morning at 36$\frac{5}{8}$ may be 52$\frac{1}{4}$ before evening. Here is the doubtful within the doubtful, and half the success of operators is in their ability to take a rapid survey of the market, and judge whether a fluctuation be final or the prelude of a corner.

The influence of legislation on prices involves similar perplexities. When Hooper's bill was reported in Congress early in 1868, and there was a general belief that its passage was certain, thus effectually closing up our national indebtedness, governments rose markedly. The subsequent death of the measure in the Senate produced a corresponding reaction. Operators in possession of Washington secrets made immense sums. When Grant's message in the fall of the same year appeared, governments, so far from bounding up, as they might naturally have been expected to do under the inspiriting effects of the Executive document, remained either stationary or with a fractional decline. A vote to increase the fare on the New York Central or to reduce it on the Illinois roads has seriously affected the Exchange at one period and been without any influence at another. The New York Legislature attempted to punish Vanderbilt for not spending money freely to defeat Jay Gould and the Erie Act. A *pro rata* freight bill was introduced and urgently pushed. Its effect, had it passed, would have been to greatly decrease the earnings of the Central. Nevertheless, in the share market Erie yielded more than either of the Vanderbilt stocks, upon reception of the news.

Brokers have a theory, that when gold is high stocks should be high; greenbacks being worth less, stocks should be worth more. A fall in gold of two per cent has, time and again, sent speculative stocks down from three to eight per cent. Yet on December 20, 1869, without any other cause at work save the heave and flux of an ordinary market, gold dropped $\frac{5}{8}$ by steady fractions through the day, while stocks rose an average of one per cent.

There is a certain grim satire in some of the influences affecting stocks. November 24, 1869, there was a rumor that the Fisk party was to be ousted from the Erie direction, and that Daniel Groesbeck had been appointed receiver. The stock of the broad gauge rose two per cent in consequence! A like result followed upon the cable despatch announcing that the English bondholders were going to institute litigation against the road.

The new Tennessee bonds at 1 P. M., December 27, 1869, were quoted at 45½. The street presently learned that a committee had been elected for the purpose of influencing Nashville legislation, so as to insure enhanced value to the securities. In two hours after the bonds were at 47.

The whisper that the directors of a company will omit the usual dividend has an instant effect in depressing stock. On November 11, 1869, Pacific Mail fell from 60¾ to 56¼, because of such a rumor. St. Paul not long since was buoyed up to 116½ by anticipations of large stock and cash dividends. When the directors had unloaded at heavy profits, these dreams were suddenly dissipated, and the shares declined to 60.

The disastrous consequences of corners have been already alluded to, but the influences of cliques upon stocks are not limited to these grand operations. When the attempt of the Erie managers to get control of the Columbus, Chicago, and Indiana Central Railroad failed ingloriously, the stock was knocked down six per cent in revenge. This was February 1, 1869, and the quotations of sales amounted to only eight or nine hundred shares, illustrating the cheap way in which prices can be changed.

The inter-sympathy between stocks is remarkable. November 6, 1869, there was a break in Chicago and Northwest. St. Paul, Hudson, Chicago and Alton, all fell. 5-20s declined 4⅛. Mississippi 6s dropped six per cent. Rock Island showed a loss of 5⅛. Central, Hudson, and Harlem are very sensitive to whatever enhances Erie.

The Cuban insurrection has at different times affected Governments; now causing a slight fall in fear of Spanish complications, and again leading to a rise, from the fact that the revolutionary party entered the market as purchasers, in order to reinvest the money previously employed in Havana trade.

In its panics, Wall Street is especially unreasonable. Indeed, there is not a safer method of profit in existence than to watch the periodical depressions of securities; and to buy, buy, buy as soon as the downward pressure is fully under way. When the White fraud was discovered in the summer of '68, the loss by forgeries was something like $ 200,000; while the shares of the six companies whose certificates had been tampered with were sold down to the equivalent of a loss of ten millions.

The mere sale of a few millions of gold by Secretary Chase, in the spring of '64, sent stocks tumbling from five to twenty-five per cent; and the gold which, in the second week of April, was held at 189, was offered on the 18th for 168, with no one to take it. It was the same way in September, 1869; the depression in stocks being due to purely artificial causes, and the purchasers who had the courage to buy at the fall insuring to themselves enormous gains.

Nor are these fluctuations below intrinsic value confined to special and sensational crises. They are a part of the history of every year. In the table given at the commencement of this chapter a basis for the judgment of values is afforded in cases where the dividend or interest is sure. Its application to Government, State, and Railroad bonds, in which the element of suspicion has the least influence, would illustrate the opportunities of speculation very forcibly. Unfortunately, such an inquiry would be complicated by the fact that in some cases coin interest is paid; while, in others, peculiar circumstances have affected confidence either advantageously or disastrously, but in ways requiring constant explanation. What is true of the more stable classes of investment is necessarily even more a fact in regard to those descriptions of stock in which either the dividend is variable or the management untrustworthy. Nevertheless, there are points in the course of prices at the New York Exchange which can be rendered clearer by a comparison with the theoretical scale of values. The year 1868 was an active one for stocks. It is, in fact, more representative than either the preceding or succeeding twelve months. The rates of the principal shares during each month are now before us. Taking bank stock, which is altogether held for investment, we find a few of the New York banks which conform with the figures of the table. Thus, subjoined are the names of four banks, the par value of whose shares is 100, on which, for the year, ten-per-cent dividends were declared. Selling at \$ $142\frac{6}{7}$, they would consequently be equivalent to an investment in the proportions of one hundred dollars at seven per cent. We give the lowest and highest bids, with the comparative cheapness and dearness of the stock, taking $142\frac{6}{7}$ as the true value.

	Lowest.		Advantage to Buyer.	Highest.			
America .	$ 136	=	$6\frac{6}{7}$	$ 145	=	$2\frac{1}{7}$	Disadvantage to buyer.
New York .	133	=	$9\frac{6}{7}$	140	=	$2\frac{6}{7}$	Advantage "
Fulton .	. 160	=		160	=	$17\frac{1}{7}$	Disadvantage "
Corn Exchange	124	=	$18\frac{6}{7}$	$135\frac{1}{2}$	=	$7\frac{3}{7}$	Advantage "

The highest sale-price of twelve other banks with par 100, and with 10 per cent dividends, is given below :—

Atlantic . .	103	Supposed advantage	to buyer	@ $142\frac{6}{7}$ =	$ $39\frac{6}{7}$
Butch. & Drovers'	135	"	"	"	$7\frac{3}{7}$
Import. & Traders'	135	"	"	"	$7\frac{6}{7}$
Commerce .	130				$12\frac{6}{7}$
Commonwealth	116				$26\frac{6}{7}$
Republic . .	$125\frac{1}{2}$				$17\frac{3}{7}$
Hanover .	117				$25\frac{6}{7}$
Market . .	116				$26\frac{6}{7}$
Mech. Bank. Asso.	117				$25\frac{6}{7}$
Mer. Exchange	120				$22\frac{6}{7}$
National .	110			" "	$32\frac{6}{7}$
St. Nicholas .	112				$30\frac{6}{7}$
Shoe & Leather	$125\frac{1}{2}$	"	"		$17\frac{3}{7}$

It should be added, that many in the above list sold from five to ten per cent lower at other sales. The figures in the last column help to illustrate a general law in stocks, namely, that whenever even the vaguest suspicion lurks about an investment, it never rises to the maximum of its dividend-bearing worth. Thus the Marine Bank declared a dividend of 16 per cent. That would have placed its genuine value at 228, but it actually sold for 150. The Chatham, with the same dividend, sold for 145. The Park Bank declared fourteen-per-cent dividend.

That would be equal to $ 200 at seven per cent, yet the stock sold no higher than 155. The Seventh Ward sold for 112 on an eight-per-cent dividend. This was $ $2\frac{2}{7}$ below the table. *Per contra*, the City, with twelve-per-cent dividend, sold for 186 – 190. The tabular value would be $171\frac{3}{7}$, giving an excess of over $ 15 on each share. The Manhattan shows a vastly greater excess in its selling value.

Passing to railroads, we will first select three whose dividends naturally kept them mainly in the hands of investors.

	Par.	Dividends.	Theoretic Value.	Lowest Sale.	Highest.
Panama . . .	100	24 per cent	$342\frac{6}{7}$	290	369
Hartford and New Haven	100	12 "	$171\frac{3}{7}$	213	225
New York and "	100	10 "	$142\frac{6}{7}$	133	159

It will readily be seen that Panama at 290 was a very cheap purchase, and that the confidence of purchasers was sufficient to carry it considerably above $ $342\frac{6}{7}$, which would be the real worth when money loans for seven per cent. New York and New Haven was at least nine per cent too low when at 133. Hartford and New Haven sold, at its lowest, for forty per cent above what a twelve-per-cent dividend would naturally appreciate a stock. Illinois Central and Hudson River might have been added to the others, but the dividend of the former road was complicated by a stock bonus, and the latter line was subjected to a speculative bull movement which gave it a fictitious value.

It may not be inadvisable, however, to test the table

by the prices of a few specially active stocks given below:—

	Par.	Dividend.	True Value.	Lowest.	Highest.
Chicago, Rock Island, and Pacific	100	10	$142\frac{6}{7}$	85	118
Chicago and Alton . .	100	10	$142\frac{6}{7}$	120	$158\frac{1}{2}$
Chicago, Burlington, and Quincy	100	10	$142\frac{6}{7}$	138	175
Cleveland, Col., Cin., and Indiana	100	7	100	75	110
Cleveland and Toledo . .	100	7	100	95	113
Dubuque and Sioux City .	100	7	100	39-50	101
Lake Shore	100	7	100	95	114
Rensselaer and Saratoga .	100	$6\frac{1}{2}$	$92\frac{6}{7}$	84	$95\frac{3}{4}$
Adams Express . . .	100	5	$71\frac{3}{7}$	46	$80\frac{1}{2}$
Western Union Telegraph .	100	4	$57\frac{1}{7}$	33	$39\frac{1}{2}$

With the exception of the first and the last stock on the list, the reader will perceive the range of prices to have been in each case above and below the standard of the seven-per-cent table. Rock Island this year labored under the disadvantage of a lawsuit, and also of a heavy new issue of shares representing construction expenses, and therefore temporarily depressing the property. Western Union was buried beneath the immense weight of the Russian Extension debt, which the directors had neatly shifted from their own shoulders to those of the shareholders. All the other properties rose or fell beyond the unit of true value calculated on a seven-per-cent basis.

We have directed attention to the apparent corroboration of the scale by the actual vibrations of the market, simply to show that there is a sense of some governing unit of value in the minds of all dealers. With the exception of a few of the banks, it has been seen that the table affords a near average of the intrinsic worth of the stock cited above. Buyers of shares at figures below the seven-per-cent unit would have been secure of ultimate profit. Holders, when the rates were above that unit, would have been prudent had they sold at once. The reader ought to thoroughly understand, however, that there is no royal road to speculation. Given all the conditions of the problem, and profits could be ciphered out with the accuracy of a mathematical demonstration. But the unknown quantities are the stumbling-blocks of system-mongers. Integrity and ability in directors, the earning capacity of the property of a corporation, the chances of the future as well as the past, are essential points to the final judgment, and the rates of the Exchange are averagely the measure of increasing or decreasing faith in the dividend worth of a security.

Successful operators unquestionably have a mental rule of valuation. By processes which they cannot explain even to themselves, they know when stock is a good purchase, and when its price is running too high. None of them would allow that a system is possible, or could perfect their combinations except by an unconscious use of this very impossibility. For the sake of illustration, therefore, and with the preliminary warning, that, at best, the sale is only approximately correct, we propose to continue our glance at the opportunities of speculation on the seven-per-cent interest basis.

Panama, in 1868, was a good investment at $342\frac{6}{7}$. A hundred shares, costing $\$34{,}285\frac{5}{7}$, would have netted twenty-four per cent in four successive payments on each certificate. Twenty-four per cent on the par of a hundred shares, and seven per cent on the selling rate, would each give $ 2,400. A capitalist having sufficient faith in this, and with money at command for purchasing and holding 100 shares even at 400 as the quotation, could easily have made six times the dividend profit by buying and selling this small even lot just ten times during the year. In January the stock was 290. In February it was 345. Buying at the former price and selling at the latter, he would have cleared $ 5,500.

In March	he could have	bought at	330	and sold at	346 =	$ 1,600
" May	"	" back at	315	" "	330¼ =	1,525
" June	"	" "	329¾	" "	339 =	925
" July	"	" "	330	and sold in Aug. at	368	3,800
" Oct.	"	" "	330	" " "	345	1,500
" Dec.	"	" "	327½	" " "	340	1,250
Giving him his money back, and a profit of				. .		$ 10,600

With the exception of the sales of May and June he would have acted throughout upon the principle that stocks quoted above their investment worth may be safely sold with a view of buying back at a great decline. It will be noticed that the highest figure of purchase in this case was 330. A twenty-per-cent margin on that price would have been $ 6,600. The operator, with that advance, could have easily performed every part of the series of transactions, and have closed them with his six thousand changed to twenty-one. A speculation on a margin, however, is more profitable in the lower-priced shares. Take Chicago and Alton. It paid ten-per-cent dividends, was well managed, and represented a property that was of growing value. One hundred shares at $ 14,200 was a good purchase. The men who went into the market with a firm faith in the worth of the stock even at 142 must have made money. They could have bought at 120 in April, and sold in August at 144. That would have been a clear gain of $ 24 on the share. What ordinary business pays such profits ? A buyer might have said in January : " I will buy whenever the stock touches 130 or falls below it. My broker shall sell at every six-per-cent rise on this, and buy again on a six-per-cent fall. I will purchase no more than I can really hold, even if it falls to zero, but will only place twenty per cent on deposit. Above 142, I will let it alone." He sends up to New York two thousand dollars, and his broker acts faithfully. Now observe the figures : January, 130 – 136 ; February, 128 – 136 ; April, 120 – 128½ ; June, 130 – 136 ; August, 145 – 138¼ ; November, 135 – 150. The other months show like vibrations, but the prices were such that the broker, with his peculiar orders, would not have been warranted in buying. Even on six per cent, however, the customer could not have failed to clear $ 3,600, besides holding his margin intact.

This is conservative speculation. There were men, that year, who bought Dubuque and Sioux City at 39, and sold it for 100. They had the courage to wait from January to September. They could have bought a thousand shares on a margin of $ 4,000, and would have been worth $ 65,000 in nine months. The stock paid seven per cent, and was therefore well worth $ 100, even to hold.

The course of Chicago, Burlington, and Quincy was a beautiful example of the advantage of solid purchases. It could have been bought in January for 138. In March and September there were semiannual five-per-cent dividends. By December the stock could have been sold out for 175; that would have given $ 37 on each share. This is the ideal; it presupposes buying at the lowest ebb, and selling just when the wave crests for a fall. Such extremes are the luck of the lottery. There is plenty of good profit open in the market, without any of these miracles. Cleveland and Toledo was cheap for any price below 100. It was dear for any price which reached much above that figure. Within 96 and 106, any one who knew about the road might have safely held the stock. A buyer, acting upon this belief, would have made thirty per cent in five transactions with certainty, so evenly did the stock fluctuate.

There are hundreds of interesting features in the prices of '68. Thus Rock Island sold down to 85 in April, and it seems incredible that its first rebound was only 93. People who knew this road, and dared to buy, even at the latter depression, could have sold in June with a profit of $ 8 on a share; in July, with a gain of $ 17; in August, with an enhancement of $ 19; or they could have held on till December, and made $ 250 on every ten shares. In Hudson, between 125 and 138, there were incessant profits; and the variations of each month would have taught an operator that these limits were to be the year's rates. An average of 62½ as a unit, with buying at not less than eight per cent below, and selling always at eight per cent above that figure, would have been assured profit to any one in Milwaukee and St. Paul. But the chances of stocks can be seen in a better light, if examined by the record of ten years. We have before us a partial registry from 1860 to 1870. It is not easy to persuade one's self, in the face of the facts revealed by this extraordinary table of prices during the past decade, that a capitalist who has a fair proportion of foresight, and is willing to wait, can fail to make more money, and make it with greater security through speculation, than by any other of the ordinary methods of investment. The venture of a month may be treacherous, but the courage of a year is golden.

In 1860 the gates of Wall Street opened to the provident an opportunity for becoming rich such as cannot be found elsewhere in history. Men could have bought Erie for 8⅛, Harlem for 8¼, Michigan Southern for 5, Cleveland and Pittsburg for the same price, Prairie du Chien for 2. Erie could have been sold in eight months at an advance of five times the purchase-money, and Harlem at three times the cost. In seven months, Prairie du Chien was worth eight times what it sold for in February. In six months, Michigan Southern was quoted at 25. Five hundred shares in February would have cost only $ 2,500; in August their owner could have sold for $ 12,500. Twenty thousand dollars in six short months converted into one hundred thousand!

And this is but half the story. Observe the table below.

	Jan. 1860.	Feb. 1860.	May. 1863.	Aug. 1863.	Mar. 1864.	June. 1864.
Erie,	$8\frac{1}{8}$		105		126	
Harlem,	$8\frac{1}{4}$			179		285
Hudson,		35	July. 180			
Michigan Central,	35				152	
" Southern,		5			April. 118	
Cleveland and Pittsburg,	$6\frac{3}{4}$				132	
Chicago and Rock Island,		$42\frac{1}{2}$		1864. Jan. 145		
Prairie du Chien,		2		90		
Del. Lack. West.,	54					Sept. 265
Cleveland and Toledo,	19				150	

The purchaser of Erie in 1860 would have found one dollar turned to twelve in May, '63. In four years, a dollar in Michigan Southern would have changed to twenty-three. Ten thousand grown to two hundred and thirty thousand! Two thousand dollars in Prairie du Chien would have become ninety thousand in '63. Ten thousand in Cleveland and Pittsburg would have bloomed out into two hundred thousand by April, '64.

The difference of gold does not account for these figures. One dollar increased to three dollars and ten cents was the utmost contrast that the gold-market afforded through all the years of the war. Even the artificial influences at work in stocks, which undoubtedly produced the extreme quotations of Harlem, Erie, and Prairie du Chien, were as nothing compared to the legitimate effects of the enhancing value of railroad property.

Moreover, it would seem as if none of the usual explanations of the depression of 1860 were sufficient to afford a basis for hesitation to invest. All the roads were poor. Many were in debt. Dividends were infrequent, and the earnings of the great lines gave no promise of increase. But even at two-per-cent dividends a year, shares were cheap at 28. At one half of one per cent, they were a fair purchase at seven. War, indeed, was imminent; but even the regular increase of population, continued emigration, and the lowest estimates of the progressive wealth of the nation, ought to have furnished a conservative basis for confidence in the inevitable increase of these securities. That they did not have that effect with the majority of investors is clear from the mere fact of such extreme quotations as are to be found in the previous page, and it is probable that the immense profit which the future disclosed really fell to the very few capitalists who chanced to have confidence as well as money. These men became directors, infused energy, prudence, and economy in the management, and in no small degree created the wealth which ultimately flowed in to them. Some of our greatest railway kings date from that period.

The low prices of the beginning of the last decade extended even to some of the most undoubted properties. Panama, in April, '61, was 97½. In July, '64, it sold for 300. Philadelphia and Reading, which dragged in '62 at 35, sold up and down in April, '64, from 165 to 125. Between '62 and '64 there was a fortune, and the fluctuations of April would have given any lucky operator a competence. Chicago and Alton sold, in '62, for 16; in '68 it reached 158½. Illinois Central in '62 sold for 60. Chicago, Burlington, and Quincy was at the same figure. In '68 the former sold for 158, and the latter for 175. In '65 both the New York and New Haven and the Harlem were subject to heavy dealings. To-day they are out of the market; one because of its large dividends, the other from its steadiness and uselessness for speculation. For six months, in '66, New York Central sold down below 100, and might have been bought in the largest quantities at 91. The purchaser, from July onward to the present day, could have always sold at a profit, and even in that year might have realized from twenty to thirty per cent.

In '66 Pacific Mail fluttered between 180 and 240. Atlantic Mail rose and fell in weekly see-saws from 108 to 136 through January and February. Pennsylvania Coal vacillated from 131 to 170. New Jersey Railroad stock waved up and down between 120 and 145. Erie pulsed from 55 to 95.

How easy it would be to fill a book with these figures! The charts teem with them. There is not a stock of genuine worth which does not indicate, by the registry, alternations of hope and fear in wide percentages and with unbounded opportunities for speculators to buy with confidence of profit. Brokers tell us that about one in a hundred buy in this manner. The ninety-nine mean to do so. They make their calculations, add up, subtract, wander hither and thither for points, try this system and that theory, are wise to the extent of their wisdom, and come forth from their ventures shorn of all their golden fleece. With a chart of prices before one, this fatality seems inexplicable. But facts are difficult matters to combat, and the facts are indubitably discouraging. There is a solution of the failure, however, which has already been suggested. These ninety-nine buy on margins, ten per cent or twenty per cent as the case may be, but always extending themselves to the utmost limit. They also buy "active" stocks, whose fluctuations are of ten to forty per cent, giving large profits if the tide runs up, but sweeping away the advances of the outsider in a moment whenever the market breaks. If they purchased "out and out," the whole aspect of things would change. The cliques could not control as at present, and speculation would become an affair of relative judgment. There would, of course, be fluctuations, since human nature remains tolerably constant in directions of companies, money-lenders, and purchasers, and shares would be buoyant or depressed beyond their just proportion. The over-confident would lose by holding, and the suspicious would sell where they ought to buy. But the average of the unlucky would surely decrease.

THE GOLD ROOM.

CHAPTER XII.

IN THE GOLD ROOM.

JUST beyond the dusty entrance to the Long Room, on New Street, is a narrow doorway leading into a grimy and fusty corridor. If a stranger continue on, he will find himself descending sundry foot-worn stairs, and finally arriving at an inner enclosure with a private passage to the Stock Exchange at the left, and a tomb-like causeway in front of him, which penetrates through to Broad Street. On dull days he might wander up and down through this perplexing labyrinth for hours without having any clearer perception of how to reach the temple of the Gold kings than upon his first ingress. If haply some broker's clerk, sympathizing with his distress, should bravely come to the rescue, he would guide him back to the twilight of the New Street corridor, and indicate with his dexter finger two doors on the left, whose sombre and inauspicious aspect would strangely contrast with the dreams of princely splendor with which dealings in gold by the hundred millions are associated in the rural mind. Nothing in fact could be so dismal in its externals, or so modestly inconspicuous in its approaches, as the famous Gold Exchange. We have alluded to two modes of entrance. One is for members, and is strictly guarded from the interior by the Peter of the coin-market. The other leads to the free gallery,—a scrimped and box-like place, mainly devoted to office-boys and mischief. There is yet another door reached by uncertain ways, where, if properly provided with tickets, one may enter and discover himself in an upper, nest-shaped eyrie, affording an excellent view of the exciting scenes below. An on-looker from this point perceives the whole contour of the chamber. In front against the New Street side is the raised dais of the officers. President John F. Underhill occupies the seat of honor. Near him is the desk of Secretary Thomas P. Akers, with an under-clerk at his side. On the right of the President is the stand of the telegraph-operator and beyond are the open doorways of committee-rooms. To his left and above is a sort of reading-room, where half a dozen city papers are on file. Before him is the fountain, shut in by a circling iron railing perhaps thirty feet in diameter, and consisting of a Cupid playing with a dolphin, from which microscopic streamlets of water fall harmlessly into the basin beneath. Its æsthetic features may be clear as a melted margin to brokers, but to ordinary eyes it is an ineffable vision of ugliness. Against the outlying rail the operators lean idly, or join in the feeble patter of offers and bids which are prelusive of the coming combat. At an active season the fountain begins to attract brokers as early as nine o'clock. But the real business of the day starts with ten A. M. By that hour the floor buzzes with the whisperings and murmurs of a hundred voices. The President rises to his feet; the gavel rings down upon the block, and the bulls and bears spring forward to the contest.

Broker. " $5\frac{1}{8}$ for fifty. $\frac{1}{4}$ for fifty, — fifty, — I 'll give $\frac{1}{4}$ for any part of a hundred."

Voice. " Sold."

The Secretary notes down $135\frac{1}{4}$ as opening price, and $100,000 as the amount sold, while the bids continue with renewing fury.

" $\frac{1}{4}$ for five hundred, — give a $\frac{1}{4}$ for —"

" $\frac{3}{8}$ for a hundred."

" Take 'em. How much ? "

" Hundred thousand, — take fifty more."

" $\frac{1}{2}$ for twenty, — a $\frac{1}{2}$, — a $\frac{1}{2}$, — a $\frac{1}{2}$, — for any part of fifty."

Other Voices. " $\frac{5}{8}$ for fifty." — " $\frac{3}{4}$ for a hundred." — " I 'll give 36 for twenty."

" Sold," — " Sold."

President. " Twenty thousand sold to Peters & Co. at 136."

Voice. " That 's my bid, Mr. President."

Second Voice. " I appeal."

President. " Is the appeal seconded ? "

Several individuals uphold the new claimant, and the question goes to vote precisely as at the Stock Board. Then the battle recommences, with perhaps an influx of bears, who knock the metal slowly down to the opening figure. In the fall the noise and bustle swells to high confusion. Twenty shout at once. The crowd sways from side to side, and the officers from the rostrum find it nigh impossible to keep abreast with the biddings.

Just outside of the extreme verge of the tumult little groups of brokers collect, talking with nervous quickness. They are borrowers, and are arranging for loans to cover the deficiency of yesterday's transactions. Here, as in stocks, the market varies, falling as low as four or five per cent, and rising to seven per cent coin interest, or to turns of from $\frac{1}{16}$ upwards, in addition.

To understand more completely the object of these conferences, it will be necessary to explain the workings of the Gold Exchange Bank and Clearing-House. For some time after the national coin currency became a salable commodity, all exchanges between buyer and seller were effected by actual transfers of gold. During the mid hour of the day the streets were thronged by boys hurrying from office to office with bags of the precious metal. These canvas sacks were marked with the figure of their contents. Quite frequently, either from carelessness or fraud, the count did not correspond with the tally. Hence constant bickerings, quarrellings, and general bad feeling among dealers. Occasionally the specie-clerks would be knocked down in the street, red pepper thrown in their eyes, and the thieves, either in light carts or, in winter time, on runners, would dash off with their spoils before the police could be warned. The occurrence of two or three raids of this kind, added to the troubles in the count of coin, led the brokers to arrange with the Bank of New York for the issue of gold certificates based on actual deposits. Dealers were provided with check-books, for which a large guaranty payment was demanded, and the certificates passed current on 'change as good deliveries in all purchases of gold. It corresponded very exactly with the Bank of Hamburg's *banco* transactions. In August, 1865, it was discovered that this certification was surrounded by great hazards. During that month Edward B. Ketchum, of the house of Ketchum, Son, & Co., Exchange Place, suddenly disappeared. The street soon rung with the news of forgeries in gold checks to the appalling amount of a million and a half. Confidence was destroyed. It became apparent that a new system must be introduced. The Gold Exchange Bank, with its associate Clearing-House, answered to all the conditions of security, and the Gold Board immediately gave it official sanction. The method of settlement under the new order of things is as follows: On or before half past twelve o'clock a statement of all the purchases or sales made by each broker on the preceding day must be rendered to the bank. If the gold bought be in excess of that sold, a check for the difference must accompany the statement. If deposits in gold or currency are not kept in the bank, the coin must be delivered at every deficiency. The Board adjourns at twelve, in order to enable tardy dealers to complete their accounts. Provided all contracts are honored, the bank must settle by two P. M. In case of default the amount in abeyance is credited or debited to the broker who suffers by the failure. The character of the paper sent in to the bank officers will be better comprehended by the subjoined illustration of the customary form:—

Statement of Jew, German, & Co. to New York Gold Exchange Bank.

Receive from	Gold.	Rate.	Currency.	
Philes and Sawes .	$ 60,000	130	$ 78,000	
Smith and Jones .	10,000	131	13,100	
Humphrey Davy .	. 15,000	130	19,500	
Winthrop Johns .	5,000	131½	6,575	
Gardner and Smith	. 20,000	130½	26,100	
Spades and Stock .	30,000	130¾	39,225	$ 182,500
	$ 140,000			

Deliver to	Gold.	Rate.	Currency.	
Doe and Roe . .	$ 30,000	132	$ 39,600	
Harvey and Elderkin	40,000	132½	53,000	
Bacon and Herring	. 20,000	132¾	26,550	
Israel and Son . .	30,000	133	39,900	
Joseph and Ishmael	. 10,000	132¼	13,225	
Balance Check .			10,225	$ 182,500
	$ 130,000			

In this instance operations covering $ 270,000 in gold are effected with no farther direct payment than that of the check for $ 10,225. Jew, German, & Co. will be credited at the Bank by the $ 10,000 of coin due them in the balance of purchases over deliveries, and the currency check makes their account good at the Clearing-House. Had the sales been more than the purchases, they would either pay in the *difference* from their bank deposit or would have borrowed it in open market on the best terms that could be secured.

It is needless to add that this beautiful arrangement by which the completion of contracts is rapidly and efficiently accomplished by the simplest figures of book-keeping, has encountered recently a great deal of newspaper criticism. The fact that the final adjustment of the statement may often be made by the transfer of a comparatively small sum of money is pointed at as a proof of the gambling tendencies of the street. That a man with a few thousand dollars, *if he can get the credit,* might buy fifty times what he had cash to pay for is unquestionable. Suppose gold at 135. A broker with a deposit of $ 5,000, his entire capital, may have noticed that for the past ten weeks gold has seldom been below 140, and in no case has fallen to 134. He studies the external causes of the decline, and is convinced that they are inadequate to effect the market except briefly. Going to the Gold Room and finding the bears hard at work forcing the metal down step by step $134\frac{7}{8}$, $134\frac{3}{4}$–$\frac{5}{8}$–$\frac{1}{2}$, at which point it turns back oscillating between $\frac{3}{4}$ and the next lower fraction; he snaps up an offer of $ 100,000 specie for $134\frac{5}{8}$, buyer 3. Gold may fall sharply to 130, and stay there for seventy-two hours. In that event he sells $ 100,000 at 130 cash, and supplements the statement to the Clearing-House with a check for $ 4,625, leaving his whole capital $ 375. Had it fallen to $129\frac{5}{8}$, he would have been left without a mill. *Per contra,* however, it is possible to conceive that the operator's prescience did not mislead him. From $134\frac{5}{8}$, the buying price, it jumped to 136, '$38\frac{1}{4}$, '40, 143, and on the morning of the third day was at 145. He sells $ 100,000 *cash* at that price, and on rendering his account to the bank he claims a credit in *differences* over and above this five-thousand-dollar capital of $10,325. So far as the machinery of the Clearing-House is concerned, it will readily be seen that if the sales and purchases were always at a profit and without default, there would be no necessity for capital on the part of any operator. Why the interests of society and of legitimate business should be better served by the conveyance of a number of bags of gold from two offices perhaps three streets apart, when the same result is reached by a half-dozen pen-strokes at the Clearing-House, is one of those metaphysical mysteries that brokers find hard to solve. Unfortunately the felicity of unvarying success is so rare that a well-authenticated instance of it is not to be found in the annals of brokerage, and for the rest the significant "Ten up" is heard too often at the Gold Board to permit any one to imagine that dealers are not thoroughly alive to the financial status of their neighbors, and by no means willing to entangle themselves in transactions with men whose capital is inadequate to meet their engagements.

Five minutes spent in the Gold Room is sufficient for a stranger to master its distinctive features. A thousand dollars constitutes the unit, and "I'll sell any part of a hundred" means that the dealer will sell any portion of $100,000. Beyond this there is nothing to explain. All the various methods of purchase or sale, the margins, loans, and every technicality of the Stock Market are equally in use with the Gold-Brokers. The usual practice of dealers, however, is to buy or sell either Cash or Regular, and then borrow the gold or greenbacks in case an operation is to be prolonged over a series of weeks. Options are employed at times very freely, but the general custom is that just noted. As from the very nature of the business there can be no daily call, the duty of the President is simply to preserve order and arbitrate in disputes. Before and after the regular session brokers frequent the chamber precisely as in the Long Room of the Stock Exchange, and till three P. M. there will always be found a more or less spirited warfare around the circuit of the fountain. The difference of one day over another is simply in the relative intensity of speculation.

When coin has other value than that belonging to the legal tender of a nation, an artificial market is inevitable. With a great people such a condition can never be permanent, and the very sense of the temporary character of the anomaly gives a feverish and fitful complexion to dealings in bullion. In every other market the commodity offered for sale has a measure of worth apart from its current price. With coin, however, the margin between par with paper and the buying rate constitutes the sole basis of its utility as merchandise. The premium is everything, and the precious metal in itself is nothing. Moreover, whether from education or from fundamental laws of trade, there has arisen an ineradicable impression that coin transactions have more of the unsubstantial than those of commerce or stocks. Gambling, or, in other words, the trade in chance, is necessarily associated more or less intimately with every human pursuit; but in gold sales it stands forth in bold relief. Chance alone creates the premium. Chance magnifies it. Chance annihilates it. With specie payments the Gold Room becomes a reminiscence. A silver-mine is opened in Nevada. Its yield is prodigious. The company earns a thousand dollars for every ten dollars spent. The stock rises by startling leaps. The shares of $10 at par sell for $100. The Mining Board is delirious. Suddenly the vein gives out utterly. The debts of the corporation equal the entire worth of all machinery. The stock whirls down to zero. Enlarge the comparison to the dimensions of the gold market, add the certainty even at highest quotation that the day must come when 0 will indicate the premium, and the reader will at once comprehend why the Gold Board for the past eight years has been the synonyme of all that is maddening, passionate, and reckless in the struggle for wealth. In that human maelstrom where nothing but money enters, where coin metal exchanges only with coin paper, where trade is stripped of all its illusions and men battle for gold, gold, gold, with a naked greed and fury that satirizes life beyond all the imaginings of the poets, it is impossible for the combatants to be other than natural, carrying their souls in their faces, revealing in every tortuous lineament the exultations and the despair of the heart. There are individuals who have staked their fortunes on the turning of a card, without a shadow of joy or anguish perceptible in their bearing. One may find dozens of operators whose interest in the shaping of the market cannot be discerned by any ordinary rules of scrutiny.

But on the genuine field-days of the Gold Room, it is hard to believe that the general aspect of the tumult is not one in which nature throws aside its veil. In the days of the war an unexpected victory converted the gold arena into a den of wild beasts. The bulls fought against the inevitable decline with the ferocity of gladiators. The chaos of voices and the stamping of feet shook the building as in an earthquake, and boomed out of the open windows into the street below like the discharge of artillery. In some respects the scenic effect resulting from important army news was marked by more startling phases than in the sharp rise or fall of artificial movements. The gloom or the gladness over success or defeat of the national flag mingled with individual passions. Men leaped upon chairs, waved their hands, or clenched their fists; shrieked, shouted; the bulls whistled "Dixie," and the bears sung "John Brown"; the crowd swayed feverishly from door to door, and, as the fury mounted to white heat, and the tide of gold fluctuated up and down in rapid sequence, brokers seemed animated with the impulses of demons, hand-to-hand combats took place, and bystanders, peering through the smoke and dust, could liken the wild turmoil only to the revels of maniacs. The anecdotes afloat regarding gold brokers and operators all have a ring of Baden Baden in them. The dial, marking the changing price of bullion, which overhung the street when the Board met in Gilpin's Reading Room, and which more recently has told its changing story to the motley crowds of New Street, always had its little band of worshippers who watched the varying figures and bet their dollars on the next quotation. The fury within changed into curious comedy without. The men who live upon each other, and adorn Broadway on bright afternoons by the gorgeousness of their waistcoats and the flashing of their jewelry, never failed to get quick wind of whatever sport was going on "down in the street." One could safely gauge the degrees of slaughter by the number of these birds of ill omen, but of festive plumage, who haunted the sidewalk, and wagered " fifty to three " that the next show of figures would be a $\frac{3}{8}$ difference, or " one hundred even that it will be down a fraction," or " six cents to cocktails for four " that there would be a bid three per cent higher in five minutes. There was a queer street man, named T——, whose line was mainly stocks, but who had a *penchant* for betting on the register. When the luck was all against him, and his exchequer was low, he would wait till the brokers came out in the afternoon, and shout to his friends, " Say, boys, let 's go over to my place and have a little cock-fight!" Frequently the gayer men would fall in with the humor of the thing and make up a party to visit his den. The birds were game. T—— knew all their points, and generally managed to pick up enough out of two or three tournaments to venture anew into the troubled waters of buyer 3 and Regular. On black Friday the throng in New Street, largely swollen by the listless " lockers-on in Vienna," had its due complement of veteran register gamblers, and the spirit of the scene was enhanced by a dim consciousness that this was to be the last great field-day. The jokes, the merry reminiscences of bygone glories, the laughter over extravagances in bettings, the shrewd prescience of some who wagered on 160, and the reckless waste of fractional currency on the part of others of the bear side, who sought to forget their greater stakes on the day's fortune by curbstone episodes, — these were a dramatic feature in that large tragedy which gave it a Shakespearian roundness. The epoch of the sidewalk gamblers is over. The old excitements have vanished. The men who gloated over the frenzied alternations between 170 and 280, and who reappeared with something of the bygone animation in the hour when the metal fluttered betwixt 160 and 133, have lost their interest in the game. And whatever the future may disclose of storm or struggle in the downward slide to specie payments will limit itself to the confines of the Gold Room and the secret counsels of our great importers. The worth of bullion will hereafter be a financial rather than a speculative problem.

CHAPTER XIII.

THE GOLD-BROKERS.

WHEN the banks of the Union refused to honor their own bills by payment in coin for the full face value, gold tremulously vibrated in small percentages for months before it began that succession of immense leaps which grew out of the first reverses of the war. On Saturday, April 18, 1862, it was at 101½; July 1 it was 108¾; July 21 it stood at 120. The disastrous campaign of the Peninsula had borne fruit! The houses in foreign trade who had bills for one hundred thousand dollars maturing found that it would require twenty thousand more to make their contracts good. It was their first contact face to face with the luxury of rebellion. New York, neither in its commerce nor its speculation, looked kindly upon the appreciation of bullion. At the Stock Exchange the bears were in scores and the bulls in half-dozens. It was the gentlemanly thing to sell gold, and the stock operators chose to be gentlemen.

On William Street, a few paces from the rooms occupied by the Regular Board, is a basement floor, now radiant with the brass-mounted counters of a flourishing lager-beer restaurant. In 1862, however, it was a dark and sombre cellar, so gloomy and forbidding in exterior and interior that its familiar title was the "Coal

Hole." * Its frequenters were mainly curbstone brokers; and the business of speculating in railway stocks, to which it was set apart, was conducted with a total absence of decorum, and a freedom from all those restraints of daily call which the Long Room of the present day exhibits. Here the bulls in gold found refuge. By December 4 they had tossed it up to 134; on January 31 of the next year they bought it at 160. These startling changes in price had an effect upon the outside public. Customers became numerous. Gold brokerage assumed a distinctive feature in the market. Speculation, which had found an incentive in the sudden appreciation in stocks, was intensified by this new and fascinating game. The gambling instinct penetrated to the national capital, and soon made that the *point d'appui* for all operations. The Washington Party, as it was styled, held the keys to the gold citadel. Members of both Houses, and of all political creeds, resident bankers, the lobby agents, clerks, and secretaries, haunted the War Department for the latest news from the seat of war. The daily registry of the Gold Room was a quicker messenger of successes or defeats than the tardier telegrams of the Associated Press. A private secretary of a high official, with no capital at all save his position, which gave him authentic information of every shaping of the chess-game of war full twenty hours in advance of the public, simply flashed the words "sell," "buy," across the wires, and trusted to the honor

* This title was first given it by Mr. Henry A. Bowen, who was then the financial editor on a leading paper.

of his broker for the rest. He never knew what he was worth till one day, with a week's vacation on his hands, he jumped into the cars, and, entering the office of his agent, saw a credit of $ 280,000 on the books. By January, 1863, the Washington speculators were at the high-tide of their winnings. They extended their operations to stocks, included merchandise in their grasp, bought exchange largely. The brokers in their employ became marked men; and operators went long or short, according to the complexion of the dealings of these favorites of fortune.

In February, 1863, Congress attempted to put a curb upon the gold gamblers. It was made penal to offer loans on bullion above par. Other fribbling difficulties were thrown in the way of traffic in coin; but the quotations were in no wise seriously affected. Gold fell and rose between 172 and 145 until July. The capture of Fort Wagner, and the strong belief that Charleston would fall into the hands of the Union, were the first vital blows to the Washington clique and their New York coadjutors. The precious metal reached 122½ before it rebounded. Foreign Exchange sharply declined. Merchants saw their stocks of goods daily lessening in value, and in despair sold bales on bales in the auction-room.

The autumn trade opened more brightly. The Petroleum mania assisted in the recovery of the market. Stocks of all kinds sold high, and were manipulated without regard to dividends, permanent value, or aught else. Gold vibrated between 140 and 169.

The bulls were seventy out of a hundred. Between September, 1863, and April of the succeeding year the speculative fever reached a height unequalled at any previous or succeeding stage of the national history. Many brokers earned from eight hundred to ten thousand dollars a day in commissions. The entire population of the country entered the field. Offices were besieged by crowds of customers. At least a hundred million of dollars were realized in sales. New York never exhibited such wide-spread evidences of prosperity. Broadway was lined with carriages. The fashionable milliners, dressmakers, and jewellers reaped golden harvests. The pageant of Fifth Avenue on Sunday, and of Central Park during week-days, was *bizarre,* gorgeous, wonderful! Never were such dinners, such receptions, such balls. Anonyma startled the city with the splendor of her robes and the luxury of her equipages. Vanity Fair was no longer a dream.

In other chapters we shall glance at the speculative career of the country from the first stock market to the beginning of the war. But the story of Wall Street during the Rebellion can best be understood from the stand-point of the gold-broker. It was the fluctuating character of bullion which caused the two great panics of the period. It was the lock-up of greenbacks — coin paper momentarily taking the place of coin metal — which led to another intermediate and less important flurry. 1864, 1868, 1869, can best be comprehended from the outlook of the Gold Room. Early in April, 1864, Secretary Chase visited New York. Determined to put a check upon what he was not alone in deeming a national disaster, he dashed aside the law requiring the creation of a sinking-fund for the redemption of the national debt, and the rule whereby custom dues are made payable in coin. It was announced that paper would be received at the rate of 165 cents to the gold dollar, and that every morning the Sub-Treasury would designate the rate at which government was prepared to sell specie for the day. On Saturday, April 16, gold opened at 189 in private sales; but the news of the resolution of the Secretary of the Treasury presently swept over the street like a tornado. By night the metal had fallen to 175. All day Sunday the city was in a tremor of excitement, and on the first day of the secular week men hurried to William Street hours before the usual time. The bulls fought against hope, but with tenacity. 170½, 170¼–⅜–½, up and down through the fractions, with resolute determination to keep the price above 170 if possible. At last the bears had hammered it down to the fatal point. A despairing bull bought $50,000 in order to check the decline, when suddenly one hundred thousand was offered at 168, and no one ventured to take it. The market was broken. The brokers forsook the Gold Room and retired to their offices. At the Stock Exchange all was confusion. Ten days before Fort Wayne had dropped from 152½ to 135; it now fell to 83. Reading, which had seen 160, was flat at 111. Panama reeled to 200. Northwest touched 24. All along the line stocks plunged downward, with fifteen per cent fall on Saturday, and from five to twenty-five per cent depression on Monday. Morse & Co., a heavy house whose operations in Fort Wayne and Rock Island were on a vast scale, announced their suspension at the close of the first call. Sam Hallett followed. Smaller firms broke by dozens. Outside operators who had made rapid and excessive fortunes were ruined in a day. Brokers' offices were filled with customers whose margins had been swept away, or whose stock had been ruthlessly slaughtered. One man, just married, whose capital of $30,000 had been risked and lost in a single bold venture, sat in his dealer's room through the long hours of Monday, unmindful of the busy stir around him, his teeth set as if in death, his eyes transfixed, his face like a winding-sheet, and nothing to indicate that his heart still continued to beat save the cold beads of perspiration on his pallid forehead. Actors and actresses who had invested their earnings lucklessly were there. Professional men came in shoals. Rough-handed and ill-humored countrymen burst into the privacy of inside rooms, and demanded instant return of their deposits. Throughout the week Wall, Broad, and William Streets were the scene of whatever is tragical and terrible in speculation.

On Tuesday, Wednesday, and Thursday the bears had the field to themselves in both markets. On Friday, however, confidence gradually restored itself. The capitalists who had foreseen the great break in stocks and had temporarily retired, now returned and bought heavily. The gold-operators renewed their attack, and compelled the Sub-Treasury to vary its rates to suit their own schemes. By Monday the 25th government discovered that it could not longer dispense with coin for custom dues, and gold jumped instantly to 182. Thwarted in his efforts, the Secretary now used his influence to secure the passage of the Gold Bill through Congress. The act came into effect June 21st. The Gold Room was at once closed, and the Stock Exchange expunged the precions metal from the daily call. On July 4th the act was repealed, as its only consequence had been to embarrass the commercial class, causing a rise in exchange and an increase from 210 to 250 in the rates of private sale. Upon the morning succeeding the national holiday the Gold Room opened anew. The next seven days the chamber rocked with the struggles of the bears, now caught in a vast network which the bull leaders had been weaving during the interval of the Gold Bill. On July 11th gold reached its highest quotation, selling at nightfall for 285. War had nothing to do with that excessive price. It was simply the culmination of a well-concerted corner. Even these figures, which will probably go down into history as the extreme point reached in gold sales, were really below the prices paid at the Room after the regular adjournment. One transaction at least on that day was for 289½. And a lot of gold amounting to $ 100,000 was bought at the extraordinary rate of 310! The purchaser was William Limerick, a banker of Lexington, Missouri, who happened to be in the city at the moment, and, believing that the country was on the edge of immense and irretrievable ruin, gave a peremptory order to his brokers to buy just as the cornering clique had given a final twist to the shorts by a sharp upward rise in the asking price. The bullion was placed in the hands of Wm. H. Pomeroy with an injunction to keep it in his safe till called for, and Limerick retired for the night with the proud consciousness that, whatever might betide the nation, he had something secure for his old age.

Heretofore the gold-brokers had had no regular government. From the Coal Hole they had moved to Gilpin's News Room, corner of William Street and Exchange Place, where any one could be admitted on payment of $ 25 a year. It was in this room that the great corner of July 11th had been brought to successful conclusion. A few months later a number of the better class of operators and dealers came together, and preliminary steps were taken for a definite organization. On the 14th of October this action bore fruit. A constitution and by-laws were approved and accepted, three hundred members paid in their subscriptions, and the new Gold Board proceeded to the election of its officers. Henry M. Bendict was chosen President, Thos. P. Akers and R. H. Foote were made First and Second Vice-Presidents, J. W. Moses was elected Secretary, and Theodore Gentil Treasurer. The new body shortly after took up its quarters in the rooms of the old Stock Board at 24 Beaver Street.

The ensuing season was signalized by a fresh accession to the speculative excitement. New operators came into the field, and old leaders greatly extended the dimensions of their transactions. Wm. L. Hoblitzel, a dashing and shrewd broker, had given the keynote to the campaign by selling a million short in one block. The gold gamblers were startled. No transaction of such huge calibre had as yet occurred. The sale was in September, and bullion fell at once to 200. Hoblitzel covered with immense profit, and the street was not slow in following up the novel example. Dr. Shelton sold $ 6,000,000 in successive strokes, and bought in at a figure which afforded a brilliant fortune. E. A. Corey was another operator of the time, whose dealings were as vast as successful. He was invariably a bear, and seldom missed his mark. Light-haired S. T. Suit, a thriving Kentucky whiskey-distiller in early days, had recently entered the street and speculated as bull, buying a sum-total of $ 10,000,000 up to the moment that Hoblitzel hammered gold down to 200, when he went into short transactions, minting money by the way. John M. Tobin and Charles Kearney also shone, buying and selling in lots of from one hundred thousand to a million. The former shortly after the capture of Atlanta bought several millions at 198 – 201, and sold a lot for 221 with consequent heavy realizations. It would be easy to fill many pages with these records of gains, darkened by occasional losses. In early spring Limerick reappears. He had been buying and buying as his resources would allow, and sending his gold to Canada from an almost insane doubt of the continuance of prosperity in the Union. The one hundred thousand which he had purchased at 310 was clung to pertinaciously until its owner was compelled to realize. It was then sold on March 14, '65, for 185! Shortly after Limerick partly retrieved his reverse by selling at 175, and covering at 144. One of the extraordinary features of the gold market at this period was the great alternations of price within the limits of single days. Thus July 12th gold was sold for 271 and 282. July 19th the range was 258–268; August 29th, 235–245; September 10th, 218–228½. The next Monday it sold for 213½ and 225. On Tuesday it was 217½–228. On the 24th the difference in the day's price was twelve per cent. November 2d it vacillated seventeen per cent. On the 9th it changed from 246 to 260. Changes of five, six, seven, and eight per cent were common.

During the winter and spring of 1864–65 the days were too short for the fervid haste of the speculators. The corridors of the Fifth Avenue Hotel were crowded nightly by eager throngs, and the barter in stocks and gold went on with almost the same intensity which characterized the down-town boards. A Mr. Gallagher saw his opportunity for coining money out of this unnatural fever, and opened an evening exchange in a room back of the hotel, where the Fifth Avenue Theatre now stands. Railways, petroleum stocks, and gold were sold at different hours of the night. He had previously established an outside Petroleum Board at the corner of Broadway and 23d Street, and ultimately the evening exchange transferred its quarters to the same spot. A blood-red transparency, announcing this strange anomaly of the century, glared out upon the great pleasure street of New York immediately after dusk, and until midnight the murmur of voices rolled out upon the sidewalk. The street became demoralized. Brokers apparently lived without sleep or rest or peace. They haunted the day boards with pallid faces and a strange glitter of the eye. High-strung, fevered in blood, craving excitement from the very exhaustion of overwork, they carried in their faces a prophecy of evil. In August the evil came. Jenkins, cashier of the Phœnix Bank, defaulted for $ 300,000, lost in gold and stocks, or spent in the mad debaucheries of the year. Close upon this came the failure of P. R. Mumford, an operator with an office at 42 Exchange Place. On the 12th he had bought $ 150,000 in gold and paid for it when delivered by checks on a bank where he had no deposit. Seven brokers suffered from this default, and the Christian world was scandalized by the fact that Mumford was a trustee of a church at Flushing, Long Island. These "irregularities" were prelusive of far more terrible revelations. Upon the 14th of the same month Edward Ketchum absconded, leaving behind him a bequest to the street in the shape of a million and a half of forged gold certificates. The failure of the house of which he was second partner followed immediately, and out of the smoke of the ruin emerged the amazing rumor that two millions and a half of State securities had been stolen from the firm. In a vain attempt to stem the tide, Ketchum, Son, & Co. had gathered up some 200,000 shares held on margin or contract, and sold them upon a falling market at Gallagher's Exchange and at the first call of the regular Board on the succeeding day. Stocks dropped from three to eight per cent, gold fell in proportion, and the days of '64 seemed on the point of returning. Sensational rumors were spread over the country by telegraph. It was whispered that D. Groesbeck & Co. were seriously involved, and the house was compelled to publish a letter from the President of the Union Bank stating that they had then on deposit $1,173,554. A prominent house issued a panic-stricken circular, announcing that thenceforward they should greatly restrict the extent of individual loans on collaterals, and that customers must accompany their orders with enhanced margins. Money grew exasperatingly tight. The banks refused to discount. Brokers slaughtered their customers' stocks without warning. As usual, also, the big leviathans of speculation came sailing into the market at its low ebb and bought heavily only to sell again a week after or as soon as the tempest had spent its force. The bears reaped millions by their opportune courage.

When the street had somewhat recovered its tone, a simultaneous attack was commenced upon the Evening Board. The banks of the city compelled their officers to sign an agreement to hold no intercourse with the men who frequented the rooms. The Stock Exchange voted unanimously to the same effect, and the Open Board adopted a similar resolution by 97 yeas against 17 nays. On August 25th the Gold Board at its first call gave the last blow to night-dealings by acceding to the general feeling, and making the frequenting of Gallagher's rooms a sufficient reason for the immediate expulsion of the offending member.* On the same day the public was informed of the capture of Ketchum, and fresh light was thrown upon the vast proportions of current speculations by his statement that only a few months before he had acquired six millions of dollars by street dealings, and that in the subsequent fall of gold from 201 to 147, incident to Sherman's successful march to the sea, this had not only disappeared, but had involved liabilities to the extent of four millions, which he had sought to protect by margins based upon his forgeries.

From '65 to '69 the Gold Board was free from the startling paroxysms of the anterior period. The daily variations were seldom more than two or three per cent. Prices ranged up and down through the months with singular evenness. Brokers contented themselves with smaller profits. Slight causes came in play to affect the market. Government was a powerful disturbing force. One Friday McCulloch employed three or four agents to sell six millions, seller 3. The buyers anticipated that the contracts would go over till Monday, when they were taken aback sharply by a demand for immediate payments. The market broke at once. Frequent raids of this kind incensed the street. On the

* The Gold Room was now in New Street, where it has since remained. The apartments had been leased the 1st of May, 1865, but were not occupied till August, as extensive repairs were found necessary. The terms of lease had a curious clause. For five years the rent was to be $25,000 annually. After 1870, and until 1875, it was to be reduced to $16,000. The lessors evidently supposed that by the present year the Gold Room would be a reminiscence.

reception of the news of the London Panic of '66, Peter Myer & Co. received orders from Washington to sell all the gold the street would take at 130, to steady the market. The price of bullion was considerably above this figure, and when the government broker went down on the pavement before the Stock Exchange at 4 P. M. to make the sales, dealers fought with each other for the privilege of purchase. At least thirty millions were sold off within little more than a half-hour. The next day ten millions additional were put into the market. This action of McCulloch unquestionably saved the Bank of England from suspension and Great Britain from an unprecedented financial revolution. Indeed, some of the ablest bankers of Wall Street are of the opinion that, if government had not interfered at this crisis, New York, in less than six months, would have been the principal financial city of the world. The forced and sudden cheapness of the precious metal made it the most profitable of exports. The bullion, when sent to London, was exchanged for American products, then selling at panic prices, and vast realizations were made by trans-shipping the wheat, cotton, lard, and other articles of commerce which had been exported from the United States during the spring. 5-20s were bought in large quantities with from fifteen to twenty per cent profit. It is a curious commentary upon the rapidity with which the British market recovered through the interposition of Mr. McCulloch, that some lots of government bonds bought at this time in London reached New York too late for profiting by the home market, and were consequently reshipped by the next steamer for England.

The Gold Board after this brief flurry lapsed into a certain degree of quiet. Bullion rose and fell in easy flights. The fall of American securities abroad, fears of Prussian or Oriental complications, heavy shipments of gold, the rumor of the fatal illness of Napolcou, have all had their effect in influencing price. Merchants and foreign bankers go into the market not infrequently to buy, and, if rates are unsatisfactory, imitate the methods of the brokers, by borrowing. Occasionally houses are caught inextricably. Not many months ago a broker, on failing for four millions and a half, disclosed his principals, who proved to be a prominent firm in the Rio Janeiro trade.

The star of Erie during the last four years has dimmed the radiance of the Gold Room. In '66 Daniel Drew achieved his grandest victory in that volatile security, tossing the stock up and down from 50 to 90, and making two fortunes out of the campaign. Twenty-four months later the purses of the street were twice wrung dry by the same skilful manipulator, assisted, or rather overshadowed, by the impulsive and wonderful operatic *impressario* Fisk. The instrument of torture was the "lock-up." Its method is simple. The firm of Fisk & Belden deposited on March 8th and 9th the sum of $3,625,000 in the Tenth National Bank, receiving certified checks therefor. Two days after David Groesbeck & Co. sent these checks to a bank as a special deposit. Meanwhile Mr. Drew, by sales of Erie, accumulated $5,000,000, which he carried immediately to Jersey City. Thus twelve millions were suddenly taken from the market. No financial centre can bear such a strain without sensible disturbance. Loans went up to one per cent a day. Stocks fell with a crash. At the end of October the operation was renewed. By deposits of greenbacks, by certifications of certifications, collusion on the part of bank directors, and limitless audacity on the part of the Erie clique, some twelve or fourteen million dollars were peremptorily "retired" from employment in the market at precisely that point of the year when the necessities of trade make heavy drafts upon the resources of the banks. The effect was unexampled. The city saw a week of unabated and hourly augmenting agony. Gold, which had adapted itself to trivial variations of an eighth or a quarter, showed two per cent depreciation. But in stocks the effect, as instantaneous as in the precious metal, was far more marked in its final results. St. Paul fell 42 per cent; Hudson dropped 15 per cent; Northwest, 19 per cent; Chicago and Alton, 15. Fort Wayne and New York Central both broke, — the former from $114\frac{1}{8}$ to $104\frac{3}{8}$, the latter from $126\frac{5}{8}$ to $117\frac{1}{2}$. It is estimated that the two lock-ups produced a depreciation of at least twenty per cent in railway property, over the country, or, stated in sum-totals, not less than two hundred millions of dollars!

The Gold Board had been comparatively untouched by this upheaval. Half its members also hold seats at the Stock Exchange, and the complications necessarily affected them seriously. But in purely gold transactions the consequences of the clique movements were inconsiderable. All through the fall and ensuing spring and summer gold slid up and down the grooves in slight changes, with fractional profits to those who followed the market with shrewdness. But none of the old spirit of the war remained with the gold-dealers, and for sharp and sudden vacillations of price they were compelled to pass from the New Street Board to the Long Room. Early in September, 1869, however, the atmosphere began to exhibit signs of an approaching tempest. It was noticed that the clearances of the Gold Exchange Bank were increasing in magnitude. The biddings at the Board grew more lively, and the evidences of a vast clique movement were plainly perceptible. Although the ostensible brokers of the league invariably sold, it was not difficult to discover that the balances of purchases, from whatever cause they might be due, were greatly in excess of sales. Nevertheless, the vast proportion of operators took the bear side. It seemed preposterous that there should be any marked change in gold values. A corner in the precious metal has been proved more than once to be feasible, but the traditions of the street are against it. For one success there have been ten failures. Nor is it necessary to go far for an explanation. In stocks one may buy up double or treble the capital stock, or double and treble the amount held by the street or within the circuit of *bona fide* delivery. But gold is like the air. London or Frankfort or San Francisco can transfer millions upon millions by flash of telegraph. The immense ocean of the Sub-Treasury may overflow. All the small sums of gold scattered throughout the banks of the United States may be tributary. The task of withdrawing and cornering coin would therefore appear comparable to the pumping out of the New York Bay by a grand combination of steam-engines. To the just scepticism with which the rumor of an impending conflict was received there was added a firm belief that the era of specie payments was not far distant, and the proposition for consolidating the national debt, with a corresponding steadiness of governments in the European money-markets, aided materially this conviction. It followed that, although during the three previous years gold had invariably mounted the register with the approach of harvest, the short interest of '69 was very great. Common belief estimates the sales for future delivery on the part of brokers and their customers at this time at an amount not less than fifty millions, one fourth of which was in the hands of three men.

On the 22d of September gold stood at 137½ when Trinity bells rung out the hour of twelve. By two it was at 139. Before night its lowest quotation was 141. This ascent, regular, unfluctuating, and evidently predetermined, carried the more alarm by the very extent of the rise. In the old Rebellion days a ten-per-cent increase in eight hours was an affair of no moment whatever. It happened every week, sometimes twice and thrice a week. But since the sharp vibrations of June 16 and 18, 1866, when gold rose and fell from 154 to 160, and again from 133 to 167¾, the utmost daily range had been two per cent, with occasional fractional additions. Three years of dull monotony, and now an advance of three and a half per cent in five hours! At the same time the Stock Market exhibited tokens of excessive febrility, New York Central dropping twenty-three per cent and Harlem thirteen. Loans had become extremely difficult to negotiate. The most usurious prices for a twenty-four hours' turn were freely paid. The storm was palpably reaching the proportions of a tempest.

Nevertheless, the brokers on the bear side strove manfully under their burden. The character and purposes of the clique were fully known. Whatever of mystery had heretofore enfolded them was now boldly thrown aside, and the men of Erie, with the sublime Fisk in the forefront of the assailing column, assured the shorts that they could not settle too quickly, since it remained with the ring, now holding calls for one hundred millions, either to kindly compromise at 150 or to carry the metal to 200 and nail it there. This threat was accompanied by consequences in which the mailed hand revealed itself under the silken glove. The movement had intertwisted itself deep into the affairs of every dealer in the street, and entangled in its meshes vast numbers of outside speculators. In borrowing or in margins the entire capital of the former had been nearly absorbed, while some five millions had been deposited by the latter with their brokers in answer to repeated calls. When Thursday morning rose, gold started at $141\frac{5}{8}$, and soon shot up to 144. Then the clique began

THE GOLD INDICATOR.

to tighten the screws. The shorts received peremptory orders to increase their borrowing margins. At the same moment the terms of loans overnight were raised beyond the pitch of ordinary human endurance. Stories were insidiously circulated exciting suspicion of the integrity of the Administration, and strengthening the belief that the National Treasury would bring no help to the wounded bears. Whispers of an impending lock-up of money were prevalent; and the fact, then shrewdly suspected, and now known, of certifications of checks to the amount of twenty-five millions by one bank alone on that day lent color to the rumor. Many brokers lost courage, and settled instantly. The Gold Room shook with the conflict, and the battle prolonged itself into a midnight session at the Fifth Avenue Hotel. The din of the tumult had penetrated to the upper chambers of journalism. Reporters were on the alert. The great dailies magnified the struggle, and the Associated Press spread intelligence of the excitement to remote sections. When Friday opened clear and calm, the pavement of Broad and New Streets soon filled up with unwonted visitors. All the idle population of the city and its neighborhood crowded into the financial quarter to witness the throes of the tortured shorts. Blended with the merely curious were hundreds of outside speculators who had ventured their all in the great stake, and trembled in doubt of the honor of their dealers. Long before 9 A. M. these men, intensely interested in the day's encounter, poured through the alley-way from Broad Street, and between the narrow walls of New Street, surging up around the doorways, and piling themselves densely and painfully within the cramped galleries of the Room itself. They had made good the fresh calls for margins up to 143, the closing figure of the night before. The paramount question now was, How would gold open? They had not many minutes to wait. Pressing up to the fountain, around which some fifty brokers had already congregated, a bull operator with resonant voice bid 145 for twenty thousand. The shout startled the galleries. Their margins were once more in jeopardy. Would their brokers remain firm? It was a terrible moment. The bears closed round the aggressors. Yells and shrieks filled the air. A confused and baffling whirl of sounds ensued, in which all sorts of fractional bids and offers mingled, till '46 emerged from the chaos. The crowd within the arena increased rapidly in numbers. The clique agents became vociferous. Gold steadily pushed forward in its perilous upward movement from '46 to '47, thence to '49, and, pausing for a brief twenty minutes, dashed on to 150½. It was now considerably past the hour of regular session. The President was in the chair. The Secretary's pen was bounding over his registry book. The floor of the Gold Room was covered with three hundred agitated dealers and operators, shouting, heaving in masses against and around the iron railing of the fountain, falling back upon the approaches of the committee-rooms and the outer entrance, guarded with rigorous care by sturdy door-keepers. Many of the principal brokers of the street were there, — Kimber, who had turned traitor to the ring; Colgate, the Baptist;

Clews, a veteran government broker; one of the Marvins; James Brown; Albert Speyer, and dozens of others hardly less famous. Every individual of all that seething throng had a personal stake beyond, and, in natural human estimate, a thousand-fold more dear than that of any outside patron, no matter how deeply or ruinously that patron might be involved. At 11 of the dial gold was 150½; in six minutes it jumped to 155. Then the pent-up tiger spirit burst from control. The arena rocked as the Coliseum may have rocked when the gates of the wild beasts were thrown open, and with wails and shrieks the captives of the empire sprang to merciless encounter with the ravenous demons of the desert. The storm of voices lost human semblance. Clenched hands, livid faces, pallid foreheads on which beads of cold sweat told of the interior anguish, lurid, passion-fired eyes, —all the symptoms of a fever which at any moment might become frenzy were there. The shouts of golden millions upon millions hurtled in all ears. The labor of years was disappearing and reappearing in the wave line of advancing and receding prices. With fortunes melting away in a second, with five hundred millions of gold in process of sale or purchase, with the terror of yet higher prices, and the exultation which came and went with the whispers of fresh men entering from Broad Street bearing confused rumors of the probable interposition of the government, it is not hard to understand how reason faltered on its throne, and operators became reckless, buying or selling without thought of the morrow or consciousness of the present.

12

Then came the terrific bid of Albert Speyer for any number of millions at 160. William Parks sold instantly two millions and a half in one lot. Yet the bids so far from yielding rose to 161, 162, 162½. For five minutes the Board reeled under the ferocity of the attack. Seconds became hours. The agony of Wellington awaiting Blucher was in the souls of the bears. Then a broker, reported to be acting for Baring and Brothers at London, sold five millions to the clique at the top price of the day. Hallgarten followed; and as the shorts were gathering courage, the certain news that the Secretary of the Treasury had come to the rescue swept through the chamber, gold fell from 160 to 140, and thence, with hardly the interval of one quotation, to 133. The end had come, and the exhausted operators streamed out of the stifling hall into the fresh air of the street. To them, however, came no peace. In some offices customers by dozens, whose margins were irrevocably burnt away in the smelting-furnace of the Gold Board, confronted their dealers with taunts and threats of violence for their treachery. In others the nucleus of mobs began to form, and, as the day wore off, Broad Street had the aspect of a riot. Huge masses of men gathered before the doorway of Smith, Gould, Martin, & Co. and Heath & Co. Fisk was assaulted, and his life threatened. Deputy-sheriffs and police-officers appeared on the scene. In Brooklyn a company of troops were held in readiness to march upon Wall Street.

When night came, Broad Street and its vicinity saw an unwonted sight. The silence and the darkness which ever rests over the lower city after seven of the evening was broken by the blaze of gas-light from a hundred windows, and the footfall of clerks hurrying from a hasty repast back to their desks. Until long after Trinity bells pealed out the dawn of a new day, men bent over their books, scrutinized the Clearing-House statement for the morrow, took what thought was possible for the future. At the Gold Exchange Bank the weary accountants were making ineffective efforts to complete Thursday's business. That toilful midnight, at the close of the last great passion-day of the bullion-worshippers, will be ever memorable for its anxieties and unsatisfying anguish.

Saturday brought no relief. The Gold Board met only to adjourn, as the Clearing-House had been incapable of the task of settling its accounts, complicated as they were by ever fresh failures. The small brokers had gone under by scores. The rumors of the impending suspension of some of the largest houses of the street gave fresh grounds for fear. The Stock Exchange was now the centre of attraction. If that yielded, all was lost. To sustain the market was vital. But whence was the saving power to come? All through yesterday shares had been falling headlong. New York Central careened to 148, and then recovered to 185¾. Hudson plunged from 173 to 145. Pittsburg fell to 68. Northwest reached 62½. The shrinkage throughout all securities had been not less than thirty millions. Would the impulse downward continue? The throngs which filled the corridors and overhung the stairway from which one can look down upon the Long Room saw only mad tumult, heard only the roar of the biddings. For any certain knowledge they might have been in Alaska. But the financial public in the quiet of their offices, and nervously scrutinizing the prices reeled off from the automaton telegraph, saw that Vanderbilt was supporting the New York stocks, and that the weakness in other shares was not sufficient to shadow forth panic. It soon became known that the capitalists from Philadelphia, Boston, and the great Western cities had thrown themselves into the breach, and were earning fortunes for themselves as well as gratitude from the money-market, by the judicious daring of their purchases. The consciousness of this new element was quieting, but Wall Street was still too feverish to be reposed by any ordinary anodyne. A run on the Tenth National Bank had commenced, and all day long a steady line of dealers filed up to the counter of the paying teller demanding their balances. The courage and the ability in withstanding the attack which were shown by the president and his associates deserve something more than praise. The Gold Exchange Bank witnessed a similar scene, angry brokers assaulting the clerks and threatening all possible things unless instantaneous settlements were made. The freedom with which the press had given details of the explosion had been extremely hurtful to the credit of many of the best houses. In a crisis like that of Black Friday the sluice-gates of passion open. Cloaked in the masquerade of genuine distrust, came forth whispers whose only origin was in ancient enmities, long-treasured spites, the soundless depths of unquenchable malignities. Firms of stanchest reputation felt the rapier stroke of old angers. The knowledge that certain houses were large holders of particular stocks was the signal of attacks upon the shares. Despite of outside orders for vast amounts, these influences had their effect upon securities, and aided to tighten the loan market. One, one and a half, two and even four per cent were the compulsory terms on which money could alone be borrowed to carry stocks over Sunday.

On Monday the 27th the Gold Board met, but only to be informed that the Clearing-House was not yet ready to complete the work of Friday. Important accounts had been kept back, and the dealings, swollen in sum-total to five hundred millions, were beyond the capacity of the clerical force of the Gold Bank to grapple with. A resolution was brought forward proposing the resumption of operations Ex-Clearing House. The measure took the members by surprise, for a moment quivered between acceptance and rejection, and then was swiftly tabled. It was an immense bear scheme, for no Exchange can transact business where its dealers are under suspicion. All outstanding accounts require immediate fulfilment. Failure to make good deliveries would have insured the instant selling out of defaulters "under the rule." As the majority of brokers were inextricably involved in the late difficulty, the only consequence would have been to throw them into bankruptcy, thus bringing some sixty millions under the hammer. The market could not have borne up under such an avalanche. It was decided that the Room should be kept open for borrowings and loans, but that all dealings should be suspended. One result of this complication was that gold had no fixed value. It could be bought at one house for 133, and at other offices sold for 139. The Board thus proved its utility at the very juncture when least in favor.

The remaining history of the panic need not long detain us. As more and more light fell upon the tactics of the ring, it was seen that the final basis of their scheme was the use of a very old trick, first put in practice long ago on the London Stock Exchange. Two dealers league together. One buys all that he can by cash or credit; the other sells proportionately. One loses heavily; the other gains vastly. The former breaks and retires; the latter remains, and secretly divides up the profits. With proper regard for that bulwark of the American people, the libel law, we shall not undertake to carry out the comparison. It may not be unfair, however, to note as an example of the proportions of the struggle, that Albert Speyer, on Friday, bought $ 47,000,000 and failed to make good his contracts; while Belden & Co. "broke" for $ 50,000,000; and several others, supposed to be acting for the clique, had obligations out for so many millions that no attempt has yet been made to give them numerical computation. As a relic of that astonishing conflict, out of which no one is supposed to have made anything, we subjoin a statement supposed to be the account current of the

Gold Bank with Smith, Gould, Martin, & Co., which has the merit of having been indorsed by the famous committee of twenty, who finally brought order out of the terrible confusion. The reader can gather from this brief paper no inaccurate idea of the magnificence of the dealings of Black Friday:—

Received from		*Delivered to*	
Wm. Heath & Co.	$6,210,000	Lockwood & Co.	$10,000
White, Morris, & Co.	400,000	Stout Thayer	20,000
Dakin & Gillespie	1,980,000	Dzondi, Springer, & Co.	50,000
E. K. Willard	5,845,000	Carver & Co.	430,000
Hodgskin, Randal, & Co.	50,000	Gibson Beadleston	75,000
Budge, Schiff, & Co.	300,000	B. K. Stevens, Jr.	25,000
Cushman & Hurlburt	50,000	Lounsbery & Fanshaw	1,700,000
S. R. Jacobs	100,000	Fanshaw & Milliken	300,000
Lange, Bolle, & Anning	50,000	Hallgarten & Co.	35,000
Dean, Maginnis, & Co.	95,000	Kamlah, Sauer, & Co.	134,000
M. Morgan's Sons	20,000	Parker Bros. & Geston	15,000
Foster & Randall	20,000	Fellows & Co.	15,000
J. & W. Seligman & Co.	225,000	Cunningham & Mead	85,000
Hallgarten & Co.	200,000	Maxwell & Graves	30,000
Domett & Nichols	10,000	Norton, Haughton, & Co.	50,000
B. Hall & Young	500,000	Taussig, Fisher, & Co.	90,000
G. H. & H. Redmond	875,000	N. R. Travers	50,000
W. C. Mumford	50,000	Gray, Prince, & Co.	1,245,000
Meyer & Greve	200,000	Chapin, Bowen, & Day	2,915,000
Kennedy & Hutchinson	100,000	Wm. Heath & Co.	200,000
Robinson, Cox, & Co.	30,000	Cushman & Hurlburt	25,000
Lees & Waller	200,000		
Reed, Leo, & Content	1,015,000		$7,499,000
Hagen & Billing	200,000	Coin due dealer	$13,151,000
E. H. Biederman	445,000	Currency due Bank	20,650,000
G. P. Persch	735,000		
Robert Waller	655,000		
Stout Thayer	90,000		
	$20,650,000		

In due season, after some anxious weeks, the Gold Clearing-House was once more in operation, and the Gold Board pursued the even tenor of its way. Shortly, upon the renewal of daily sessions, at a large gathering of the members, a resolution was quietly passed declaring that at some future moment, to be hereafter determined, the Board reserved the right to incorporate in its dealings government securities and exchanges. Specie payments will, therefore, not put an end to the Gold Room.

The members of the Board are now four hundred and eighty in number. The large proportion have connection with the Stock Exchange, and what has been said respecting the frolicsome spirit of the dealers in stocks applies with even greater emphasis to the gold-brokers. The gayety with which they welcomed last Christmas-eve, in a grand carnival of drums, fifes, tin-trumpets, gongs, and vocal music, exemplifies the delightful *abandon* which lurks beneath the hard exterior of the bullion-operators. One of the curious features of the Board is in its officers. Thomas A. Hoyt, the active Vice-President, is a Presbyterian clergyman. Thomas P. Akers, the Secretary, has been a member of Congress from Tennessee, and gained great repute in former years by his eloquent labors as a Methodist preacher. Tall and broad-shouldered, he has a muscular energy which Morrisey can scarcely surpass, and on dull days he amuses the idle crowd around the fountain when the Board is not in session, by taking a fair-sized man lightly in the palm of his hand and holding him at arm's-length, while he himself sits quietly in his chair.

A very considerable amount of the business of the Gold Board at present is in orders from the South. Some four hundred telegrams arrive daily with commissions from this and other sections. During the panic double the number were received. William Bird, who sold three million dollars short in September, is now one of the largest operators. But the dealings of Trevor and Colgate, and Henry Clews, are also notably extensive.

The steady decline of gold during recent months, amounting to a fall of more than one half the average premium of 1869, has given a certain feverishness to the market; but its most notable effect is seen in the diminished value of membership of the Board. Seats that once cost five hundred dollars were sold in March, 1870, for a fifth of that sum. With government 6s of 1881 at $116\frac{7}{8}$, when bullion sells at $114\frac{3}{8}$, — the figures of March 3d, — it is not surprising that veteran dealers should begin to discount the day of specie payments, and trim their sails accordingly.

CHAPTER XIV.

THE MINING BOARD.

IN the good year 1854, when the Kyle and Schuyler forgeries and the "drop" in railroad shares were agitating the Stock Exchange, there were two or three brokers in Wall Street who did not care a sixpence for the tumult. They were deep in mining securities, and the fluctuations of the market had little effect upon their substantial commodities. Copper was the leading fancy, and the profits in that direction were literally immense. We have before us a statement of the prices of Lake Superior Mining Stock at this period, which is worthy of reproduction: —

	Shares.	Paid in.	Par Value.	Bids in '54.	Value of Mine.
Boston & Pittsburg	6,000	$18½	$111,000	145	$870,000
Minnesota . .	3,000	22	66,000	175	525,000
North American	10,000	17	170,000	75	750,000
National . .	10,000	3	30,000	32	320,000
Clark . . .	20,000	1	20,000	10	200,000
Rockland .	20,000	1	20,000	12	240,000

Scrutinize these figures closely. An investment of ten thousand dollars would have made the lucky speculator a prince among his fellows. It is the very multiplication-table of wealth! How much of this was due to "washings" at Share Boards? Rumor is silent; but at all events New York was innocent of any such speculative manœuvre. George F. Riley, Ralph King, John Simpkins, and R. H. Richard were in those days the principal mining-brokers. But they had no regular place of meeting or definite organization. All the business was done in offices. In fact the first Mining Board in this city dates no further back than 1857.

Tradition is very vague in details regarding this Board. It was started at 29 William Street. The stocks dealt in were of different complexion from those in the table just presented. The call contained the names of companies whose property was in North Carolina gold and copper mines, Georgia gold-mines, Tennessee and Maryland copper, New York and Pennsylvania copper and lead mines. On glancing at the localities, and contemplating the actual mineral yield of these sections during the past dozen years, one is thrown into an abyss of compassion for the unhappy purchasers of stock. Dealers must have developed a volume of imagination in their speculations sufficient in a purely literary direction to have created half a dozen first-class epics. Fulton Cutting, Talmadge & Mawley, and R. L. Cutting have the credit of being in the forefront of the operations. The times were, however, inauspicious; and six months brought the board to a sudden end.

In 1859 a fresh board was inaugurated. Its earlier sessions were held in the rear of Talmadge & Mawley's office, No. 25 William Street. Two months later it had already outgrown its narrow quarters, and, crossing the street, found shelter at No. 24. Mr. Talmadge was elected President. The dealings consisted of such substantial stocks as the copper-mines of Lake Superior along with Will-of-the-wisp North Carolina and Georgia gold and copper mines, and Tennessee copper shares. The real object of the Board was to work off these latter fantasies. A little nest of Baltimore operators, who found themselves altogether too heavily weighted by the commodities, had conceived the idea of creating a mining *furor* in New York. Hence the organization. All the leading manipulators of '57 were in the scheme. Seton & Wainwright and Ashley & Norris were also prominent. Two of the liveliest stocks were the North State Gold and Copper Company and the Gardner Hill Gold and Copper Company. Both the mines were in Guilford County, North Carolina, about seven miles from Greensboro'. Veterans in the business remember the old McCulloch mine. The North State Company had purchased this very property for only $ 1,200, and now placed it upon the market as the modern Eldorado, — so rich in gold-veins and copper-leads that the capital stock could not be a dollar under a million! Accordingly 200,000 shares were issued at five dollars par. The auction-hammer pattered; the brokers "washed" the new issue up and up, until large quantities were actually sold at $ 4. The Gardner Hill Company had much the same history, except that the first cost was $ 30,000. The capital was a million in five-dollar shares; and under clever management a very considerable number of sales took place at eight dollars. That price would have made the mine worth $ 1,600,000, giving the promoters, who had paid only thirty thousand dollars in cash, the neat net profit of a million and a half, with seventy thousand thrown in as contingent expenses! Naturally, with such glittering prospects of sudden opulence, the Board was fostered by every appliance which could decoy outsiders.

The next year a Mr. Clayton of Baltimore was appointed President. For Treasurer, a leading operator, one Charles Kowalski, a Pole, was selected. The election of Lincoln, and the war-cloud in the South soon threw the Guildford County stocks into disfavor. The shares fell to fractions of zero; and Kowalski, driven crazy by misfortune, jumped off a dock and so closed his account with this world. The affairs of the organization were at once wound up, and on dividing the assets it was discovered that the Treasurer had used up all the funds in a frantic attempt to "cover."

The regular Stock Exchange, for the next three or four years, was the scene of what little activity prevailed in mining matters. "Mariposa" was the principal fancy. The history of that stock in which Colonel Fremont, Morris Ketchum, the state of California, and other powers, political, legislative, and financial, figured largely, has been told so often that any further comment would be superfluous. It was one of those securities in which "bear" operations were profitable and "bull" movements disastrous. Copake Iron was another fantasy. In January, '66, it reached 0½, and thereafter ceased being quoted. Mining stocks, however, were never popular among the heavy railroad brokers; the calls were slurred over, and the opportunity for speculation lost, in the hurry for the larger prizes of Pacific Mail, Erie, Michigan Southern, and the rest. When the tide of popular investment, therefore, had begun to buoy up mining shares, the brokers in this merchandise determined to make a third attempt for a Board of their own.

On March 21, 1864, forty-one gentlemen met in the office of J. B. Norris, and subscribed their names as members of the Mining Board of New York. The President elect was John Simpkins. Nearly all connected with it had seats in the regular Stock Exchange. The fee for admission was placed at $250, and the earlier sessions were held at the old rooms of the Gold Board, corner of Williams Street and Exchange Place. Next it migrated to 12 Wall Street, and again to No. 7 New Street, in a dingy and dreary room, whose only merit was its very cheap rent. Minnesota was one of the leading shares, and the agile bulls tossed it up to $109. Another was Evergreen Bluff, which sold as high as $17. Both have long since gone out of sight, and their holders draw dividends from Dreamland. The same may be said of Caledonia copper, which reached $10, and then exploded. Quincy and Central were also favorites; the former running up to 95, and the latter to 70. One can buy them now for 25 and be sure of three dollars in annual dividends, until the trustees deem best to "pass" them.

The call of the Board embraced other stocks of sterling value; but, in general, the great companies, whose mills and mines have been coining gold and silver for the world at the rate of a hundred million of dollars a year, are under the control of men who keep their own secrets, and prefer to sell their shares, if at all, by private hands. There has never been any such representative stock organization, in New York, for the sale of legitimate mining securities, as exists for governments, State bonds, and railroad property. Chestnut Street, Philadelphia, State Street, Boston, and the financial quarter of San Francisco, all equal or eclipse the metropolis in this important department.

While the mining-brokers were maintaining a deceptive vigor, and the shuttlecock game of bids and offers was played with waning zest, the Petroleum mania burst out in Western Pennsylvania, and spread like a prairie-fire through the Atlantic cities. The features of that curious frenzy are still fresh in every memory. Probably swift wealth never fell upon a class of people whose education was so preternaturally insufficient for the new cares and duties which opulence brings in its train. The world has known enough of the vulgar rich, but ordinarily these are individual cases. The oil wells of West Virginia and the Alleghany River Valley floated a whole community upon their surface, and poured into New York a most astonishing description of Crœsuses. They thronged the principal hotels, chiefly those with marble fronts. The air of fashionable restaurants was laden with the essential oils of kerosene. Gallic waiters were feed liberally for bringing on strange French dishes, and then feed with even greater liberality for carrying them away. Husbands, wives, and daughters, accustomed to the fare which Dickens thought indigenous in his tour through the Far West, gave orders for what they did not want in a language which they did not comprehend, and which became equally incomprehensible to others when transformed by agricultural pronunciation. There was a melancholy as well as comical aspect in that sudden, fresh butterfly life, never quite able to free itself of the traces of its origin. The tragic romance of some of these owners of petroleum farms, who spent fortunes even quicker than they acquired them, is one of the darkest shadows of the excitement. But in 1865 they were in their fullest bloom; and the rumor of vast riches open to any one who chose to invest in oil stock soon created a crowd of brokers eager to assist the outside public. The organization of a Petroleum Board followed soon after, the first meeting taking place the 31st of October, 1865, at 16 Broad Street. Samuel B. Hard was elected President, and Edmund C. Stedman, the poet broker, Secretary.

The earlier sessions of the Board were comparatively quiet. Only eleven stocks were upon the call. They included Central, for which 75 was bid, while holders demanded 90; Germania, which started at $1\frac{7}{8}$, and soon became the Erie of Petroleum; Titus, $7\frac{1}{2}$; Manhattan, 2; Rynd Farm, $5\frac{1}{2}$ to 6; Buchanan Farm, $3\frac{1}{2}$; Noble and Delameter Rock Oil, 4; Knickerbocker, $2\frac{1}{8}$; Highgate, $1\frac{3}{4}$; together with McKinley and Clifton of indifferent reputation. Gradually, under the clever manipulation of operators, the Board grew into a distinct feature of the street. New members from the Stock Exchange became subscribers, and readily paid the $ 250 initiation-fee. The farther the oil-fever spread, and the wilder the stories of the profits in certain shares, the greater the interest evinced by outsiders. The rooms were frequently thronged. Half the promoters of companies had such faith in their own stock as to hold it with blind pertinacity, and this very confidence was an additional lure to the public at large. The brokers made large commissions. Orders came in from all quarters; and the operations were marked by all the peculiarities of the regular Exchange. One of the shrewdest and most versatile speculators was Ulrich de Comeau. He had a singularly quick and retentive memory, and great power of mental combination; a man who relished turf-sports, knew all the points of a horse, and seldom failed to estimate accurately the degree of speculative bottom in each new petroleum fancy. Just at the right moment he retired from the Board and purchased an Illinois stock farm with a portion of his oil profits. Other prominent operators were J. E. Morris, E. C. Stedman & Co., Col. J. Turner, Hard, Kendall, Geo. F. Riley, F. A. Artault. Many of them were new to the business, but not a few were veterans of the street. At the height of the excitement the call contained the names of some thirty-five companies; corners were frequent, and large sums changed hands in the dexterous manipulation of values. Excelsior was a leading football selling up to $ 17, with daily and wide fluctuations. Where the sale value of a stock was small, the equipoisè was kept up by the largeness of the bids. Shade River was a favorite, with offers at $7; Oil Creek at $4 was another. These three stocks are now completely out of sight, or unsalable. The fate of some of the other active shares may be seen in the subjoined table:—

Companies.	Bids, 1865.	1869.
Bennehoff Run	$21	$0.40
United States	40	0.80
Pithole	18	1.50
Central	100	0.75
Rynd Valley	8	0.35

On the 1st of January, 1866, the Mining and Petroleum Exchanges were amalgamated under the title of the Petroleum and Mining Board. A room in the new Stock Exchange was leased at an extravagant rent, the fee was raised to $1,000, and many new members from the Open and Regular Boards were admitted. Speculation under the changed auspices sensibly increased, and for a year the rooms were the scene of genuine excitement. There was a fine exaggeration and a beautiful disregard of ordinary notions regarding what constitutes proprietorship, in the creation of not a few of the corporations which now appeared on the list. To buy land for $2,000 and then issue shares for $600,000 was a conservative process compared to some of the antics of these imaginative speculators. Magnificent bubbles were blown into prismatic and profitable radiance with nothing more substantial than borrowed phials of oil and deeds of property, whose only value consisted in the durable nature of the parchment and the abundant stamps wherewith they were adorned. The Napoleon Oil Company was a notable example of this class. It claimed to have ownership of extensive lands in Kentucky, and by the versatile combinations of operators a corner was effected carrying the shares from $ 2 up to $ 32. Men who had agreed to deliver 10,000 certificates for $ 30,000 at buyer's option could make their contracts good only by paying $ 320,000 to the controlling clique. Brokers everywhere were on the verge of ruin. A few appealed to the courts, and on investigation it was proven that the company had no real estate, no oil shafts, nothing but an office, a small accumulation of petroleum in exquisite glass cans, and a bountiful supply of audacity to which of course no mercantile value could be affixed!

Some of the mining companies had scarcely a better basis. Three fancies, in particular, commanded the market by their large dividends and magnificent pretensions. One was the New York and Nevada Gold and Silver Mill and Mining Company; another, the New York and Washoe Mining Company. The third bore the name of the New York and Reese River Company. The capital stock of the first was $ 660,000; of the second, $ 1,000,000; of the last, $ 1,500,000. George A. Freeman was President, and John J. Osborn was Treasurer of each of these corporations. William H. Forbes, likewise a trustee in each, formed with the others a majority of the triple management. There was still a fourth company, called the New York and Santa

Fé Mining Company of Nevada, of which these three gentlemen were sole trustees, and which represented a paid-up capital of over $700,000. The shares of this latter stock were also quoted on the Boards; but as in full bulk the capital was $5,000,000, an inauspicious weakness disclosed itself. Presently came litigation, merciless scrutiny, and an explosion of indignation not lessened by the sharp decline of all four "securities." The facts revealed to the startled Santa Fé shareholders were remarkable as illustrations of how speculation is fostered. Not one of the three first corporations, whose titles we have already given at length, had either earned a dollar or possessed an available fraction of a dollar in its treasury. $512,000 had been paid in gold as dividends. Reese River took three per cent; Washoe, five per cent; Nevada, ten per cent. The buyers of these stocks had exulted over lavish distributions of the precious metal, salable at the Gold Room for 150, although the mines had yielded no auriferous fruitage, and the mills had not made enough to cover the running expenses. It was either the most wonderful example of alchemy or — something else, to be found in history. Investigation exploded the alchemy theory. All that had happened was simply, that, as Freeman, Osborne, and Forbes were controlling trustees of the four companies, and as they felt bound to do what they could for their fellow-men by fulfilling the natural expectation for profits, — rendered essentially difficult by the non-existence of said profits, — *they had taken the cash capital of Santa Fé and paid it out in dividends to the stock-*

holders of the other corporations. It was probably in a somewhat similar manner that the ancient Egyptians were able to make bricks without straw!

Bled in such various ways, twisted by corners, and caught by the manifold subtleties of complaisant and astute trustees, the operators both inside and outside began to lose heart. By the summer of 1867 the business of mines and oil-wells had so far decreased that half the brokers withdrew. The Board, as usual in every period of depression, began a fresh pilgrimage, first occupying a chamber in New Street, and next the ground-floor of 37 Broad Street, where the sessions are still held. The character of some of the investments in which it deals may be judged by a statement of prices at two different dates: —

Companies.	1866.	1870.
Consolidated Gregory	$21.00	$1.70
Smith & Parmelee	15.00	1.80
Quartz Hill	6.00	0.75
Grinnell	3.00	0.40
Benton	2.50	0.12

The one hundred and eighty Mining Companies now in this city represent about two hundred millions of capital, and there are about thirty-five millions invested in petroleum. In the fever days of '65 and '66 the nominal capital of both interests was $400,000,000. But whatever is of genuine value in these stocks may safely be assumed as held in private hands, and seldom presented for sale in the eddying uncertainties and speculative quicksands of the Broad Street Board.

CHAPTER XV.

BEFORE 1837.

IN the good old days of knee-breeches and shoe-buckles, when Washington was President, and Continental money was worth a trifle more as currency than as waste paper, some twenty New York dealers in public stock met together in a broker's office, and signed their names in the bold, strong hand of their generation to an agreement of the nature of a protective league. This document is still extant, and declares that "we the subscribers, brokers for the purchase and sale of public stock," agree to do business for customers at not less than one fourth of one per cent, and to give preference to each other in all transactions. Leonard Bleecker leads off among the signers, and one finds such other solid names as Hugh Smith, Bernard Hart, the McEvers, John Henry, Seixas, and Hardy. The date of this curious paper is May 17, 1792.

The volume of business of all these primitive New York brokers could not have been much above that of even the poorest first-class Wall Street house in our time. The Revolutionary "shin-plasters," as the irreverent already styled them, were spread over the land in such plenty that there were a hundred dollars to each inhabitant. Something was to be made, therefore, from the fluctuations to which they were unhappily liable. Indeed, one of the greatest broker firms of subsequent years derived its capital from the lucky speculations of its senior member in this currency.

The war of 1812 gave the first genuine impulse to speculation. Government issued sixteen million treasury notes, and put loans amounting to one hundred and nine millions on the market. There were endless fluctuations, and the easy-going capitalists of the time managed to gain or lose handsome fortunes. Bank stock was also a favorite investment. An illustration of one of the sources of money-making to brokers at this period is found in the fact, that United States 6s of 1814 were at 50 in specie and 70 in New York bank currency.

Our present governments at par in gold, 140 in greenbacks, would be an exact parallel. In 1816 one could count up two hundred and eight banks, with a capital of $ 82,000,000. When the peace of Utrecht was declared, they all began to fail, East and West. Forty millions of dollars were blotted out in a few months. There was an immense amount of depreciated paper afloat. Philadelphia especially suffered.

Meanwhile the little league of New York brokers gradually increased in numbers and in a sense of their importance. They met during stormy or wintry days in a chamber of the old Tontine coffee-house, high up under the eaves. On pleasant afternoons they consulted in solemn manner on the open pavement of Wall Street, down where the New York *Courier and Enquirer* building once stood. As yet nothing but the signatures on a strip of parchment united them. Philadelphia, in this respect was far ahead of Gotham, having a thorough stock organization, president, secretaries, and all the paraphernalia of an Exchange. One day in 1817 the New York stock-dealers met in the room of an associate, and voted to send a delegate over on the stage line to investigate the system adopted in the rival city. Tradition informs us that Mr. Will Lawton, just married and quite ready for a bridal trip, was finally selected for the mission. The visit was successful; and immediately upon the return of this committee of one, the draft of a constitution and by-laws, framed from that of the Philadelphia Board,* received the final approbation of a sufficient number of the brokers to enable the New York Stock Exchange to become a definite fact. Three years after, on the 21st of February, 1820, this preliminary code of rules received a thorough revision, and the organization was strengthened by the

* Why New York should have been dependent upon its sister community for suggestions concerning stock brokerage, and why the delegate sent forward should have been so kindly received, are puzzling questions in view of a certain affair that took place about this time. A ship had arrived with great news from London, leading to an immediate rise in stocks. When the stage set out for Philadelphia, it carried among its passengers three of the smartest operators on Manhattan Island. At Powles Hook the lumbering coach became suddenly disabled, and a delay of two or three hours was the consequence. The New-Yorkers hired a post-chaise, drove full speed over the rest of the route, and quietly bought up all the floating stock in Philadelphia. When the mail arrived the Quakers were fiercely indignant, and declared that there had been a collision with the stage-driver. The suspicion, it should be added, was not without good grounds.

accession of some of the heaviest capitalists in the city. Indeed, with 1820 the real history of the Exchange may properly be said to commence. Then it was that Nat Prime, John Ward, and others, kings of the street, made the Board the vehicle of their stock transactions. The United States Bank with its branches was already in operation; and some eighty millions in stock, representing so much fresh capital in the hands of the new incorporations which had taken the place of the old war banks, afforded frequent opportunities for speculation. In this very year of the revision we find in the New York *American* a fierce paragraph upon the progress of share gambling, *apropos* of the fluctuation of United States Bank stock from 103 to 106, the "shorts" having hastened to cover, for fear of a momentary "corner."

In 1822 the *Daily Advertiser* notes the fact, that on April 10th bank stock sold at 9¼ before 11 A. M., at 10¾ by noon, and 9¼ at 2 o'clock. Between 1 and 2 P. M. the news of the "Cambria" was published, announcing that English five per cents were to be reduced to four per cents, and that the Bank of England had lowered its interest correspondingly. "What a pity it is," cries the editor, "that even the price of our stocks is to be regulated by the jobbers of 'Change Alley, in London!" "All that mainly interests us," continues the high-spirited writer, "from a public revenue for the support of the nation down to a pair of shovels and tongs for our private chimney-corners, so much rests on foreign acts and actors that a noble, generous home feeling cannot be fully entertained in the hearts of our citizens." We quote these words that the reader may participate in the thrill of "home feeling" which must have come over the editor only three weeks later. For on May 1st, without the interposition of either "'Change Alley" or English ships, an immense "bear" pressure in Wall Street forced holders of hypotheticated stock to throw it over at once, and carried bank shares from 110 to 98. All the New York, Philadelphia, and Baltimore banks stopped discounting. The London jobbers could not have done better.

Of the gossip of the Stock Exchange in those days very little has come down to us. Membership cost $100, and there was plenty of blackballing. No broker was allowed to leave the room during sessions. If a message came to a broker there was always a fine to pay. In 1824 Warren's offices were hired at a rent of $500 a year. J. W. Bleecker was long the President. When he went out of office old Nat Prime moved that two services of silver-plate should be voted him, with a hundred fresh-minted dollars in them. The Board promptly acted on this Prime suggestion.

It was not until the finger-hand of the century dial had reached its first quarter that the United States plunged fairly into speculation. In 1825 the race began, and, judging from incidents gleaned here and there from old papers, the start was what boating-men call a "spurt." In Providence, R. I., for example, on April 22d books were opened for subscriptions to the Blackstone Canal. The capital was fixed at $500,000, and only about two thirds of this could be taken by Providence people. Nevertheless, by nightfall the subscriptions had reached $1,127,900! New York showed an even more astonishing proof of flush times and speculative eagerness. The Water Works Company was authorized to hold two millions of capital, and ten millions were subscribed. The Morris Canal and Banking Company, whose capital was fixed at $1,000,000, had twenty millions of subscriptions! In Philadelphia the Bank of Southwark opened its books on a certain day to the public, and the rush of capitalist subscribers was like a mob. Noses were smashed, hats jammed in, and the police court was at work over the wounded for weeks after. They did business on margins even then, and this fever for acquiring certificates of shares doubtless owed its intensity to the fact that only a small instalment was required on the first payment. Everybody hoped that by the second call they could sell out at a profit.

England is scandalized at some of the developments of Wall Street speculation; but there is not a trick or scheme in the entire history of New York stock-jobbing that cannot be illustrated by dozens of London examples. This very American fever of '25 was calmness itself compared to the fiery pulse-beat of speculation with which all England was throbbing. Merchants and clerks, wives and widows, the judge on the bench, the jury in the box, the lawyer and his client, doctors and patients, the clergy, the aristocracy, and even their flunky servitors, all hung upon the action of the London Exchange. Men paid 35 as a premium for United Mexican mining shares in December, '24, and by January sold them out at 155. The subscribers for Real del Norte paid down £70. By December the same shares sold for £550, and in January of the next year they were at £1350. There were 624 new joint-stock companies organized in Great Britain within 1824–25, and the news of vast profits coming by every mail to America fed the flame of home speculation. Moreover, the corporations which were already under way in the United States paid profits which might well have driven ordinary people into mild insanity. From five to ten per cent semiannual dividends were repeatedly declared by Insurance Companics, and strangely enough they kept up this pace year by year. In 1828 the Ocean Insurance Company of New York netted the holders of its stock twenty per cent. The American Insurance Company, likewise a Manhattan institution, paid twelve per cent each half-year, and in '29 declared a fifteen-per-cent semiannual dividend. Items of this character were copied from one journal to another, and disposed all who had money to seek equally promising investments. When the railroad movement began, the country was, therefore, fully prepared to help it on. State legislatures, eager to avoid taxation and to aid internal improvements, also availed themselves of the tendencies of the times, and issued bonds by the million. By 1838 there were at least one hundred and seventy-five millions of these securities, — sixty millions for banks, forty millions for railroads, fifty millions for canals, and the rest for turnpikes, etc. All these bonds found their way first or last to the New York Stock Exchange. The brokers also had their hand upon all the new railroad stocks, bank scrip, and the shares of all sorts of minor companies. In 1870 Wall Street does more than two hundred times the business that was then carried on. But considering their capital, the brokers of thirty-five or forty years ago were wide-awake men. There were king operators in those days. Samuel J. Beebe was one of them. J. W. Bleecker was another. Jacob Barker was very famous. He was always ready to lend money on good collaterals, doing it through the New York Exchange Bank, which the brokers called Jacob's Bank. His transactions in United States Bank were often immense. Nicholas Biddle and his operations in the same stock are already history. The last week of March, 1833, closed one of his campaigns. The street was heavily short of bank stock, which had been sold down to 102. As the day of settlement approached there were frantic efforts to break the market. The bears flooded New York with sensation rumors. President Jackson's proclamation was surreptitiously obtained and published. It was all in vain. Up went United States Bank to 110–111, and "the street" lost $350,000.

In '34 Biddle created an artificial pressure by calling in his temporary advances to the banks. The Jackson organs claimed that it was in order to coerce Congress. By July the stringency in money reached its climax, and thereafter the bank loans rose from forty-seven to sixty-three millions.

The next time that the bears availed themselves of Jackson, it was with a far different result. The Presidential attack soon told heavily upon all descriptions of securities. Subjoined is a partial table of the rapid depreciation:—

	1833. August.	1833. December.	1834. Jan. 3.	1834. Jan. 17.
Life & Trust Co. . . .	160	139½		
Mohawk & Hudson R. R. .	136	101¼	80	94
Del. & Hudson Canal . .	125	99	91	73
Boston & Prov. R. R. .	111¼	92	90	89
Saratoga Railroad . .	128	108½	105	103
Morris Canal & Bank Co. .	88	41		
Harlem Railroad . . .	95	70		

By January 25th stocks were still lower. The money-market was exceedingly stringent. Failures among brokers were frequent, and one house suspended with liabilities amounting to eight hundred thousand dollars.

In 1835, as was intimated in a previous chapter, everybody played high cards in the street. The Stock Board suspended twice. The "corners" of that year have not been equalled since for audacity. When the pressure on Harlem occurred, it is alleged that the United States Branch Bank helped to tighten the screws by making a sudden demand on the Manhattan (or, as the brokers called it, the British Marquis) Bank for $400,000 in specie. That bank drew on others; the purse-strings closed and it was impossible to borrow money. The subjoined contrast of a few stocks will illustrate the activity of the market at this period:—

	Nov 25, '34.	April 25, '35.
Morris Railroad	70	200
Harlem Railroad	64	105
Dry Dock Bank	118	145
Del. & Hudson Canal . .	72	113

When the great fire of December broke out and burnt the old Merchants' Exchange, where the Stock Board met, there were several heavy speculative movements under way, and it was deemed indispensable to save the records. One brave fellow went in among the blazing rafters, seized the big iron box, where they were kept, and bore it safely out. The Board voted a generous reward at its very next meeting.

Not the least interesting feature of that time was the prevalence of human weakness, incident to the desire for money. Early in the year there was a movement in favor of enlarging the capital stock of Harlem. The lobby went up to Albany in force. On April 16th the bill came before the Senate, and a Mr. Kemble made a vigorous speech in opposition. The next day the lobby returned to New York by boat, fully convinced that the measure had failed. The news reached Wall Street, and Harlem bounded up. At the top of the market a broker, whose name has not been caught up by the amber of history, sold 800 shares. His principal was Kemble, who had despatched a message with the order by the same boat which had borne the announcement of the death of the bill. There were no telegraph-wires in those days, and on the 16th, while his Harlem was selling off in the city, Kemble resuscitated the measure at Albany, and carried it through by a handsome majority. Only four persons understood this keen manœuvre, which even James Fisk, Jr., must allow was contemptible, seeing that Kemble's profit, all told, amounted to only $ 2,239! Doing business in such a small way, it was among the sure eventualities of life that he should be discovered. The four men who were in the secret were Kemble, his broker, Bishop, also of the Senate, and H. Bartow, Cashier of the Albany Commercial Bank. The latter placed the resources of his institution at the command of Kemble and Bishop. False entries were made, losses were covered up, and by October of this year the firm of Kemble & Bishop had managed to speculate away in Long Island and Harlem some $130,000. Naturally the bank was also a sufferer to just this amount, and the sleepy directors finally discovered the deficit. Bartow, the defaulter, was arrested. The Legislature, in fierce indignation, held a court of investigation, and Kemble was expelled from the Senate. Bishop, meanwhile, had prudently resigned.

What is encouraging in this story is the action of the Legislature; but even here tradition is so far unkind as to attribute it quite as much to partisanship as to higher motives, the Jackson papers declaring that it was a subterfuge of the Federals in order to gain two fresh votes in the Senate. Shall we believe this, and relinquish all faith in a Golden Period of Statesmanship? Judging from other facts, mankind was certainly not much better then than now. There was Federal Dr. Watkins, who defaulted, about this time, for five thousand dollars of government money, and a Jackson land-officer out West, who failed to account for sixty-three thousand dollars belonging to the nation. In '27, Kane, Secretary of the National Insurance Company, lost sixty thousand dollars one Christmas-eve, at the gambling-table, and the next day the directors discovered his account short $180,000. They threw him into prison, and the following morning he was found dead. His mistress revelled in dresses and jewelry; and when the officers of the law swooped down upon her sinful luxury, they seized a jingling purse out of which rolled some five thousand Spanish dollars. Then there were Rathbun of Buffalo, and Wilding, and shoals of lesser defaulters.

The men of those days knew everything. At the Stock Board "washing" was a frequent artifice. One day the members detected this in a transaction upon Catskill Railroad shares. The offending brokers, named respectively Tolman and Robinson, were compelled to discover their principals. Each gave the name of Alexander Hamilton, the son of New York's greatest statesman! This was in May, 1832. In Augusta, Georgia, a corporation was chartered with the condition that no stockholder should own more than forty shares. Six lawyers formed between each other forty-eight firms, and subscribed for $400,000 of stock. There was fierce excitement, penetrating to the remotest plantations. Finally the courts took hold of it, and the lawyers were nonsuited. We might fill a dozen pages with like incidents.

Speculation was running riot up and down the whole country. Maine was delirious over gigantic land-schemes. All through the West the national government was selling its public domain, and the farmer dropped his ploughshare to speculate in yet untilled fields. The Land

Office at Washington sold forty millions' worth of the public territory between '35 and '36· Purchasers paid cash to the utmost extent of their resources. The government agents deposited the money in local banks. Then the land-buyers came in as borrowers, giving their note, and putting the loan into still fresh property. And this process continued until the utmost limit of credit had been passed. Chicago imported wheat from Europe, paying twenty-two dollars for a barrel of flour. The entire agricultural population almost forgot seed-time and harvest in its haste for sudden riches. Meanwhile commerce itself was under high pressure. An unlimited chain of credits stretched from London bankers to New York importers, thence to jobbers, to the rural retailers, and on to farmers, who trusted in the crops which they hardly deigned to cultivate. In '36 this perilous condition of affairs reached its climax. Finance was at the mercy of the skies. Twenty days of excessive rain, twenty days of insufficient sunshine, would destroy the harvest on which the whole sequence of trade relations depended. The rain came, the sunshine did not come; and the failure of harvest, heightened by the diminished area of cultivation, plunged America and Europe into the panic of '37· The West failed for hundreds of millions. The real-estate bubble burst in a day. In New York one merchant who had speculated madly in land saw his danger on the very edge of the storm, risked and lost a million and a half of dollars, and came forth into the calm of '38 with the bulk of his wealth intact.

CHAPTER XVI.

FROM '37 TO '60.

THE Stock Market had only an incidental connection with the crash of '37. That event was purely commercial in character, but its consequences penetrated deeper. All over the country the banks closed their doors. The first suspension was on the 11th of May. In three years sixty banks sank from sight, dragging one hundred and thirty-two million dollars into the vortex. Everybody was bankrupt, and, in the settlement of debts, out of $440,000,000 the creditor class could only realize about one cent in the dollar, the rest disappearing in collectors' fees, brokers' commissions, and the costs of courts, lawyers, and juries. The States came to the rescue. Stay laws were passed. Insolvent banks were allowed to issue inconvertible bills, by special enactment. The paper epoch having once set in, half the legislatures busied themselves in creating a vast bonded indebtedness.

New York City, at this stage of the crisis, undertook two offices. Its banks determined upon resumption; its great bankers and brokers undertook to float the new State securities upon the market.

Old Sam Ward was a leading mind in the former movement. He was a hard-money man, and thoroughly hated suspension. James Gore King, his partner, was a congenial spirit. In London the latter had the reputation of a Midas. Representing to the directors of the Bank of England the urgent necessity for immediate action, he succeeded in borrowing the equivalent of $5,000,000 in specie. This formed the basis for a return to coin payments. In season and out of season, the tireless presence of Ward strengthened faltering managers, and encouraged them to withstand the immense pressure of the outside cities, whose paper currency would necessarily be affected by gold resumption in New York. Gallatin resigned the Presidency of the Bank of Commerce. Sam Ward promptly accepted the invitation to fill the vacancy. It was a perilous position, and he stood to his work night and day. The walls of the bank had been newly plastered. Partly from overwork, partly from this subtle dampness, the inflammatory gout with which he was afflicted became intensified. All through the spring of '39 he fought the disease within and the clamor for suspension that came up from without. In July his doctors told him there was no hope unless he paused instantly. Then he yielded, and sought rest in Newport.

When the history of money-marts is fully told, there should be a chapter upon money martyrs. The indefatigable member of the great house of Prince, Ward, & King was fated. The Philadelphia banks, after some ineffective efforts at solvency, had suspended. They now threatened New York with instantaneous ruin, if it did not imitate their example. Back from Newport, over the painful turnpike-roads, came the President of the Bank of Commerce. His return infused confidence. All the other directors agreed to stand by their positions, and in a great meeting, in a certain historic parlor, each bank in turn pledged itself to pay gold over the counter to the last dollar. Then, at last, Old Sam Ward, having won his victory, went back to his island retreat, took to his bed instantly, and died within a few weeks. He had sacrificed himself to resumption!

While the clink of silver and gold was heard in city vaults, down in the door-guarded mysteries of the Stock Exchange the brokers were selling Michigan's, Louisiana's, Mississippi's, and other bonds, which had been created by legislatures, in order to buoy up the paper notes of their local banks, — paper floated upon paper. Some of these securities were already stale at the Board. Tradition is obscure concerning the secrets of many of the older bonded issues, but there is good reason for believing that in some few cases the States were victims to the shrewdness and unscrupulousness of New York capitalists. Thus, Indiana credited the Morris Canal Company with a million of its bonds, and when that great corporation failed, the State had not a dollar to show for its indebtedness. Michigan let the same company have five millions. The United States Bank took these bonds as collaterals, and placed them in the French and English markets. Michigan claimed that it had risked everything and gained nothing. Illinois, Arkansas, Florida, Pennsylvania, Mississippi, had each a similar tale. To penetrate into the real truth of all this bond business would now be next to impossible. There is no question but that Wall Street made and lost a vast deal of money through them.

Eventually, as we all know, repudiation set in, and as a large proportion of the securities had found their way across the water, the financial reputation of the country received a serious blow. At least one hundred and fifty-four millions, lent the South and West by England and the Eastern States, were thus lost. Especially in respect to the Mississippi bonds, foreign opinion was outraged; and whatever may have been the defence of other States, the action of the Mississippi Legislature was certainly flagrant enough to merit all the outburst of sarcasm and contempt with which it was visited. The story, in brief, was as follows: The crisis of '37 had nearly ruined the country. Mississippi, in particular, was a community of paupers. Everybody wanted money. The planters were at the last extremity for need of it. Finally, the State voted five millions of bonds as a basis for a State Bank. The directors of the newly chartered institution came at once to New York to sell the securities. There was not a respectable house to be found which would take them short of ten per cent discount. Then they crossed over to Philadelphia. Mr. Biddle received them warmly, and agreed to take the issue at par, provided the bonds were made payable in London, at the rate of 4 *s.* 6 *d.* to the dollar. They were to have a million in specie, three million eight hundred and fifty thousand dollars in exchange on New Orleans, and one hundred and fifty thousand dollars in notes of the Merchants' Bank of the same city. This was to be paid in instalments, beginning November, '38, and closing July, '39. The bargain was concluded; and, on receiving the securities, the United

States Bank immediately forwarded them to the great house of Hope & Co., Amsterdam, who sold them all over Europe. The money thus obtained, and lent freely to planters and merchants, restored Mississippi to more than its old prosperity. The State Bank, at Jackson, having been managed with an imbecility passing belief, subsequently failed, throwing the whole weight of the indebtedness on the people. Then, for the first time, Mississippi discovered that it had been unjustly dealt with. A pamphlet was put forth containing the best illustration of the Pogram style that is to be found in our political literature. Amid its abounding rhetoric the only semblance of an excuse for the repudiation which it purported to defend was that, in establishing the rate of sterling payment, a slight percentage below par had resulted! The best answer to this document, — beyond question the most scandalous publication in the financial or political history of the world, — was made by the *Democratic Review*, whose national politics were those of the repudiators. That able periodical proved, by unimpeachable figures, that the Jackson Bank had actually realized on the sale of bonds the sum of $ 5,086,667.19, every dollar of which had been in use in Mississippi!

European publicists were unbounded in invective over the gigantic swindle; but English anger became suddenly diverted to Pennsylvania, whose Legislature soon after imitated the example of its Western sister by wholesale repudiation of its own securities. The keen sarcasms of Sydney Smith upon America are still read by thousands in this country who have quite forgotten the circumstances which inspired them. Nor can there be much profit in recurring to the dreary scandal and shame of that time. It is sufficient to know that by '44, Pennsylvania, Maryland, Florida, Louisiana, Mississippi, Illinois, Indiana, Michigan, and Arkansas were all delinquent in meeting their indebtedness. The banks which they had coddled and fattened with bonds were all bankrupt, owing more than a hundred millions. Such of the States as sought to partially retrieve their honor found that it could only be accomplished by a payment of double their loans, so effectively was their credit shattered. At the Stock Exchange the securities were quoted so low that only the most reckless of speculators would touch them, and Wall Street, whatever may have been its previous gains, preferred the worst of railroad stock to the best of the repudiated fancies. How considerably brokers had been victimized by the immense fluctuations in these State debts was curiously proved in 1840. Upon a vote of inquiry it was ascertained that year that the treasury of the Board held $20,000 in accumulated fines. This sum was at once distributed among sitting members as a loan without interest, and not to be called in except after sixty days' notice. Only ninety-one members were entitled to a share in the division. Of these, twelve alone had escaped failure in the previous five years. Thirty had suspended in the fall of '39.

It is an interesting fact that while popular loans were thus universally discredited, the United States Stocks invariably sold above the market. At the height of speculative distrust, some three millions and a half of Sixes, coming suddenly upon the public, were bought up in a day at 103.

For the succeeding decade the history of the Stock Exchange is that of railway interests. But to enter upon the details of that movement would absorb space which will be filled more to the satisfaction of the reader in a description of the first great share panic in New York. This dates with 1853–54. All the principal main lines of to-day were by that time on the share list. For ten years there had been a plethora of money. California poured an incessant tide of wealth into the city, and intensified the speculative fever. Brokers grew rich on all sides. The attractions of the market drew in poets, historians, novel-writers, doctors, and lawyers. Bids and offers resounded from curb to curb at nightfall. The old code of 1820 was still in force. Membership cost $ 400. The Vice-President's salary was $ 2,000. Many people preserved the ancient habit of keeping personal records of the daily sales at the Exchange, and the books containing these entries were always to be found in every important office for the inspection of customers. Every month there were accessions to the ranks. Moreover, the "outside" Board was becoming a power. There were two hundred "regular" brokers; but the irregular, curbstone, outside phalanx was far more numerous. They leased a room below the Stock Exchange, and constant communication was kept up between the rival bodies. The New York *Herald*, betwixt jest and earnest, asserted that the curbstone men were held in better repute in matter of contracts than their competing brethren.

The banks aided speculation with a free hand. Brokers with only $1,500 on deposit would draw checks for $100,000 or even $300,000 which were promptly certified by paying tellers. From '51 to '53 twenty-seven new banks had been organized in the city. Hence competition, a relaxation of the scrutiny of securities, and an eagerness for call loans. The weekly average of loans, or promissory notes and stocks, was from ninety-five to a hundred millions. Even the staid conservative banks lent money freely. In June, '53, *Hunt's Merchant's Magazine* sung a pæan over the fiscal year which had just closed. "In commercial activity, and in wide-spread prosperity," it cried, "it has never been equalled since the formation of the Federal Union."

July followed, and the sky was still bright. Six per cent, or at lowest five per cent, was current interest in New York, while in London capital could not command more than one and a half or two per cent per annum. England, therefore, forgot its old fears, and had again become a buyer. It absorbed our governments, and such stable State securities as those of New York and Massachusetts. Then it began to purchase railroad bonds. In those days railway companies issued enough stock to pay for right of way, and then put forth bonds to cover the expense of construction. The London capitalists took the best of these bonds. The home public bought the second class, and in short any class. Merchants, everybody, invested, holding all they could carry upon margins. The money-centres of the seaboard were overburdened by a surfeit of gold. Deposits were on the increase. They fluctuated from forty-nine to fifty millions, rising sometimes even higher. Naturally the banks were made unduly confident, and were prepared to loan on almost any description of paper. Half the houses in foreign trade had their capital in bonds. Some even invested three times their real capital, hypothecating as fast as they bought, and drawing nine, eight, or seven per cent interest on securities, which, as collaterals, could procure loans at four per cent. Clerks who could not raise even a hundred dollars freely speculated, and brokers took their orders without question, so absolutely plentiful were loans.

Meanwhile there was the shadow of a war-cloud over Europe. English bankers became timid, and sent their securities to New York for realization. Breadstuffs went up, alarming London capital still more. Money in the metropolis caught the alarm. Deposits decreased. Heavy importations came due, and the United States Treasury was filled with specie accumulating from the receipts of the Custom-House. By August the banks had reached the point where an immediate calling in of loans was indispensable. For a month the speculative element attempted to breast the tide; but the bears were in the street, stocks fell ten per cent a day, it was impossible to make good the money which they had borrowed. The banks were left with a vast load of shares and bonds, every day diminishing in value. The subjoined table illustrates the depression in some of the steadier classes of stock:—

Panama, Jan. 1, '53=140;	July 1=122½;		Sept. 1=108;		Dec. 1=96		
6th Av. R.R., Apr. 1=120	"	118	"	109½	"	98	
Del. & Hudson Canal Co.	"	120½	"	118	"	104½	
Harlem	"	65	"	56	"	55¾	
Hudson	"	72¼	"	68¾	"	67½	
Erie	"	80	"	74½			

The Parker Vein Coal Co., among the "fancies," was 67 on the first day of the year. In June it was 32; in August, 20; in December, 7½. Erie, in this exhibit, presents a firmer front than either Hudson or Harlem.

If the merchants of New York in this year 1870 wish to warn the banks against call loans, by which our present mercantile trade is imperilled, let them organize a subscription for an accurate history of banking in the metropolis during 1853–54. The directors of the lending banks, with all their capital out in advances, and the cash deposits perceptibly decreasing, saw themselves on the brink of failure unless they continued to lend on doubtful security or sold this dead weight of bonds. When they went into the market, however, they suddenly discovered their dilemma. The Stock Exchange may almost be said to have disappeared. All that excited buying and selling, that maelstrom of contending passion, that whirl and tide of money-getting, had vanished as if in a dream. Wall Street was as sombre as a plague-stricken city. Brokers flitted in and out like uneasy ghosts. The outside speculative world had shrunk back aghast: and the brokers only operating upon margins were like an army despoiled of its implements of warfare. Beyond their margins, their only capital was their credit, —the banks were their capital!

Nothing saved the banks in this crisis but the good fortune of the great merchant houses. Neither jobbers nor wholesale firms who had limited themselves to legitimate trade suffered. The demand for breadstuffs abroad had given an impetus to commerce, and in the agricultural sections the retail trade was rich, and made constant remittances. Confidence was restored. Deposits again became heavy, the specie balance was favorable, and by private sale or by reasonable extensions of credit the banks succeeded in relieving themselves of their burden.

The end, however, was not reached. The spring trade of '54 opened gloomily. Large quantities of goods were slaughtered in auction-rooms. In June it was discovered that the Parker Vein Company had flooded the market with an immense and unauthorized issue of stock. The first of the next month New York was startled by the intelligence that Robert Schuyler, President of the New York and New Haven Railroad, had been selling some 20,000 illegal shares at par, — and was now a defaulter for two millions. Almost simultaneously it was asoertained that Alexander Kyle, Secretary of the Harlem Railroad Company, had made an issue of forged stock to the amount of $ 300,000. Other developments of breaches of trust came flocking from the inland cities. A fierce panic filled the air. Clerks, accountants, bank-officers, were all under suspicion.

It was the time of the year when the "solid" men were out of town on vacations. The banks, again embarrassed, knew not which way to turn. Several Western banks suspended, and a few just established in the city were forced to the same course. The best indorsed paper could not be discounted for less than fifteen per cent.

The Stock Exchange was the scene of fierce tumult. The bulls shivered and the bears were jubilant. It was loudly asserted that the old-established banks had exaggerated the crisis in order to buy in a cheaper market. Not merely "fancy," but the most unquestioned securities felt the pressure. In Hartford and New Haven there were capitalists who had ventured to make loans in the previous winter, when New York lenders had refused. They now were weighted down with a million and a half of bonds, which were selling in the street for almost any price. The depression was enormous, taking the whole market through, although we are without a basis for accurate estimate.

Fortunately it was an epoch of great elasticity. By winter affairs assumed a more natural condition. In the summer of '55 speculation became again buoyant. The West turned anew to landed property. Vast sums were made in town lots. Men bought in the spring, giving their notes, and sold out in November with large margins of gain. Crops were abundant. Railroad earnings were good, and the bulls took courage. For two years there were enormous fortunes realized by the capitalists who had dared to buy in the cheap market of '54. One of the remarkable features of the Exchange was the high range of United States securities. Even the panic scarcely affected them. All through the vacillations of '53, six per cents remained steadfast between 121¾ and 123. They were exceedingly sought after from abroad.

Had government exhibited the same conservatism in respect to other classes of security, the shadow which was shortly to descend upon the country might have been robbed of half its gloom. Congress, however, was disposed to fan the speculative flame. Unusual land-grants were made to railroad companies. Prominent officials were more than suspected of stock jobbery, and State legislatures derived no inconsiderable inspiration from Washington for questionable charters and open bribery. Lines of roads were laid out to suit the interest of capitalists, who were not merely willing but prompt to pay lobby agents for every sacrifice of public to individual advantage. Bonds by the million were guaranteed, and bonds by the hundred millions were floated in the market at all possible shades of discount.

The great New York operators varied their speculations according to the opportunities of the market. But the special favorite of the time was the old New York and Erie. This road was only completed in '51, and its finances were in a comparatively healthy condition. Daniel Drew had commenced his career as director as far back as '52, and the broad gauge rose and fell with magnificent opportunities for gain under his unique manipulations. William M. Tweed, who had quit the chair business for a broker's office in '51, managed within a few months to sink his little fortune in the Erie maelstrom, and his recent profitable connection with Messrs. Fisk & Gould may be ascribed to a natural desire to retrieve the old reverses.

Jacob Little still frequented Wall Street, losing and

winning with the coolness of a veteran player. His operations dated back to '34, and the Morris Canal Company corner was one of his brilliant achievements. He has the reputation of having invented short sales, using options, however, as the vehicle of his manipulations. The street was always in conspiracy against him, frequently causing him heavy losses, and twice breaking him. Never was there a bear so invincible in the face of defeat. Other leaders were George Law, who handled Panama deftly; and Dean Richmond, who swayed the fortunes of New York Central.

Vanderbilt was already looming up upon the horizon. It was an epoch of giants, and the Stock Exchange reeled under the heavy blows of alternate bull and bear. Nelson Robinson was one of the shrewdest and keenest operators. He had been in "the street" since '45, and never made less than $50,000 a year even in his worst speculations. During '53 and '54 the tremendous vicissitudes of stocks affected his nerves. His family implored, his doctor insisted. At last he yielded and retreated into the country. But it is impossible for men who have once mastered the science of stock manipulation to resist its allurements. In '56 he returned. All the brokers welcomed him. Erie and Central felt the subtle presence of the leader. His combinations were wonderful. One Saturday, after a week of intense exertion, he left at night for home. The next day he sat in his pew at church, with his brain feverish over new and magnificent projects. Friends congratulated him, as the congregation poured out, upon his healthy appearance. Ten minutes after he was struck by apoplexy, and in six hours was dead. The times were prolific of similar tragedies. Guano speculations, sugar, cotton, land operations, sent men into insane asylums or brought life to a full stop. The fever of the day seemed to know no limit. It penetrated to the poultry-yard. There were hen-brokers in New Orleans, Boston, and London. A pair of Cochin China fowl were valued at $ 700. Gray Chittagongs sold for $ 50. Shanghaes commanded $ 100. One man in Boston sold $ 23,000 worth of "fancy" poultry stock in '53. This was the parody of speculation, but it illustrates even in its absurdity the tendency of the period. As many as two hundred thousand individuals are said to have been holders of stocks or bonds. All the old established roads paid handsome dividends. Competing lines now came into the market. The rivalry led to low prices. Some of the railways were built through mortgage bonds; others by State, city, or county guaranties. These were sold at from five to fifty per cent discount,* and the whole country came forward as buyers. Agents crossing the Atlantic with five millions of scrip sold the entire bulk in two months.

* In the just irritation felt against railway directors for their immense hydraulic operations, by which the capital stock of the great trunk lines has been "watered" to the extent of $ 100,000,000 within the past eight or nine years, the public should not lose sight of the fact that the original cost of railways was greatly enhanced by the difficulty projectors met with in floating these bonds; loans, interest and commissions, absorbing a very heavy percentage of the amount of money which the securities represented on their face.

The banks helped forward the speculative mania. From December, 1854, to August, 1855, they increased their loans to the amount of twenty millions. From February, 1856, to August, 1857, the daily credits ranged from one hundred to one hundred and twenty two million dollars. The keen manœuvres of the Stock Market under these happy auspices were beyond all precedent. Loud complaints came from England of the scandalous bear manipulations of the street. The London *Times* (July 7, '57) thundered out anathemas at the New York operators, who sought to bring on a panic by offering to sell Hudson, then quoted at 89, for 20, seller 12 months. These men lost hundreds in order to make thousands. The action of the New York and New Haven Railroad in repudiating the issues of Schuyler was as little understood abroad as it was relished by Vanderbilt at home; and the *Times* found language inadequate to express its indignation of a certain bank president who borrowed money in England and plead usury as an excuse for non-payment; and of the "pious" head of an American Trust Company who had persisted in retaining possession of funds obtained from London, in order to spend them in years of litigation with English shareholders.

This tendency toward sharp and unscrupulous bear tactics was largely due to the presence of new men, known popularly as the "Observatory," who had come from the West with large accumulations of capital, and with a predetermination to break the market. They played recklessly and for high stakes. Nevertheless, the aspect of the financial sky was such that everybody predicted, if not fair weather, yet nothing worse than squalls. Brokers coolly quoted the slight downward fluctuations of stocks as proof that panic was impossible, since it could only originate from London, and the capitalists of that city were not likely to send back the many hundred millions of American securities which they held to certain sacrifice in the New York market. The bears persisted in plying the hammer, but they had nearly reached the point at which they proposed a change of tactics, and a sharp advance. Just at this stage, when the banks,—alarmed by the loan statement of the first week of August, in total $122,077,252,—called in the comparatively insignificant margin of a million, "the street" was startled by the rumor of "irregularities" on the part of prominent railroad officials. A break of one or two per cent in some of the more active shares resulted, and the still further decrease of a million in loans helped to give an unsettled aspect to the market.

The state of affairs at this critical juncture was briefly as follows: The bears had depressed prices where they were willing to buy, but had not bought. The bulls had been waging a losing battle for months, and were still endeavoring to carry a heavy weight of stocks which had sunk below the estimates on which they had been hypothecated, and were now almost down to the low-water mark of their margins. The banks had lent money beyond what was safe, and were forced into slow contraction, lest any sudden rigidity should destroy not only their customers but the market for their collaterals. A few weeks might change everything. If no great failure occurred, the danger could be securely tided over. The banks were generously cautious. Brokers were endeavoring to force stocks into a healthier position. It was one of those crises where an inopportune event would be only the first step in an immense succession of disasters.

Such an event was a part of destiny. On the 24th of August the Ohio Life Insurance and Trust Company closed its doors to the public. This institution, with its principal office in Cincinnati and a branch at New York, had been doing an immense business in banking and general collection through the West. The cashier in the metropolis had advanced large sums of money on shares and bonds. An imperative call on the part of depositors compelled him to insist upon the immediate return of the advances made to brokers. The latter could not comply. The condition of the market made it impossible to realize upon the securities. There was, therefore, no alternative but suspension, and the lowest estimates of the failure were above three millions.* The announcement came upon the city like a whirlwind. Bank presidents lost their heads. Loans were cut down at the rate of four millions a week. Crowds of mer-

* The subsequent closing of the Cincinnati offices augmented the liabilities to five millions. Much of this was squandered illegally by the managing trustees, but the exact facts were carefully concealed from the public, from a belief on the part of stockholders that the truth would only add to the alarm while decreasing their chance of recovering something from the ruin.

chants gathered at every discount day only to have their paper thrust back upon them with scarcely an explanation. The telegraph was spreading half-truths and wild rumors over the whole country. Journals, in the interest of men who prey upon panic, caught up every whisper, misstated and exaggerated printed list of failures, and ran up their editions to thousands upon thousands. While the commercial world was thus being swept forward into illimitable ruin, the storm had already burst upon Wall Street and was carrying everything before it. The board was like a gathering of demons. Bull and bear came in personal contact, and fierce blows mingled with the ceaseless rapping of the President's hammer and the terrible slaughtering of every description of security. The great mass of brokers found it impossible to return their loans. Many were swamped by time contracts. Dozens "broke" every day. The whole talk of the money market was of the rottenness in the conduct of corporations. It was asserted that the directors of Western railways had been hiring funds at the rate of twenty-five per cent per annum with which to pay dividends, — that one of the best known lines had been drawn into an over-issue of stock to the detriment of bondholders and in violation of their charter. It became more and more understood that the collapse of the Ohio Trust Company was due to wild advances to the Cleveland and Pittsburg Railroad, and other doubtful stocks. Under the impetus of this universal and justifiable distrust shares went down, down, down. It was impossible to borrow upon them except at ruinous usury.

Panama fell twenty per cent in four weeks; in two months it had fallen thirty per cent. Illinois Central dropped forty-two per cent. Milwaukee and Mississippi fell thirty-six per cent in ten days. Erie declined twenty per cent, and New York Central twenty-four per cent. Rock Island went down thirty-four per cent before it turned. Delaware and Hudson Canal sunk in leaps of twenty per cent, measuring forty per cent of decline by October 13th. Galena and Chicago was quoted thirty-four per cent lower in the second week of October than in the last week of August. Reading was in the same plight. Missouri 6s and Virginia 6s both declined twenty per cent. Railway bonds went the way of stocks. Bank shares had the same fate.

On Friday, September 25th, the Bank of Pennsylvania suspended, followed the next day by the other Philadelphia banks. Baltimore, Washington, and the lesser cities yielded to the example, and by the middle of October the New York banks had refused further payments of coin. The stock-brokers now saw the opportunity for revenge. When the call of banks began it was the signal of assault. The Bank of America was forced down thirty-four per cent, the Bank of Commerce thirty-five per cent; Park Bank sold down forty-four per cent; the Metropolitan, fifty per cent. A bank whose shares a month or two before were at par went plunging under the auctioneer-gavel to thirty-five. The bears were gleeful, and their faces radiant with smiles.

United States 6s of '68 felt the effect of the universal decline, and Howell Cobb, then Secretary of the Treasury, promptly came into the market and bought up several millions. The savings-banks which had used governments as the basis of their business were thus supplied with gold, and succeeded in withstanding the daily run upon their resources. It is a curious circumstance, in view of our present Gold Board, that silver during this period sold at a discount for paper, and one half of one per cent was the highest price which gold reached even at the white heat of the crisis.

The catastrophe of '57 illustrates what might have been the fate of the country in '69, if the whole nation had not grown wiser and our banking community clearer-sighted. The crash began with the Stock Market. It would have ended there, had not two things supervened. The New York banks withdrew eleven millions of loans in three weeks. August 22d they were lending $ 120,000,000, October 24th, only $ 95,500,000. Such an alarming shrinkage, attended by the suspension of specie payments and the sensationalism of the telegraph and daily press, destroyed confidence everywhere, and threw the paper of the oldest and most reputable mercantile houses into the same contempt with the certificates of rotten and bankrupt corporations. But, in addition to this cause, there was another quite as vital and as immediate in its effects. The entire country was in stocks. The farmer, the country lawyer, jobbers, heavy domestic dealers, the whole foreign trade, were more or less holders of shares, bonds, county, city, or State paper. These they used as capital, drew therefrom dividends or interest, raised money for immediate needs by hypothecation, and, in a word, based their business movements upon the belief that this property could always be converted into coin or employed as collaterals. The panic in the Stock Market destroyed the former hope; the panic in the banks put an end to the latter anticipation. The money of the West and the Middle States had gone into stocks, and stocks had now gone to the dogs.

In '69 these conditions were reversed. The general public no longer held securities, with the exception of governments. If men bought it was on margins, and with the intention of selling upon the first rise. With ten per cent of their capital they controlled the same speculative profits which would have been theirs if the shares had been bought out and out. Here and there, in communities comparatively untainted by the fever for stock manipulation, the certificates of local manufacturing and railroad corporations were used as an investment; but this description of property neither constituted the full bulk of assets nor was liable to the ordinary fluctuations of the market. The preponderating mass of the shares dealt in on the Stock Exchange was in the street, passed from broker to broker, was used by the great operators like the pawns in a game of chess. The September gold gale swept away the margins of outside speculators, but left their remaining capital intact. Moreover, the brokers, schooled by the artificial "lock-ups" of money in the preceding year, were better able to resist the attack; and the banks, in drawing in their loans, exhibited unusual prudence and conservatism. The pressure in the loan market continued only a few days and then sensibly relaxed. The West suffered by the decreased value of its products, and merchants in the foreign trade were temporarily affected by the condition of exchange, and the variable value of the only legal currency for the payment of custom dues. The spasm limited itself almost exclusively to Wall Street and to the corresponding speculative centres of Philadelphia, Boston, and Baltimore. Such stocks as had genuine investment value were bought up at once by capitalists all over the Union, the moment the line of depression had reached a point where they could profitably be held. The very fact of this immediate influx of money is a further proof of the difference between the two crises. But it is in the results of '57 that the impropriety of its comparison to '69 is clearly shown. Factories at that period were everywhere shut up. Employees and domestic servants were dismissed by thousands. In New York City alone twenty thousand men and women lost their places in a fortnight. The country dealers found it impossible to meet their indebtedness. Liabilities incurred when wheat was two dollars a bushel were now to be met with wheat at seventy-five cents. Merchants, banks, all trades and professions, were in sore distress. The mails were weighted down by letters pleading for help. Twenty tons of these clamorous missives went out of the New York post-office in one day. Nothing but favoritism could secure help from the banks. In Philadelphia a merchant who had made ineffectual efforts to obtain advances on prime paper drew up a thirty days' note for five dollars, went to his neighbors and secured sufficient first-class indorsements to cover the back. He then pinned on a ten-dollar bill of his bank as collateral and presented it for discount. The President smiled grimly at the delicate hint.

The press of the time overflowed with anecdotes illustrating the popular feeling against the great financial corporations, and their "unjustifiable" slaughtering of collaterals. A Chicago bank had ordered a lot of corn which had been hypothecated to be sent to a house at Oswego for instant sale. As the firm failed to remit the money, the Chicago president concluded to take a trip over the railroad and inquire into matters. The dialogue which ensued upon his arrival is thus stated:—

Chicago Financier. "Is Mr. H—— at home?"

H. "That 's my name, sir: take a seat."

C. F. "My name is Mr. ——, of Chicago, and I 've come for the 15,000 bushels of wheat I sent you the other day."

H. "Have not got it, sir; it 's been sold."

C. F. "Very well, then. I want the money for it."

H. "I have n't got the money, sir."

C. F. "What has become of it, sir?"

H. "I have paid my debts with it."

C. F. (In great indignation.) "You are a scoundrel, sir."

H. (With hauteur.) "Very likely, and maybe there 's a pair of us. I 'm sorry my carriage is not here, as I should like to show you about the city."

The Chicago bank president "left," naturally in no happy mental condition.

The belief that the panic was attributable to the great diminution in discounts and call loans was shared not merely by journalists and the general mercantile class. Nathan Appleton, himself a bank director so far back as 1814, wrote to the Boston *Advertiser*, October 12, 1857, that the further contraction of New York banks, after the alarm incident to the failure of the Ohio Trust Company ought naturally to have died out, assuredly "brought about the present disastrous crisis."

We have already lingered too long upon the commercial phases of the panic, although it would be easy to fill a dozen pages with characteristic stories of runs on the banks, of the troubles of traders who drew out their deposits in specie and then passed sleepless nights in guarding their uncomfortable wealth, of young merchants and manufacturers who preserved their credit by efforts and accidents which have all the coloring of romance. The fate of the steamship Central America was a curious episode of the times. She was on the California line, and her arrival was anxiously anticipated in New York, as her heavy freight of gold would have sensibly relieved the market. On Saturday the 12th of September, — three weeks after the city had been thrown into wild confusion by the financial tornado, and men grew pale and weary of life in the struggle for money, — the officers of the steamer discovered that she had sprung aleak in stress of weather. They were already far out on the Atlantic. Every effort to stop the influx of water proved unavailing. In a few hours the ship would founder. The passengers were at once notified to put themselves in readiness for the boats.

Then ensued one of those scenes in which the emptiness of wealth discloses itself, as in sudden new light, to even the dullest of mankind. The waves were high, the distance from shore so great as almost to forbid hope. All were huddled together in the cabin, — a few women, one or two tourists; but mainly stalwart men who had risked fever and years of desolate toil for the loved ones of a home whose sunny brightness was fading away forever. Every one had money: some, thousands; many, their ten thousands. A bronzed-faced miner, catching the impulse of the moment, opened his carpet-bag, weighted with freshly minted dollars, and strewed its contents over table and chairs, beseeching his terror-stricken comrades to help themselves. The crazed crowd, half unconscious of the satire, began to imitate the example. Purses, through whose meshes gleamed hundreds upon hundreds of gold-pieces, were tossed from hand to hand. The sofas were covered with piles of coin in which no one cared to confess ownership. One individual, lifting a huge canvas-sack, poured out ten thousand dollars of gold-dust, until the carpet was thick with precious metal. This man, through strange fortune, was almost the only one of the little gathering who reached land in safety, after they had taken to the boats; and the simple story of that hour, coming from his lips, gave point to hundreds of sermons, and to abundant editorials from those pleasant newspaper optimists who discover an advantage even in the fact of "hard times."

If it were possible to know the secret history of many of the great commercial houses which failed during the panic, a vast number of new illustrations of the connection of the Stock Market with the financial depression would come to light. The chief partner of one firm, early in '56, became so overwrought by the immense risks and profits of business that he lost his mind. His own share in the house was two millions and a half. Before winter the balance-sheets showed a clear gain, in a single season, of $ 1,300,000. The victim of trade was put in an insane asylum. In a few months he died. On examining his assets there were found ten thousand shares of Illinois Central, which sold at the time of his derangement for 140. As all the instalments had not been paid in, the real value then was about $ 800,000. In October, 1857, the heirs put them in the market, and realized only fifty thousand dollars!

Illinois Central had become a bankrupt road; yet even in failure its shares were in high repute, compared to other Western securities. The Chicago, St. Paul, and Fond du Lac Railroad Company went under with a crash this year, its stock being quoted down in the lower numerals, and its bondholders foreclosing. William B. Ogden was the leading spirit in this road, and is understood to have lost and recovered several millions in the vicissitudes of the company. In '59 the famous Chicago and Northwest Line was created out of its ruins; but during the *interregnum* the bonds of the company, as well as the certificates of indebtedness of cities, counties, and States throughout the West, were in ill odor on the Stock Exchange. Whole bales of worthless paper of this character were piled away in New York brokers' and bankers' offices. The luckless victims of over-confidence found language fail them to express their indignation. On a certain day in November, while the street was still prostrate under the collapse of August, there entered one of the offices which had dealt most heavily and fatally in Western stock a nattily dressed young man from a remote section of Wisconsin. The banker recognized him at once. "Well, Williams, why are you here?" "Just to have you help me negotiate some bonds. Our county has elected me agent. We have printed off certificates to be issued for the purpose of building a new county-house and jail. They gave me the choice of banker, and so I concluded to let you have the job. See here, now, the discount is perfectly awful," — and the confident capitalist-borrower from Wisconsin began to unfold his budget, and whisper the terms on which the little affair was proffered. The Wall Street veteran first shaped his mouth into a sharp significant whistle, then slowly rose from his chair, his face assuming the utmost solemnity and severity. "Now, Williams, if you care to take advice, you will put those bonds in your pocket, and yourself in the cars, and when you reach home you will toss all that waste paper in the fire. If your county wants money, it better tax itself for it. New York won't risk more cash in wildcat Western county-houses any longer; and, hist! you can't disappear too soon, for if they get wind of what you 're after hereabouts, they 'll —" Before he could finish his sentence Williams had seized his hat, edged off toward the door leading into the outer vestibule, and was bowing himself out in a most comical condition of terror. The banker, from whom we have the anecdote, adds that the Wisconsin county agent lingered some thirty-six hours longer about town, and then departed with such mental illumination as effectually cured him of all further attempts at bond negotiations.

From the spring of '58 to '60 the Stock Board very slowly recovered its old tone. The bear element, especially the Observatory, was in its glory. Brokers had become fearful of forced quotations. "Washing" had been a constant trick before the panic, and bids were now closely scrutinized. The evidences of mismanagement and fraud in great corporations, of the bribery of journals, of jobbing in Congress, before the crash, were now cropping out in all directions. Companies which had contrived, by great sacrifices, to hold out during the panic, began to disclose their weakness when the subsidence of excitement seemed to give a safe opportunity for frankness. Not a few succumbed; among them New York and Erie, which in '59 failed to pay the interest on its mortgages, and was subjected to instant foreclosure and the appointment of a receiver. Rev. Mr. Cuyler visited the Board about the time of the Erie "break," and reported his views to a religious paper. The sessions were then held in Exchange Place. The clerical on-looker took a cheerful view of things, and was confident that a fair proportion of these keen stock-heroes were not unfitted for spiritual communion. He saw one hundred and twenty men sitting at tables, with hats on head and books in hand. When favorite stocks were called a broker would spring up, fling himself into the middle of the room "shaking his finger violently, gesticulating, shouting, vociferating 'I'll take you up,' 'Seventy-five for the lot,' 'That's my bid,' 'Seller thirty days.'" Of the *Ursa Major* of Erie we are told, "His financial fame is world-wide. While the bids are made, the workings of his countenance remind us of Brougham in the House of Lords. He steps out from his desk and snaps his finger toward another broker, calling out, 'I'll take your lot at thirty days.'" The picture has the truth of a photograph, but since the war brokers jumble up their bids in fewer words, and with more precision than is indicated in the phrase attributed to the king bear.

What was the full value of the stocks and bonds dealt in at this time by the Stock Exchange? It is a question difficult of answer, as no complete statement is extant, and the labor of separating the additions of indebtedness, through stock watering and new issues of bonds in the last ten years, would be very great. To estimate it at one sixth of the present bulk of securities would be to do more than justice to the past. One ninth would be more nearly accurate. It should further be noted, that all the great stocks and State or railroad securities were then at a far larger percentage below par than they are now above. The actual capital invested was, therefore, disproportionately small. Probably where one hundred millions are now employed, not ten million was then in use. An able writer of the period predicted that the wonderful phenomenon of the Paris Bourse and the London Stock Exchange would find no analogue in America. We had no great titled or moneyed aristocracy concentrating the whole wealth of the nation at one point, drawing their resources from remote regions and spending them in one metropolis. There was no such centralization of government or State debts as would enable New York to compete with European finance, nor any "field for those extensive combinations which, as in the case of the elder Baring, would yield a profit of a million and a half in three days." Times have bravely changed since this prophecy was written. Jay Cooke can match the story of Baring. Vanderbilt at one stroke in '68 made more than either of the Rothschilds ever earned in any single speculation. In one decade New York has attained precisely the central figure which the fine reasoning of ten or twelve years ago proved to be impossible; and the impulse toward far higher grandeur through suboceanic cables and trans-continental railroads has scarcely begun to disclose its immense force.

Governments in '59 were a very insignificant item, but there was, nevertheless, a certain significance in the character of the holders. Two thirds of our national debt was in foreign hands! In that year any one fortunate enough to be allowed access to the Sub-Treasury's books would have found among the chief names of creditors only a few Americans of note, — George Peabody, John J. Astor, William B. Astor, and Jacob Little.

A key to this may be discovered in the fact, that, when Congress went into the market about this period to borrow a few millions, it could not place the loan except by twelve per cent discount. Outside of the country, however, such a man as John Lloyd (Lord Overstone) held $ 350,000. Lord Elgin was down for $ 17,000. Baring Brothers, the Rothschilds of both Paris and London, the nobility of Spain, Italy, Russia, and England were buyers. Asiatics and West-Indians were found on the list. Macaulay began with $ 5,000 and ended with $ 30,000. De Tocqueville, Scribe the dramatic author, Pouchouke the Paris publisher, Sontag, Paul Julien, and other minor celebrities, were creditors. When war came these securities were returned in hot haste; but the inevitable tendency of Europe for American investments was shown by an almost immediate reabsorption, and in the subsequent popular subscription throughout Germany and Holland for the 5-20s.

Our commercial classes had become exceedingly cautious at the close of the last decade. Trade turned to the South in consequence of the general distrust of the West. As a result of the prevalent timidity there was very little mercantile paper afloat, and the banks were compelled to restrict their loans from the absence of anything which would authorize discounting. Money was, therefore, more than ever a "drug" in the market. Vast quantities of specie were collected in New York. The bank vaults overflowed with it. This plethora reached its height in February, 1861, and the final suspension of coin payments was unquestionably delayed by this cause.

In a previous chapter we have called attention to the low state of railroad stocks in 1860.* Vast fortunes

* The annexed table of prices during 1859, 1860, and 1861 at the Stock Exchange will be of value as indicating the average low range at which securities sold and the degree of upward fluctuations effected by bull operators :—

	1859.		1860.		1861.	
	Lowest.	Highest.	Lowest.	Highest.	Lowest.	Highest.
Indiana 5 per cent .	85	93	86	93	75	93
Tennessee 6 per cent .	86¼	93⅞	64	93	34¼	77
Virginia 6 per cent .	92½	99½	73	95	36	80
N. Carolina 6 per cent	94½	101¼	77½	100	44	82½
Missouri 6 per cent .	80½	87¼	61	84⅞	35	72
Louisiana 6 per cent .	90	96	94	99½	45	77½
California 7 per cent	80	86½	82	95	71½	88
Reading	35½	54¾	29½	49¼	29½	47¾
Michigan Central .	38	54¼	35	73½	39¾	61½
Michigan Southern .	4	21½	5	25	10¼	20⅛
Panama . . .	113½	137¾	106	146½	97½	121
Illinois Central . .	53	72	51¼	89½	55½	88½
New York Central .	69	86	69	92⅛	68	82½
Erie	4	17¼	8⅛	43	17	40½
Hudson River .	30	42¾	35	66	31½	49¼
Harlem	9	14¼	8	23½	8¾	17
Harlem preferred .	33	44¼	27	55	20½	43
Cleveland and Pittsburg	6	10	5	15½	6½	17
Cleveland and Toledo .	16½	33⅛	18⅝	49½	20½	38⅜
Cleveland, Col. and Cin.	91	100	86	99½	90	102
Galena and Chicago	60½	77½	55	82¾	55	74½
Rock Island . . .	55⅝	71	42½	84¼	30¾	62
Chi., Bur., and Quincy	48½	61	40	92¾	51	78½
Mil. and P. du Chien .	3	13½	1½	16¼	9	23
Canton Company .	16½	20	14	23½	8	15
Pennsylvania Coal .	79½	85¾	73½	88¼	72	81
Del. & Hudson Co. .	87	101	80	101½	72	92
Cumberland preferred .	11	24½	8	17½	4	9¼
Pacific Mail . .	67¼	93½	70	107½	50	100

were open to any one who chose to invest. Yet stocks which sold for a song remained stationary for months, and exhibited immaterial appreciation even in '62. That year there was a sharp upward movement. The rise in gold and the great expansion of legal tender were unquestionably the source of the speculative excitement; but it was not less due to an obscure cause, the origin of which dates back to '57. The country had been importing and manufacturing heavily. The crash threw this vast surplus stock into the auction-room. Even as late as 1860 the slaughtering of dry goods continued, and servant-girls found it easy to dress in fine silk and satin. Retailers and jobbers throughout the rural districts bought immense supplies, and for two years were able to rely upon their home stock without recourse to the city. When the swelling tide of greenbacks flowed in, agricultural products went up, and farmers' families, with more money in hand than ever before, thronged the adjacent villages and towns, and stripped the shop-shelves of even their stalest goods. The dealers instead of buying again proportionately, contented themselves with purchasing small quantities, and invested the main bulk of their profits in the stock market. The stagnancy which New York merchants experienced in '63 finds its solution in this fact; and the judiciousness of the country speculators was shown in the great increase in the average wealth of traders throughout the Union, fortunes of fifty thousand being less common in 1860 than those of one hundred thousand in 1865.

CHAPTER XVII.

PROSPECTIVE.

THREE billion of dollars, invested in securities to which the New York Stock Exchange in this year of grace 1870 affixes its daily stamp of value, is a sum-total which may well confuse the imagination. It exceeds the sale worth of all the cotton, corn, wheat, oats, buckwheat, barley, potatoes, rye, hay, and dairy produce of the Union during 1869, together with the earnings of all our fisheries, and the manufactories in iron, leather, wool, cotton, and paper in the same period. The yearly fluctuations of some of the active stocks are equal to what in the grain market would make a barrel of flour worth at one time $12, again $9, and the next day $4 or $6. Western Union has sold for 250, and is now quoted at 32. Wheat, subject to similar vacillations, would bring in the farmer $1.25 a bushel at one season, and 15 cents a bushel at another. And although such startling vibrations are not the rule of the Share Board, the ordinary changes which mark its weekly business, if transferred to the departments of industry or agriculture, would affect ceaseless and terrible derangements.

However slight may be the direct interest of the great producing class in these phenomena of the Stock Market, the secondary and less obvious consequences of traffic in the evidences of investment reach far into the affairs of every household in the nation. The future of our paramount money-mart is, therefore, of exceeding importance not less to the farmer and artisan than to the capitalist and statesman.

In approaching a subject involving so much and penetrating so deeply, it is desirable to disembarrass the mind from certain prejudices. There is, for example, a vast amount of pure speculation in Wall Street. Without entering into the metaphysics of speculation itself, or endeavoring to discover whether there be a profession or pursuit in life free from the active element of hazard, it cannot be unjust to call attention to the large arena over which this impropriety has extended. "Corners" are not original with stock-brokers. In '68 the principle was applied to corn in Chicago. In '65 it was put in operation upon wheat in California. Years before it was employed in the same way in Australia. Ouvrard, the great stock-operator of Europe in the last century, began his career by contracting for all the paper which should be manufactured in France for the two years succeeding 1789. The Revolution had just broken forth, and he saw instantly that in pamphlets, newspapers, etc., the demand would be immense. Starting with 5,000 francs, this corner made him a capitalist. His next operation displayed even higher prescience. France protected the products of her colonies. The Revolution was laying the train for a ruinous explosion in St. Domingo. Coupling the two facts, he went to Bordeaux, and in conjunction with a large importing-house, bought coffee and sugar in immense quantities. At one venture he cleared nearly a million francs, and immediately reinvested it, purchasing the entire annual yield of the colony. He was at once the heaviest capitalist in Paris. The city of Mexico is on an island in the midst of a lake. Francis Baring, son of Lord Ashburton, while there as a tourist, saw the opportunity for a startling speculation, and in a few days possessed himself in fee simple of the entire shore circuit of the water. The whole cost was £200,000, and of this he paid one fifth on the spot. Had not Baring Brothers been frightened by the daring scope of the scheme,—their timidity leading them to order its immediate abandonment,—this operation would probably have resulted in enormous profits. The most audacious and lucrative of all the speculations of the Rothschilds was outside of the London Stock Exchange. This house, through shrewd diplomacy, obtained the control of the only quicksilver-mines in Europe. The price of the lively metal was raised to an extortionate figure. So excessive was the selling rate that all Christendom, in eagerness to obtain cheap calomel, fell to scraping the backs of old mirrors. Political economy gives to the class of men who make these vast combinations the name of monopolists. But they are simply speculators in successful corners, including in their grasp commodities of far more vital importance to the public than are paper values.

Wall Street sells what it has not in hand, but what it believes can be obtained at a lower price before the time of delivery. All our great grain-merchants, cotton-factors, wholesale dealers in certain descriptions of manufactured goods, do the same. Heavy settlements were made during the war by prominent New York houses who had agreed to deliver paper and woollens to a fixed amount and within a given time, but were victims of the sudden summer drouth which stopped the mills of New England for several weeks. Operations in copper and coal under precisely the same conditions as exist in short sales are very common, and not infrequently come to light in lawsuits, where the decision of court is almost invariably against the contracting party. We call attention to these facts, not to defend speculation, but to show that the methods of the Stock Market are coextensive with trade, and have their origin, not in any particular school, or rather in the universal school whose first primary lesson is, "Make money."

Moreover, although it is hard to disassociate the two in the mind, there is an essential distinction between the cliques and the brokers. The latter are sometimes the instruments of the former; but it nevertheless remains true that the street itself is not in sympathy with the great operators. The latter rob the brokers by destroying their customers. To use the slang of the financial quarter, they "milk the street." Except in one particular, the New York brokers really stand in the position of conservators of speculation. They sell "proxies" on the stock which by the luck of the market falls in their hands. In Cleveland and Pittsburg and in Erie this open barter has been one of the scandals of the times. Naturally, the more entirely an active stock is bought at the Exchange, the greater the opportunity for irresponsible leaders to secure control of important corporations. Were this vice of wide extent, the street would become the Pretorian Guard of our railway financiers; and that it is less common, and is becoming more generally accepted as disreputable by the influential and controlling members of the Stock Board, is indubitable. Apart from this, all the worst evils of stock manipulations have their birth and abiding-place in the secret counsels of the Rings and Cliques, — of that association of railway, steamship, and telegraph directors, presidents, and heavy shareholders, who find it consonant with their consciences and their purses to water stock, pay dividends out of capital, to invent that anomalous feature in finance known as capitalized earnings, to utter unauthorized new stock, to "pass" dividends in order to break the market; in a word, to do everything which will keep them outside of prison-bars by means of shrewd lawyers and complaisant judges, if only in doing all this they can manage to make three dollars grow where but one grew before. The annals of American financiering are not particularly exhilarating. The exhibition of fraud in high places, and of effrontery on the part of responsible managers, bordering upon the sublime, which has characterized the past few years, is not calculated to inspire over-confidence in the future. Yet even here we are not without consolations. If the present is dark, was the past brighter? If speculation in the United States has discouraging aspects, are the records of the London Stock Exchange and the Paris Bourse clean of stain? The English papers have recently been laden with fierce denunciations of the New York Stock Market, and it cannot be gainsaid that their criticisms are just and opportune; but the inference underlying these reproaches, the implication that British capitalists are guileless, and that stock-jobbery is a modern and American invention, is sadly inconsistent with facts. In the old South Sea days, £574,000 were paid to influence votes and secure the enlargement of franchise by a single company. During the railway fever of 1824–25, newspaper exaggerations, neatly cooked reports, captivating prospectuses, were the main machinery of speculation. The press was bought up by the gift of options in shares which were sold out at a premium. The London *Morning Chronicle* remarked: "We blush to say few editors of newspapers in the metropolis are not to be found in the list of those benefited." In John Francis's "History of English Railways," one will find a hundred illustrations of the keenness of cockney railway cliques. One road, in 1845, placed certificates of stock in the hands of an agent. This broker, by order of directors, bought large amounts of scrip through time sales. When the shorts tried to get the paper and thus meet their contracts, they were informed that the company would make no issue for the present! Of course the premium had to be paid over, and the short interest suffered proportionately. Another company invited applications for shares. The number was to be limited. Deposits on stock were fixed at 22 shillings. The directors bought fifty times the amount to be issued, and 'Change Alley was cornered at once. Perhaps the most signal example of the corner in London speculation is afforded by the operations of a clique in the Huddersfield, Halifax, and Bradford Union Railroad during 1845. No scrip had appeared; nevertheless, a vast number of shares were sold for future delivery at 20 and 30 *s.* The entire capital stock was only 15,000, but the shorts held 75,000 shares. The line was looked upon as a failure, and every one was counting on a fortune by the fall. Suddenly it was announced that this road was to be amalgamated with the West Riding Union Line, one of the most popular fancies in the market. At a jump the stock of Huddersfield, Halifax, and Bradford Union went to £15. The speculators were ruined, and the brokers were all deeply involved. The Stock Exchange, the day after the news, shook with the wild encounter of bull and bear; and so inextricably was "the city" involved that the rooms of the Board were closed for a week to repair losses. The mere *bagatelle* of five million dollars threw the London Exchange into a six days' confusion; and yet the English journals are scandalized that the business of the New York Gold Room should be deranged by transactions covering one hundred times that amount!

That acme of gambling, the sale of privileges, called succintly in Wall Street by the name of "puts" and "calls," is an old English speculative invention. They "carry" stock perpetually, styling the act "continuation." Gold corners are a part of the history of the London Exchange. The first attempt of the Bank of England to renew specie payments after the Continental war with Napoleon was frustrated by British operators. During the Crimean campaign the London banks depended upon the receipts of bullion from Australia and California for their preservation from suspension. Sometimes the ships were delayed, throwing the money-market into a whirl of excitement. "Capitalists," said Chapman, the manager for Overend, Gurney, & Co., in his testimony before the Parliamentary committee, — "capitalists availed themselves of these crises to make enormous profits out of those who fell victims to them. There cannot be a doubt of it." "There is more than one capitalist who can withdraw from the circulating medium £1,000,000 or £2,000,000 of notes, if they have an object to attain by it, — to knock down the funds and create a scarcity. One morning there was a great demand for money in the Stock Exchange; nobody knew how it was. A person came and asked me whether I would lend money. I said, 'Certainly.' He said, 'I will take £50,000 of you at seven per cent.' I was astonished. Our rate of money was much below that. I said, 'You shall have it.' Shortly the man returned and borrowed £50,000 at seven and a half; next £100,000 at eight, and finally much more at eight and a half. It afterwards turned out that there had been a sudden withdrawal from the market which created the great pressure." As first-class bills in 1852 could be discounted for one and three quarters per cent, the rise to eight and a half was something as extraordinary as the high rates of interest in New York at the spring and fall stringency of '68. It is needless to note in passing, that the affair detailed by Mr. Chapman was the "lock-up" pure and simple, — an invention absurdly attributed to recent American financiering.

It would be easy to multiply these illustrations. The record of English speculation is crowded with examples of the most rapid and ruinous fluctuations in price, of a frenzy for "stock gambling" extending to all classes, and carried to a pitch of madness beyond the imagination of a veteran New York broker. Crossing the Channel, one finds at the French capital all the tactics and strategy of a great money-market in high perfection. The *Parquet* constitute the "regular" dealers. The *Coulisse* are the curbstone brokers. Cash sales are infrequent, and almost the whole bulk of business is in that *Rouge et noire* branch of stock speculation, the "privilege." The technical name is *Marché à prime,* and on the 15th and 30th of every month the owner of this call must decide whether he takes the stock or not. At all events he must pay the premium. Under these auspices the scenes of the Paris Bourse are characterized by an *abandon* and recklessness which leave nothing for the student of human nature to desire. There are money stringencies, fierce panics, overselling of the market, grand combinations, gigantic failures. Every year has its fringe of defalcations. Every stock has a history of sharp rise and fall. If we go to Vienna we shall find a city whose market has hardly recovered from the terrific domestic revulsion of '69· Amsterdam, Hamburg, Trieste, Smyrna, Marseilles, Madrid, Odessa, all witness the same capacity for high speculation, stock-jobbing, and financial irregularities.

The bearing of these facts upon Wall Street finance must be apparent to the least thoughtful. They prove that speculation in the United States has nothing unique, peculiar, or unparalleled. They furthermore afford room for a conjecture that much of the present exaggeration of stock manipulation is ephemeral, a part of the national education, one of those diseases which attack the young, and, though not wanting in pain and discomfort, are nevertheless not fatal nor of long continuance. Despite the speculative opportunities of London and the European towns, the controlling influences are conservative; and in New York since the war there are not a few evidences that the current is setting in a wholesome direction. The rule in force at the Stock Exchange, rendering a registry of shares obligatory on corporations, is a measure whose influence cannot be overestimated. Even the infamies of Erie have not been without a certain advantage, and the very height of recent disorders would seem to indicate that the poison in the financial system is working to a head. A probable consequence will be the establishment of more rigorous guaranties, and the enforcement of restrictions which will give to a large proportion of the stock list a greater defined value.

The enlargement of the scope of the New York Stock Exchange greatly depends at present upon Europe. We are a borrowing nation. The Panama Railroad is the nearest approach to a strictly non-national security on the list of the Exchange. All else is rigidly domestic. Our growth through foreign connections hinges, therefore, upon the repute of our stocks and bonds abroad. Germany, Holland, and England hold already about one billion of American securities in governments, railway bonds and stocks, State stocks. In the face of current speculative demoralization, this is a wonderful exhibit. With the increase of a healthier tone in our finance, and the creation of fresh safeguards upon the management of corporations, thereby rendering dividends more secure and permanent, the confidence in American stock interests will expand proportionately. The suboceanic cables have even now linked the finances of the two worlds. New York brokers pay a million a year for telegrams from London alone. This constant intercourse requires simply a deeper faith in the substantial character of the commodities dealt in upon the Broad Street Exchange to open out very wide results. Out of the ten billion dollars of stocks and funds on the list of the London Stock Board, American securities amount to a few insignificant millions. At the Paris Bourse the Southern Pacific Railroad is the only stock from the United States privileged to daily quotation. The great bulk of the United States bonds and shares owned abroad are bought and sold only through private bankers. Confidence will change all this. New York will act with Europe. The excitement at one point will be quieted by the repose at another. In the September gold flurry, it was a despatch from London quite as much as the message from Washington which checked the bullion conspiracy. The knowledge that Wall Street was calm under the news of the Overend, Gurney, & Co. failure of '66 did much to lessen the progress of panic in the English financial capital. It remains for the brokers of the Stock Exchange to decide whether they will seek the petty profits of a speculation marred by grave faults, or will cast their influence still farther and with more strenuous emphasis against the encroachment of the cliques. The former means isolation. The latter will be prelusive of an expansion in international relations which will make New York imperial, and Wall Street, what its pivotal position demands and allows, the paramount financial centre of the globe.

THE END.

Cambridge: Electrotyped and Printed by Welch, Bigelow, & Co.

Spotted something that isn't quite right?

Let us know and we'll fix it for future reprints.
And as a thank you for your diligence, we'll
send you a free Sothis book of your choice.

publisher@sothis.press

This page intentionally left blank

Except of course for that line above. And this one.
And whilst we have your attention, perhaps you'd
like to follow us on Instagram @sothis.press. Go on.

Made in the USA
Monee, IL
08 November 2026

67812139R00215